WITHDRAWN

THE JEWS AND MODERN CAPITALISM

By WERNER SOMBART

TRANSLATED, WITH NOTES, BY

M. EPSTEIN

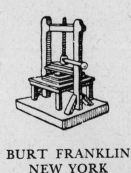

BURT FRANKLIN
NEW YORK

Published by BURT FRANKLIN
235 East 44th St., New York, N.Y. 10017
Originally Published: London 1913
Reprinted: 1969
Printed in the U.S.A.

Library of Congress Card Catalog No.: 79-80240
Burt Franklin: Research and Source Works Series 366
Judaica Series 7

CONTENTS

CHAPTER III

THE QUICKENING OF INTERNATIONAL TRADE

CHAPTER IV

THE FOUNDATION OF MODERN COLONIES

CHAPTER V

THE FOUNDATION OF THE MODERN STATE

CHAPTER VI

THE PREDOMINANCE OF COMMERCE IN ECONOMIC LIFE

CHAPTER VII

THE GROWTH OF A CAPITALISTIC POINT OF VIEW
IN ECONOMIC LIFE

PART II

THE APTITUDE OF THE JEWS FOR MODERN CAPITALISM

CHAPTER VIII

THE PROBLEM

CHAPTER IX

WHAT IS A CAPITALIST UNDERTAKER ?

CHAPTER X

THE OBJECTIVE CIRCUMSTANCES IN THE JEWISH APTITUDE FOR MODERN CAPITALISM

CHAPTER XI

THE SIGNIFICANCE OF THE JEWISH RELIGION IN ECONOMIC LIFE

CHAPTER XII

JEWISH CHARACTERISTICS

PART III

THE ORIGIN OF THE JEWISH GENIUS

CHAPTER XIII

THE RACE PROBLEM

CHAPTER XIV

THE VICISSITUDES OF THE JEWISH PEOPLE

TRANSLATOR'S INTRODUCTORY NOTE

WERNER SOMBART is undoubtedly one of the most striking personalities in the Germany of to-day. Born in 1863, he has devoted himself to research in economics, and has contributed much that is valuable to economic thought. Though his work has not always been accepted without challenge, it has received universal recognition for its brilliance, and his reputation has drawn hosts of students to his lectures, both at Breslau, where he held the Chair of Economics at the University (1890–1906), and now in Berlin at the Handelshochschule, where he occupies a similar position.

But Sombart is an artist as well as a scholar; he combines reason with imagination in an eminent degree, and he has the gift, seldom enough associated with German professors, of writing in a lucid, flowing, almost eloquent style. That is one characteristic of all his books, which are worth noting. The rise and development of modern capitalism has been the theme that has attracted him most, and his masterly treatment of it may be found in his *Der moderne Kapitalismus* (2 vols., Leipzig, 1902). In 1896 he published *Sozialismus und soziale Bewegung*, which quickly went through numerous editions and may be described as one of the most widely read books in German-speaking countries.[1] *Die*

---

[1] An English version was prepared by the present writer and issued by Messrs. J. M. Dent & Co. in 1909, under the title *Socialism and the Social Movement*.

deutsche Volkswirtschaft im 19*ten Jahrhundert* appeared in 1903, and *Das Proletariat* in 1906.

For some years past Sombart has been considering the revision of his *magnum opus* on modern capitalism, and in the course of his studies came across the problem, quite accidentally, as he himself tells us, of the relation between the Jews and modern capitalism. The topic fascinated him, and he set about inquiring what that relationship precisely was. The results of his labours were published in the book [1] of which this is an English edition.

The English version is slightly shorter than the German original. The portions that have been left out (with the author's concurrence) are not very long and relate to general technical questions, such as the modern race theory or the early history of credit instruments. Furthermore, everything found within square brackets has been added by the translator.

My best thanks are due to my wife, who has been constantly helpful with suggestions and criticisms, and to my friend Leon Simon for the verse rendering on p. 208.

M. E.

London, *April* 21, 1913.

---

[1] *Die Juden und das Wirtschaftsleben.* Leipzig: Duncker und Humblot. 1911.

PART I

THE CONTRIBUTION OF THE JEWS
TO MODERN ECONOMIC LIFE

CHAPTER I

INTRODUCTORY

Two possible methods may be used to discover to what extent any group of people participated in a particular form of economic organization. One is the statistical; the other may be termed the genetic.

By means of the first we endeavour to ascertain the actual number of persons taking part in some economic activity—say, those who establish trade with a particular country, or who found any given industry—and then we calculate what percentage is represented by the members of the group in which we happen to be interested. There is no doubt that the statistical method has many advantages. A pretty clear conception of the relative importance for any branch of commerce of, let us say, foreigners or Jews, is at once evolved if we are able to show by actual figures that 50 or 75 per cent. of all the persons engaged in that branch belong to either the first or the second category named. More especially is this apparent when statistical information is forthcoming, not only as to the number of persons but also concerning other or more striking economic factors—*e.g.*, the amount of paid-up capital, the quantity of the commodities produced, the size of the turnover, and so forth. It will be useful, therefore, to adopt the statistical method in questions such as the one we have set ourselves. But at the same time it will soon become evident that by its aid alone the complete solution cannot be found. In the first place, even the best statistics do not tell us everything; nay, often the most important aspect of what we are trying to discover is omitted. Statistics are silent as to the dynamic effects which strong individualities produce in economic, as indeed in all human life—effects which have consequences reaching far beyond the limits of their immediate surroundings. Their actual importance for the general tendency of any particular development is greater far than any set of figures can reveal. Therefore the statistical method must be supplemented by some other.

But more than this. The statistical method, owing to lack of information, cannot always be utilized. It is indeed a lucky accident that we possess figures recording the number of those engaged in any industry or trade, and showing their comparative relation to the rest of the population. But a statistical study of this kind, on a large scale, is really only a possibility for modern and future times. Even then the path of the investigator is beset by difficulties. Still, a careful examination of various sources, including the assessments made by Jewish communities on their members, may lead to fruitful results. I hope that this book will give an impetus to such studies, of which, at the present time, there is only one that is really useful—the enquiry of Sigmund Mayr, of Vienna.

When all is said, therefore, the other method (the genetic), to which I have already alluded, must be used to supplement the results of statistics. What is this method? We wish to discover to what extent a group of people (the Jews) influence or have influenced the form and development of modern economic life—to discover, that is, their qualitative or, as I have already called it, their dynamic importance. We can do this best of all by enquiring whether certain characteristics that mark our modern economic life were given their first form by Jews, *i.e.*, either that some particular form of organization was first introduced by the Jews, or that some well-known business principles, now accepted on all hands as fundamental, are specific expressions of the Jewish spirit. This of necessity demands that the history of the factors in economic development should be traced to their earliest beginnings. In other words, we must study the childhood of the modern capitalistic system, or, at any rate, the age in which it received its modern form. But not the childhood only : its whole history must be considered. For throughout, down to these very days, new elements are constantly entering the fabric of capitalism and changes appear in its characteristics. Wherever such are noted our aim must be to discover to whose influence they are due. Often enough this will not be easy ; sometimes it will even be impossible ; and scientific imagination must come to the aid of the scholar.

Another point should not be overlooked. In many cases the people who are responsible for a fundamental idea or innovation in economic life are not always the inventors (using that word in its narrowest meaning). It has often been asserted that the Jews have no inventive powers ; that not only technical but also economic discoveries were made by non-Jews alone, and that the Jews have always been able cleverly to utilize the ideas of others. I dissent from this general view in its entirety. We meet with Jewish inventors in the sphere of technical science, and certainly in that of economics, as I hope to show in this work. But even if the assertion which we have mentioned were true, it would prove nothing against the view that Jews have given certain aspects of economic life the specific features they bear. In the economic world it is not so much the inventors that matter as those who are able to apply the inventions : not those who conceive ideas (*e.g.*, the hire-purchase system) as those who can utilize them in everyday life.

Before proceeding to the problem before us—the share of the Jews in the work of building up our modern capitalistic system—we must mention one other point of importance. In a specialized study of this kind Jewish influence may appear larger than it actually was. That is in the nature of our study, where the whole problem is looked at from only one point of view. If we were enquiring into the influence of mechanical inventions on modern economic life the same would apply : in a monograph that influence would tend to appear larger than it really was. I mention this point, obvious though it is, lest it be said that I have exaggerated the part played by the Jews. There were undoubtedly a thousand and one other causes that helped to make the economic system of our time what it is. Without the discovery of America and its silver treasures, without the mechanical inventions of technical science, without the ethnical peculiarities of modern European nations and their vicissitudes, capitalism would have been as impossible as without the Jews.

In the long story of capitalism, Jewish influence forms but one chapter. Its relative importance to the others I shall show in the new edition of my *Modern Capitalism*, which I hope to have ready before long.

This *caveat* will, I trust, help the general reader to a proper appreciation of the influence of Jews on modern economic life. But it must be taken in conjunction with another. If on the one hand we are to make some allowance, should our studies apparently tend to give Jews a preponderating weight in economic affairs, on the other hand, their contribution is very often even larger than we are led to believe. For our researches can deal only with one portion of the problem, seeing that all the material is not available. Who to-day knows anything definite about the individuals, or groups, who founded this or that industry, established this or that branch of commerce, first adopted this or that business principle? And even where we are able to name these pioneers with certainty, there comes the further question, were they Jews or not?

Jews—that is to say, members of the people who profess the Jewish faith. And I need hardly add that although in this definition I purposely leave out any reference to race characteristics, it yet includes those Jews who have withdrawn from their religious community, and even descendants of such, seeing that historically they remain Jews. This must be borne in mind, for when we are determining the influence of the Jew on modern economic life, again and again men appear on the scene as Christians, who in reality are Jews. They or their fathers were baptized, that is all. The assumption that many Jews in all ages changed their faith is not far fetched. We hear of cases from the earliest Middle Ages; in Italy, in the 7th and 8th centuries; at the same period in Spain and in the Merovingian kingdoms; and from that time to this we find them among all Christian nations. In the last third of the 19th century, indeed, wholesale baptisms constantly occurred. But we have reliable figures for the last two or three decades only, and I am therefore inclined to doubt the statement of Jacob Fromer that towards the end of the twenties in the last century something like half the Jews of Berlin had gone over to Christianity.[1] Equally improbable is the view of Dr. Werner, Rabbi in Munich, who, in a paper which he recently read, stated that altogether 120,000 Jews have been baptized in Berlin. The most reliable figures we have are all against such a likelihood. According to these, it was in the nineties that apostasy on a large scale first showed itself, and even then the highest annual percentage never exceeded 1·28 (in 1905), while the average percentage per annum (since 1895) was 1. Nevertheless, the number of Jews in Berlin who from 1873 to 1906 went over to Christianity was not small ; their total was 1869 precisely.[2]

The tendency to apostasy is stronger among Austrian Jews, especially among those of Vienna. At the present time, between five and six hundred Jews in that city renounce their faith every year, and from 1868 to 1903 there have been no less than 9085. The process grows apace ; in the years 1868 to 1879 there was on an average one baptism annually for every 1200 Jews ; in the period 1880 to 1889 it was one for 420–430 Jews ; while between 1890 and 1903 it had reached one for every 260–270.[3]

But the renegade Jews are not the only group whose influence on the economic development of our time it is difficult to estimate. There are others to which the same applies. I am not thinking of the Jewesses who married into Christian families, and who, though they thus ceased to be Jewish, at any rate in name, must nevertheless have retained their Jewish characteristics. The people I have in mind are the crypto-Jews, who played so important a part in history, and whom we encounter in every century. In some periods they formed a very large section of Jewry. But their non-Jewish pose was so admirably sustained that among their contemporaries they passed as Christians or Mohammedans. We are told, for example, of the Jews of the South of France in the 15th and 16th centuries, who came originally from Spain and Portugal (and the description applies to the Marannos everywhere) : " They practised all the outward forms of Catholicism ; their births, marriages and deaths were entered on the registers of the church, and they received the sacraments of baptism, marriage and extreme unction. Some even took orders and became priests."4 No wonder then that they do not appear as Jews in the reports of commercial enterprises, industrial undertakings and so forth. Some historians even to-day speak in admiring phrase of the beneficial influence of Spanish or Portuguese "immigrants." So skilfully did the crypto-Jews hide their racial origin that specialists in the field of Jewish history are still in doubt as to whether a certain family was Jewish or not.5 In those cases where they adopted Christian names, the uncertainty is even greater. There must have been a large number of Jews among the Protestant refugees in the 17th century. General reasons would warrant this assumption, but when we take into consideration the numerous Jewish names found among the Huguenots the probability is strong indeed.6

Finally, our enquiries will not be able to take any account of all those Jews who, prior to 1848, took an active part in the economic life of their time, but who were unknown to the authorities. The laws forbade Jews to exercise their callings. They were therefore compelled to do so, either under cover of some fictitious Christian person or under the protection of a "privileged" Jew, or they were forced to resort to some other trick in order to circumvent the law. Reliable authorities are of opinion that the number of Jews who in many a town lived secretly in this way must have been exceedingly large. In the forties of last century, for example, it is said that no less than 12,000 Jews, at a moderate estimate, were to be found in Vienna. The wholesale textile trade was at that time already in their hands, and entire districts in the centre of the city were full of Jewish shops. But the official list of traders of 1845 contained in an appendix the names of only sixty-three Jews, who were described as "tolerated Jewish traders,"

and these were allowed to deal only in a limited number
of articles.7

But enough. My point was to show that, for many
and various reasons, the number of Jews of whom we hear
is less than those who actually existed. The reader
should therefore bear in mind that the contribution of
the Jews to the fabric of modern economic life will,
of necessity, appear smaller than it was in reality.

What that contribution was we shall now proceed
to show.

CHAPTER II

THE SHIFTING OF THE CENTRE OF ECONOMIC LIFE SINCE THE SIXTEENTH CENTURY

ONE of the most important facts in the growth of modern economic life is the removal of the centre of economic activity from the nations of Southern Europe—the Italians, Spaniards and Portuguese, with whom must also be reckoned some South German lands—to those of the North-West—the Dutch, the French, the English and the North Germans. The epoch-making event in the process was Holland's sudden rise to prosperity, and this was the impetus for the development of the economic possibilities of France and England. All through the 17th century the philosophic speculators and the practical politicians among the nations of North-Western Europe had but one aim : to imitate Holland in commerce, in industry, in shipping and in colonization.

The most ludicrous explanations of this well-known fact have been suggested by historians. It has been said, for example, that the cause which led to the economic decline of Spain and Portugal and of the Italian and South German city states was the discovery of America and of the new route to the East Indies ; that the same cause lessened the volume of the commerce of the Levant, and therefore undermined the position of the Italian commercial cities which depended upon it. But this explanation is not in any way satisfactory. In the first place, Levantine commerce maintained its pre-eminence throughout the whole of the 17th and 18th centuries, and during this period the prosperity of the maritime cities in the South of France, as well as that of Hamburg, was very closely bound up with it.   In the second place, a number of Italian towns, Venice among them, which in the 17th century lost all their importance, participated to a large extent in the trade of the Levant in the 16th century, and that despite the neglect of the trade route.   It is a little difficult to understand why the nations which had played a leading part until the 15th century—the Italians, the Spaniards, the Portuguese—should have suffered in the least because of the new commercial relations with America and the East Indies, or why they should have been placed at any disadvantage by their geographical position as compared with that of the French, the English or the Dutch.   As though the way from Genoa to America or the West Indies were not the same as from Amsterdam or London or Hamburg !   As though the Spanish and Portuguese ports were not the nearest to the new lands—lands which had been discovered by Italians and Portuguese, and had been taken possession of by the Portuguese and the Spaniards !

Equally unconvincing is another reason which is often given.   It is asserted that the countries of North-Western Europe were strong consolidated states, while Germany and Italy were disunited, and accordingly the former were able to take up a stronger position than the latter.   Here, too, we ask in wonder whether the powerful Queen of the Adriatic was a weaker state in the 16th century than the Seven Provinces in the 17th ?   And did not the empire of Philip II excel all the kingdoms of his time in power and renown ?   Why was it, moreover, that, although Germany was in a state of political disruption, certain of its cities, like Hamburg or Frankfort-on-the-Main, reached a high degree of development in the 17th and

18th centuries, such as few French or English cities could rival ?

This is not the place to go into the question in all its many-sidedness. A number of causes contributed to bring about the results we have mentioned. But from the point of view of our problem one possibility should not be passed over which, in my opinion, deserves most serious consideration, and which, so far as I know, has not yet been thought of. Cannot we bring into connexion the shifting of the economic centre from Southern to Northern Europe with the wanderings of the Jews ? The mere suggestion at once throws a flood of light on the events of those days, hitherto shrouded in semi-darkness. It is indeed surprising that the parallelism has not before been observed between Jewish wanderings and settlement on the one hand, and the economic vicissitudes of the different peoples and states on the other. Israel passes over Europe like the sun : at its coming new life bursts forth ; at its going all falls into decay. A short résumé of the changing fortunes of the Jewish people since the 15th century will lend support to this contention.

The first event to be recalled, an event of world-wide import, is the expulsion of the Jews from Spain (1492) and from Portugal (1495 and 1497). It should never be forgotten that on the day before Columbus set sail from Palos to discover America (August 3, 1492) 300,000 Jews are said to have emigrated from Spain to Navarre, France, Portugal and the East ; nor that, in the years during which Vasco da Gama searched for and found the sea-passage to the East Indies, the Jews were driven from other parts of the Pyrenean Peninsula.[7A]

It was by a remarkable stroke of fate that these two occurrences, equally portentous in their significance—the opening-up of new continents and the mightiest upheavals in the distribution of the Jewish people—should have coin-

cided.   But the expulsion of the Jews from the Pyrenean
Peninsula did not altogether put an end to their history
there.   Numerous Jews remained behind as pseudo-
Christians (Marannos), and it was only as the Inquisition,
from the days of Philip II onwards, became more and
more relentless that these Jews were forced to leave
the land of their birth.[8]   During the centuries that
followed, and especially towards the end of the 16th,
the Spanish and Portuguese Jews settled' in other
countries.   It was during this period that the doom of
the economic prosperity of the Pyrenean Peninsula was
sealed.

With the 15th century came the expulsion of the Jews
from the German commercial cities—from Cologne
(1424-5), from Augsburg (1439-40), from Strassburg (1438), from Erfurt (1458), from Nuremberg
(1498-9), from Ulm (1499), and from Ratisbon (1519).

The same fate overtook them in the 16th century in a
number of Italian cities.   They were driven from Sicily
(1492), from Naples (1540-1), from Genoa and from
Venice (1550).   Here also economic decline and Jewish
emigration coincided in point of time.

On the other hand, the rise to economic importance, in
some cases quite unexpectedly, of the countries and towns
whither the refugees fled, must be dated from the first
appearance of the Spanish Jews.   A good example is that
of Leghorn,[9] one of the few Italian cities which enjoyed
economic prosperity in the 16th century.   Now Leghorn
was the goal of most of the exiles who made for Italy.
In Germany it was Hamburg and Frankfort[9A] that
admitted the Jewish settlers.   And remarkable to relate,
a keen-eyed traveller in the 18th century wandering all
over Germany found everywhere that the old commercial
cities of the Empire, Ulm, Nuremberg, Augsburg,
Mayence and Cologne, had fallen into decay, and that

the only two that were able to maintain their former splendour, and indeed to add to it from day to day, were Frankfort and Hamburg.[10]

In France in the 17th and 18th centuries the rising towns were Marseilles, Bordeaux, Rouen—again the havens of refuge of the Jewish exiles.[11]

As for Holland, it is well-known that at the end of the 16th century a sudden upward development (in the capitalistic sense) took place there. The first Portuguese Marannos settled in Amsterdam in 1593, and very soon their numbers increased. The first synagogue in Amsterdam was opened in 1598, and by about the middle of the 17th century there were Jewish communities in many Dutch cities. In Amsterdam, at the beginning of the 18th century, the estimated number of Jews was 2400.[12] But even by the middle of the 17th century their intellectual influence was already marked ; the writers on international law and the political philosophers speak of the ancient Hebrew commonwealth as an ideal which the Dutch constitution might well seek to emulate.[13] The Jews themselves called Amsterdam at that time their grand New Jerusalem.[14]

Many of the Dutch settlers had come from the Spanish Netherlands, especially from Antwerp, whither they had fled on their expulsion from Spain. It is true that the proclamations of 1532 and 1539 forbade the pseudo-Christians to remain in Antwerp, but they proved ineffective. The prohibition was renewed in 1550, but this time it referred only to those who had not been domiciled for six years. But this too remained a dead letter : "the crypto-Jews are increasing from day to day." They took an active part in the struggle for freedom in which the Netherlands were engaged, and its result forced them to wander to the more northerly provinces.[15] Now it is a remarkable thing that the brief space during which Antwerp became the commercial centre and the money-market of the world should have been just that between the coming and the going of the Marannos.[16]

It was the same in England. The economic development of the country, in other words, the growth of capitalism,[17] ran parallel with the influx of Jews, mostly of Spanish and Portuguese origin.[18]

It was believed that there were no Jews in England from the time of their expulsion under Edward I (1290) until their more or less officially recognized return under Cromwell (1654–56). The best authorities on Anglo-Jewish history are now agreed that this is a mistake. There were always Jews in England ; but not till the 16th century did they begin to be numerous. Already in the reign of Elizabeth many were met with, and the Queen herself had a fondness for Hebrew studies and for intercourse with Jews. Her own physician was a Jew, Rodrigo Lopez, on whom Shakespeare modelled his Shylock. Later on, as is generally known, the Jews, as a result of the efforts of Manasseh ben Israel, obtained the right of unrestricted domicile. Their numbers were increased by further streams of immigrants including, after the 18th century, Jews from Germany, until, according to the author of the *Anglia Judaica*, there were 6000 Jews in London alone in the year 1738.[19]

When all is said, however, the fact that the migration of the Jews and the economic vicissitudes of peoples were coincident events does not necessarily prove that the arrival of Jews in any land was the only cause of its rise or their departure the only cause of its decline. To assert as much would be to argue on the fallacy " post hoc, ergo propter hoc." Nor are the arguments of later historians on this subject conclusive, and therefore I will not mention any in support of my thesis.[20]   But the opinions of contemporaries always, as I think, deserve attention. So I will acquaint the reader with some of them, for very often a word suffices to throw a flood of light on their age.

When the Senate of Venice, in 1550, decided to expel the Marannos and to forbid commercial intercourse with them, the Christian merchants of the city declared that it would mean their ruin and that they might as well leave Venice with the exiles, seeing that they made their living by trading with the Jews. The Jews controlled the Spanish wool trade, the trade in Spanish silk and crimsons, sugar, pepper, Indian spices and pearls. A great part of the entire export trade was carried on by Jews, who supplied the Venetians with goods to be sold on commission ; and they were also bill-brokers.[21]

In England the Jews found a protector in Cromwell, who was actuated solely by considerations of an economic nature. He believed that he would need the wealthy Jewish merchants to extend the financial and commercial prosperity of the country. Nor was he blind to the usefulness of having moneyed support for the government.[22]

Like Cromwell, Colbert, the great French statesman of the 17th century, was also sympathetically inclined towards the Jews, and in my opinion it is of no small significance that these two organizers, both of whom consolidated modern European states, should have been so keenly alive to the fitness of the Jew in aiding the economic (*i.e.*, capitalistic) progress of a country. In one of his Ordinances to the Intendant of Languedoc, Colbert points out what great benefits the city of Marseilles derived from the commercial capabilities of the Jews.[23] The inhabitants of the great French trading centres in which the Jews played an important rôle were in no need of being taught the lesson ; they knew it from their own experience and, accordingly, they brought all their influence to bear on keeping their Jewish fellow-citizens within their walls. Again and again we hear laudatory accounts of the Jews, more especially from the inhabitants of Bordeaux. In 1675 an army of mercenaries ravaged Bordeaux, and many of the rich Jews prepared to depart. The Town Council was terrified, and the report presented by its members is worth quoting. " The Portuguese who occupy whole streets and do considerable business have asked for their passports. They and those aliens who do a very large trade are resolved to leave ; indeed, the wealthiest among them, Gaspar Gonzales and Alvares, have already departed. We are very much afraid that commerce will cease altogether." [24] A few years later the Sous-Intendant of Languedoc summed up the situation in the words " without them (the Jews) the trade of Bordeaux and of the whole province would be inevitably ruined." [25]

We have already seen how the fugitives from the Iberian Peninsula in the 16th century streamed into Antwerp, the commercial metropolis of the Spanish Netherlands. About the middle of the century, the Emperor in a decree dated July 17, 1549 withdrew the privileges which had been accorded them. Thereupon the mayor and sheriffs, as well as the Consul of the city, sent a petition to the Bishop of Arras in which they showed the obstacles in the way of carrying out the Imperial mandate. The Portuguese, they pointed out, were large undertakers ; they had brought great wealth with them from the lands of their birth, and they maintained an extensive trade. " We must bear in mind," they continued, " that Antwerp has grown great gradually, and that a long space of time was needed before it could obtain possession of its commerce. Now the ruin of the city would necessarily bring with it the ruin of the land, and all this must be carefully considered before the Jews are expelled." Indeed, the mayor, Nicholas Van den Meeren, went even further in the matter. When Queen Mary of Hungary, the Regent of the Netherlands, was staying in Ruppelmonde, he paid her a visit in order to defend the cause of the New Christians, and excused the conduct of the rulers of Antwerp in not publishing the Imperial decree by informing her that it was contrary to all the best interests of the city.[26] His efforts, however, were unsuccessful, and the Jews, as we have already seen, left Antwerp for Amsterdam.

Antwerp lost no small part of its former glory by reason of the departure of the Jews, and in the 17th century especially it was realized how much they contributed to bring about material prosperity. In 1653 a committee was appointed to consider the question whether the Jews should be allowed into Antwerp, and it expressed itself on the matter in the following terms : " And as for the inconveniences which are to be feared and apprehended in the public interest—that they (the Jews) will attract to themselves all trade, that they will be guilty of a thousand frauds and tricks, and that by their usury they will devour the wealth of good Catholics—it seems to us on the contrary that by the trade which they will expand far beyond its present limits the benefit derived will be for the good of the whole land, and gold and silver will be available in greater quantities for the needs of the state." [27]

The Dutch in the 17th century required no such recommendations ; they were fully alive to the gain which the Jews brought. When Manasseh ben Israel left Amsterdam on his famous mission to England, the Dutch Government became anxious ; they feared lest it should be a question of transplanting the Dutch Jews to

England, and they therefore instructed Neuport, their ambassador in London, to sound Manasseh as to his intentions. He reported (December 1655) that all was well, and that there was no cause for apprehension. "Manasseh ben Israel hath been to see me, and did assure me that he doth not desire anything for the Jews in Holland but only for those as sit in the Inquisition in Spain and Portugal." [28]

It is the same tale in Hamburg. In the 17th century the importance of the Jews had grown to such an extent that they were regarded as indispensable to the growth of Hamburg's prosperity. On one occasion the Senate asked that permission should be given for synagogues to be built, otherwise, they feared, the Jews would leave Hamburg, and the city might then be in danger of sinking to a mere village.[29] On another occasion, in 1697, when it was suggested that the Jews should be expelled, the merchants earnestly entreated the Senate for help, in order to prevent the serious endangering of Hamburg's commerce.[30] Again, in 1733, in a special report, now in the Archives of the Senate, we may read : "In bill-broking, in trade with jewellery and braid and in the manufacture of certain cloths the Jews have almost a complete mastery, and have surpassed our own people. In the past there was no need to take cognizance of them, but now they are increasing in numbers. There is no section of the great merchant class, the manufacturers and those who supply commodities for daily needs, but the Jews form an important element therein. They have become a necessary evil." [31] To the callings enumerated in which the Jews took a prominent part, we must add that of marine insurance brokers.[32]

So much for the judgment of contemporaries. But as a complete proof even that will not serve. We must form our own judgment from the facts, and therefore our first aim must be to seek these out. That means that we must find from the original sources what contributions the Jews made to the building-up of our modern economic life from the end of the 15th century onward—the period, that is, when Jewish history and general European economic progress both tended in the same direction. We shall then also be able to state definitely to what extent the Jews influenced the shifting of the centre of economic life.

My own view is, as I may say in anticipation, that the importance of the Jews was twofold. On the one hand, they influenced the outward form of modern capitalism ; on the other, they gave expression to its inward spirit. Under the first heading, the Jews contributed no small share in giving to economic relations the international aspect they bear to-day ; in helping the modern state, that framework of capitalism, to become what it is ; and lastly, in giving the capitalistic organization its peculiar features, by inventing a good many details of the commercial machinery which moves the business life of to-day, and by co-operating in the perfecting of others. Under the second heading, the importance of the Jews is so enormous because they, above all others, endowed economic life with its modern spirit ; they seized upon the essential idea of capitalism and carried it to its fullest development.

We shall consider these points in turn, in order to obtain a proper notion of the problem. Our intention is to do no more than ask a question or two, and here and there to suggest an answer. We want merely to set the reader thinking. It will be for later research to gather sufficient material by which to judge whether, and to what extent, the views as to cause and effect here propounded have any foundation in actual fact.

CHAPTER III

THE QUICKENING OF INTERNATIONAL TRADE

THE transformation of European commerce which has
taken place since the shifting of the centre of economic
activity owed a tremendous debt to the Jews. If we
consider nothing but the quantity of commodities that
passed through their hands, their position is unique.
Exact statistics are, as I have already remarked, almost
non-existent ; special research may, however, bring some
figures to light that will be useful. At present there
is, to my knowledge, only some slight material on this
head, but its value cannot be overestimated.

It would appear that even before their formal admission
into England—that is, in the first half of the 17th
century—the extent of the trade in the hands of Jews
totalled one-twelfth of that of the whole kingdom.[33]
Unfortunately we are not told on what authority this
calculation rests, but that it cannot be far from the truth
is apparent from a statement in a petition of the merchants of London. The question was whether Jews
should pay the duty on imports levied on foreigners.
The petitioners point out that if the Jews were exempted,
the Crown would sustain a loss of ten thousand pounds
annually.[34]

We are remarkably well informed as to the proportion
of trading done by Jews at the Leipzig fairs,[35] and as
these were for a long period the centre of German commerce, we have here a standard by which to measure its

intensive and extensive development. But not alone for Germany. One or two of the neighbouring countries, especially Bohemia and Poland, can also be included in the survey. From the end of the 17th century onwards we find that the Jews take an increasing share in the fairs, and all the authorities who have gone into the figures are agreed that it was the Jews who gave to the Leipzig fairs their great importance.[36]

It is only since the Easter fair of 1756 that we are able to compare the Jewish with the Christian traders, as far as numbers are concerned, for it is only from that date that the Archives possess statistics of the latter. The average number of Jews attending the Leipzig fair was as follows:—

1675–1680	... ...	416	1767–1769	... ...	995
1681–1690	... ...	489	1770–1779	... ...	1652
1691–1700	... ...	834	1780–1789	... ...	1073
1701–1710	... ...	854	1790–1799	... ...	1473
1711–1720	... ...	769	1800–1809	... ...	3370
1721–1730	... ...	899	1810–1819	... ...	4896
1731–1740	... ...	874	1820–1829	... ...	3747
1741–1748	... ...	708	1830–1839	... ...	6444

Note especially the speedy increase towards the end of the 17th and 18th centuries and also at the beginning of the 19th.

If we glance at the period 1766 to 1839, we see that the fairs were visited annually by an average of 3185 Jews and 13,005 Christians—that is to say, the Jews form 24·49 per cent., or nearly one-quarter of the total number of Christian merchants. Indeed, in some years, as for example between 1810 and 1820, the Jewish visitors form 33⅓ per cent. of the total of their colleagues (4896 Jews and 14,366 Christians). This is significant enough, and there is no need to lay stress on the fact that in all probability the figures given in the table are underestimated.

The share taken by Jews in the commerce of a country may sometimes be ascertained by indirect means. We know, for example, that the trade of Hamburg with Spain and Portugal, and also with Holland, in the 17th century was almost entirely in the hands of the Jews.[37] Now some 20 per cent. of the ships' cargoes leaving Hamburg were destined for the Iberian Peninsula, and some 30 per cent. for Holland.[38]

Take another instance. The Levant trade was the most important branch of French commerce in the 18th century. A contemporary authority informs us that it was entirely controlled by Jews—" buyers, sellers, middlemen, bill-brokers, agents and so forth were all Jews." [39]

In the 16th and 17th centuries, and even far into the 18th, the trade of the Levant as well as that with, and *via*, Spain and Portugal, was the broadest stream in the world's commerce. This mere generalization goes far to prove how pre-eminent, from the purely quantitative point of view, the Jews were in forwarding the development of international intercourse. Already in Spain the Jews had managed to obtain control of the greater portion of the Levant trade, and everywhere in the Levantine ports Jewish offices and warehouses were to be found. Many Spanish Jews at the time of the expulsion from Spain settled in the East ; the others journeyed northwards. So it came about that almost imperceptibly the Levantine trade became associated with the more northerly peoples. In Holland, more especially, is the effect of this seen : Holland became a commercial country of world-wide influence. Altogether, the commercial net, so to say, became bigger and stronger in proportion as the Jews established their offices, on the one hand further afield, on the other in closer proximity to each other.[40] More particularly was this the case when the Western Hemisphere—largely through Jewish influence—was drawn into the commerce of the world. We shall have more to say on this aspect of the question in connexion with the part the Jews played in colonial foundations.

Another means by which we may gain a clear conception of what the Jews did for the extension of modern commerce is to discover the kind of commodities in which they for the most part traded. The quality of the commerce matters more than its quantity. It was by the character of their trade that they partially revolutionized the older forms, and thus helped to make commerce what it is to-day.

Here we are met by a striking fact. The Jews for a long time practically monopolized the trade in articles of luxury, and to the fashionable world of the aristocratic 17th and 18th centuries this trade was of supreme moment. What sort of commodities, then, did the Jews specialize in? Jewellery, precious stones, pearls and silks.[41] Gold and silver jewellery, because they had always been prominent in the market for precious metals. Pearls and stones, because they were among the first to settle in those lands (especially Brazil) where these are to be found ; and silks, because of their ancient connexions with the trading centres of the Orient.

Moreover, Jews were to be found almost entirely, or at least predominantly, in such branches of trade as were concerned with exportation on a large scale. Nay, I believe it may with justice be asserted that the Jews were the first to place on the world's markets the staple articles of modern commerce. Side by side with the products of the soil, such as wheat, wool, flax, and, later on, distilled spirits, they dealt throughout the 18th century specially in textiles,[42] the output of a rapidly growing capitalistic industry, and in those colonial products which for the first time became articles of international trade, viz., sugar and tobacco. I have little doubt that when the history of commerce in modern times comes to be written Jewish traders will constantly be met with in connexion with enterprises on a large scale. The references which quite by accident have come under my notice are already sufficient to prove the truth of this assertion.[43]

Perhaps the most far-reaching, because the most revolutionary, influence of the Jews on the development of economic life was due to their trade in new commodities, in the preparation of which new methods supplanted the old. We may mention cotton,[44] cotton goods of foreign make, indigo and so forth.[45] Dealing in these articles was looked upon at the time as " spoiling sport," and therefore Jews were taunted by one German writer with carrying on "unpatriotic trade " [46] or " Jew-commerce, which gave little employment to German labour, and depended for the most part on home consumption only." [47]

Another great characteristic of " Jew-commerce," one which all later commerce took for its model, was its variety and many-sidedness. When in 1740 the merchants of Montpelier complained of the competition of the Jewish traders, the Intendant replied that if they, the Christians, had such well-assorted stocks as the Jews, customers would come to them as willingly as they went to their Jewish competitors.[48] We hear the same of the Jews at the Leipzig fairs : " The Jewish traders had a beneficial influence on the trade of the fairs, in that their purchases were so varied. Thus it was the Jews who tended to make trade many-sided and forced industry (especially the home industries) to develop in more than one direction. Indeed, at many fairs the Jews became the arbiters of the market by reason of their extensive purchases." 49

But the greatest characteristic of " Jew-commerce " during the earlier capitalistic age was, to my mind, the supremacy which Jewish traders obtained, either directly or by way of Spain and Portugal, in the lands from which it was possible to draw large supplies of ready money. I am thinking of the newly discovered gold and silver countries in Central and South America. Again and again we find it recorded that the Jews brought ready money into the country.50 The theoretical speculator and the practical politician knew well enough that here was the source of all capitalistic development. We too, now that the mists of Adam Smith's doctrines have lifted, have realized the same thing. The establishment of modern economic life meant, for the most part, and of necessity, the obtaining of the precious metals, and in this work no one was so successfully engaged as the Jewish traders. This leads us at once to the subject of the next chapter, which deals with the share of the Jews in colonial expansion.

CHAPTER IV

THE FOUNDATION OF MODERN COLONIES

WE are only now beginning to realize that colonial expansion was no small force in the development of modern capitalism. It is the purpose of this chapter to show that in the work of that expansion the Jews played, if not the most decisive, at any rate a most prominent part.

That the Jews should have been keen colonial settlers was only natural, seeing that the New World, though it was but the Old in a new garb, seemed to hold out a greater promise of happiness to them than cross-grained old Europe, more especially when their last Dorado (Spain) proved an inhospitable refuge. And this applies equally to all colonial enterprises, whether in the East or the West or the South of the globe. There were probably many Jews resident in the East Indies even in mediæval times,[51] and when the nations of Europe, after 1498, stretched out their hands to seize the lands of an ancient civilization, the Jews were welcomed as bulwarks of European supremacy, though primarily they came as pioneers of trade. In all likelihood—exact proofs have not yet been established—the ships of the Portuguese and of the Dutch must have brought shoals of Jewish settlers to their respective Indian possessions. At any rate, Jews participated extensively in all the Dutch settlements, including those in the East. We are told that Jews were large shareholders in the Dutch East

India Company.52 We know that the Governor of
the Company who, "if he did not actually establish the
power of Holland in Java, certainly contributed most to
strengthen it," 53 was called Cohn (Coen). Furthermore, a glance at the portraits of the Governors of the
Dutch colonies would make it appear that this Coen
is not the only Jew among them.54 Jews were also
Directors of the Company ; 55 in short, no colonial
enterprise was complete without them.56

It is as yet unknown to what extent the Jews shared in
the growth of economic life in India after the English
became masters there. We have, however, fairly full
information as to the participation of the Jews in the
founding of the English colonies in South Africa and
Australia. There is no doubt that in these regions (more
particularly in Cape Colony), well-nigh all economic
development was due to the Jews. In the twenties and
thirties of the 19th century Benjamin Norden and Simon
Marks came to South Africa, and " the industrial
awakening of almost the whole interior of Cape Colony "
was their work. Julius Mosenthal and his brothers
Adolph and James established the trade in wool, skins,
and mohair. Aaron and Daniel de Pass monopolized the
whaling industry ; Joel Myers commenced ostrich
farming. Lilienfeld, of Hopetown, bought the first
diamonds.57 Similar leading positions were occupied
by the Jews in the other South African colonies, particularly in the Transvaal, where it is said that to-day twenty-
five of the fifty thousand Jews of South Africa are
settled.58 It is the same story in Australia, where
the first wholesale trader was Montefiore. It would
seem to be no exaggeration therefore that " a large
proportion of the English colonial shipping trade was
for a considerable time in the hands of the Jews." 59

But the real sphere of Jewish influence in colonial

settlements, especially in the early capitalistic period, was in the Western Hemisphere. America in all its borders is a land of Jews. That is the result to which a study of the sources must inevitably lead, and it is pregnant with meaning. From the first day of its discovery America has had a strong influence on the economic life of Europe and on the whole of its civilization ; and therefore the part which the Jews have played in building up the American world is of supreme import as an element in modern development. That is why I shall dwell on this theme a little more fully, even at the risk of wearying the reader.[60]

The very discovery of America is most intimately bound up with the Jews in an extraordinary fashion. It is as though the New World came into the horizon by their aid and for them alone, as though Columbus and the rest were but managing directors for Israel. It is in this light that Jews, proud of their past, now regard the story of that discovery, as set forth in the latest researches.[61] These would seem to show that it was the scientific knowledge of Jewish scholars which so perfected the art of navigation that voyages across the ocean became at all possible. Abraham Zacuto, Professor of Mathematics and Astronomy at the University of Salamanca, completed his astronomical tables and diagrams, the *Almanach perpetuum*, in 1473. On the basis of these tables two other Jews, Jose Vecuho, who was Court astronomer and physician to John II of Portugal, and one Moses the Mathematician (in collaboration with two Christian scholars), discovered the nautical astrolabe, an instrument by which it became possible to measure from the altitude of the sun the distance of a ship from the Equator. Jose further translated the Almanack of his master into Latin and Spanish.

The scientific facts which prepared the way for the

voyage of Columbus were thus supplied by Jews. The money which was equally necessary came from the same quarter, at any rate as regards his first two voyages. For the first voyage, Columbus obtained a loan from Louis de Santangel, who was of the King's Council ; and it was to Santangel, the patron of the expedition, and to Gabriel Saniheg, a Maranno, the Treasurer of Aragon, that the first two letters of Columbus were addressed. The second voyage was also undertaken with the aid of Jewish money, this time certainly not voluntarily con- tributed. On their expulsion from Spain in 1492, the Jews were compelled to leave much treasure behind ; this was seized by Ferdinand for the State Exchequer, and with a portion of it Columbus was financed.

But more than that. A number of Jews were among the companions of Columbus, and the first European to set foot on American soil was a Jew—Louis de Torres. So the latest researches would have us believe.[62]

But what caps all—Columbus himself is claimed to have been a Jew. I give this piece of information for what it is worth, without guaranteeing its accuracy. At a meeting of the Geographical Society of Madrid, Don Celso Garcia de la Riega, a scholar famous for his researches on Columbus, read a paper in which he stated that Christobal Colon (not Columbus) was a Spaniard who on his mother's side was of Jewish descent. He showed by reference to documents in the town of Pontevedra, in the province of Galicia, that the family of Colon lived there between 1428 and 1528, and that the Christian names found among them were the same as those prevalent among the relatives of the Spanish admiral. These Colons and the Fonterosa family inter- married. The latter were undoubtedly Jews, or they had only recently been converted, and Christobal's mother was called Suzanna Fonterosa. When disorders broke

out in the province of Galicia the parents of the discoverer of America migrated from Spain to Italy. These
facts were substantiated by Don Celso from additional
sources, and he is strengthened in his belief by distinct
echoes of Hebrew literature found in the writings of
Columbus, and also because the oldest portraits show him
to have had a Jewish face.

Scarcely were the doors of the New World opened to
Europeans than crowds of Jews came swarming in. We
have already seen that the discovery of America took
place in the year in which the Jews of Spain became
homeless, that the last years of the 15th century and
the early years of the 16th were a period in which
millions of Jews were forced to become wanderers, when
European Jewry was like an ant-heap into which a stick
had been thrust. Little wonder, therefore, that a great
part of this heap betook itself to the New World, where
the future seemed so bright. The first traders in
America were Jews. The first industrial establishments
in America were those of Jews. Already in the year
1492 Portuguese Jews settled in St. Thomas, where they
were the first plantation owners on a large scale ; they set
up many sugar factories and gave employment to nearly
three thousand negroes.[63] And as for Jewish emigration to South America, almost as soon as it was
discovered, the stream was so great that Queen Joan
in 1511 thought it necessary to take measures to stem
it.[64] But her efforts must have been without avail, for
the number of Jews increased, and finally, on May 21,
1577, the law forbidding Jews to emigrate to the Spanish
colonies was formally repealed.

In order to do full justice to the unceasing activity of
the Jews in South America as founders of colonial
commerce and industry, it will be advisable to glance
at the fortunes of one or two colonies.

The history of the Jews in the American colonies, and therefore the history of the colonies themselves, falls into two periods, separated by the expulsion of the Jews from Brazil in 1654.

We have already mentioned the establishment of the sugar industry in St. Thomas by Jews in 1492. By the year 1550 this industry had reached the height of its development on the island. There were sixty plantations with sugar mills and refineries, producing annually, as may be seen from the tenth part paid to the King, 150,000 arrobes of sugar.[65]

From St. Thomas, or possibly from Madeira,[66] where they had for a long time been engaged in the sugar trade, the Jews transplanted the industry to Brazil, the largest of the American colonies. Brazil thus entered on its first period of prosperity, for the growth of the sugar industry brought with it the growth of the national wealth. In those early years the colony was populated almost entirely by Jews and criminals, two shiploads of them being brought thither annually from Portugal.[67] The Jews quickly became the dominant class, " a not inconsiderable number of the wealthiest Brazilian traders were New Christians."[68] The first Governor-General was of Jewish origin, and he it was who brought order into the government of the colony. It is not too much to say that Portugal's new possessions really began to thrive only after Thomé de Souza, a man of exceptional ability, was sent out in 1549 to take matters in hand.[69] Nevertheless the colony did not reach the zenith of its prosperity until after the influx of rich Jews from Holland, consequent on the Dutch entering into possession in 1642. In that very year, a number of American Jews combined to establish a colony in Brazil, and no less than six hundred influential Dutch Jews joined them.[70] Up to about the middle of the 17th century all the large sugar plantations belonged to Jews,[71] and contemporary travellers report as to their many-sided activities and their wealth. Thus Nieuhoff, who travelled in Brazil from 1640 to 1649, says of them :[72] "Among the free inhabitants of Brazil that were not in the (Dutch West India) Company's service the Jews were the most considerable in number, who had transplanted themselves thither from Holland. They had a vast traffic beyond the rest ; they purchased sugar-mills and built stately houses in the Receif. They were all traders, which would have been of great consequence to the Dutch Brazil had they kept themselves within the due bounds of traffic." Similarly we read in F. Pyrard's *Travels* [72] : "The profits they make after being nine or ten years in those lands are marvellous, for they all come back rich."

The predominance of Jewish influence in plantation development outlasted the episode of Dutch rule in Brazil, and continued, despite the expulsion of 1654,[73] down to the first half of the 11th century.[74] On one occasion, "when a number of the most influential merchants of Rio de Janeiro fell into the hands of the Holy Office (of the Inquisition), the work on so many plantations came to a standstill that the production and commerce of the Province (of Bahia) required a long stretch of time to recover from the blow." Later, a decree of the 2nd March 1768 ordered all the registers containing lists of New Christians to be destroyed, and by a law of 25th March 1773 New Christians were placed on a footing of perfect civic equality with the orthodox. It is evident, then, that very many crypto-Jews must have maintained their prominent position in Brazil even after the Portuguese had regained possession of it in 1654, and that it was they who brought to the country its flourishing sugar industry as well as its trade in precious stones.

Despite this, the year 1654 marks an epoch in the annals of American-Jewish history. For it was in that year that a goodly number of the Brazilian Jews settled in other parts of America and thereby moved the economic centre of gravity.

The change was specially profitable to one or two important islands of the West Indian Archipelago and also to the neighbouring coastlands, which rose in prosperity from the time of the Jewish influx in the 17th century. Barbados, which was inhabited almost solely by Jews, is a case in point.75 It came under English rule in 1627 ; in 1641 the sugar cane was introduced, and seven years later the exportation of sugar began. But the sugar industry could not maintain itself. The sugar produced was so poor in quality that its price was scarcely sufficient to pay for the cost of transport to England. Not till the exiled " Dutchmen " from Brazil introduced the process of refining and taught the natives the art of drying and crystallizing the sugar did an improvement manifest itself. As a result, the sugar exports of Barbados increased by leaps and bounds, and in 1661 Charles II was able to confer baronetcies on thirteen planters, who drew an annual income of £10,000 from the island. By about the year 1676 the industry there had grown to such an extent that no fewer than 400 vessels each carrying 180 tons of raw sugar left annually.

In 1664 Thomas Modyford introduced sugar manufacturing from Barbados into Jamaica,76 which in consequence soon became wealthy. Now, while in 1656, the year in which the English finally wrested the island from Spain, there were only three small refineries in Jamaica, in 1670 there were already 75 mills at work, many of them having an output of 2000 cwts. By 1700 sugar was the principal export of Jamaica and the source of its riches. The petition of the English merchants of the colony in 1671, asking for the exclusion of the Jews, makes it pretty plain that the latter must have contributed largely to this development. The Government however, encouraged the settlement of still more Jews, the Governor in rejecting the petition remarking [77] that " he was of opinion that his Majesty could not have more profitable subjects than the Jews and the Hollanders ; they had great stocks and correspondence." So the Jews were not expelled from Jamaica, but " became the first traders and merchants of the English colony." [78] In the 18th century they paid all the taxes and almost entirely controlled industry and commerce.

Of the other English colonies, the Jews showed a special preference for Surinam.[79] Jews had been settled there since 1644 and had received a number of privileges—" whereas we have found that the Hebrew nation . . . have . . . proved themselves useful and beneficial to the colony." Their privileged position continued under the Dutch, to whom Surinam passed in 1667. Towards the end of the 17th century their proportion to the rest of the inhabitants was as one to three, and in 1730 they owned 115 of the 344 sugar plantations.

The story of the Jews in the English and Dutch colonies finds a counterpart in the more important French settlements, such as Martinique, Guadeloupe, and San Domingo.[80] Here also sugar was the source of wealth, and, as in the other cases, the Jews controlled the industry and were the principal sugar merchants.

The first large plantation and refinery in Martinique was established in 1655 by Benjamin Dacosta, who had fled thither from Brazil with 900 co-religionists and 1100 slaves.

In San Domingo the sugar industry was introduced as

early as 1587, but it was not until the " Dutch " refugees from Brazil settled there that it attained any degree of success.

In all this we must never lose sight of the fact that in those critical centuries in which the colonial system was taking root in America (and with it modern capitalism), the production of sugar was the backbone of the entire colonial economy, leaving out of account, of course, the mining of silver, gold and gems in Brazil. Indeed, it is somewhat difficult exactly to picture to ourselves the enormous significance in those centuries of sugar-making and sugar-selling. The Council of Trade in Paris (1701) was guilty of no exaggerated language when it placed on record its belief that " French shipping owes its splendour to the commerce of the sugar-producing islands, and it is only by means of this that the navy can be maintained and strengthened." Now, it must be remembered that the Jews had almost monopolized the sugar trade ; the French branch in particular being controlled by the wealthy family of the Gradis of Bordeaux.[81]

The position which the Jews had obtained for themselves in Central and South America was thus a powerful one. But it became even more so when towards the end of the 17th century the English colonies in North America entered into commercial relations with the West Indies. To this close union, which again Jewish merchants helped to bring about, the North American Continent (as we shall see) owes its existence. We have thus arrived at the point where it is essential to consider the Jewish factor in the growth of the United States from their first origins. Once more Jewish elements combined, this time to give the United States their ultimate economic form. As this view is absolutely opposed to that generally accepted (at least in Europe), the question must receive full consideration.

At first sight it would seem as if the economic system of North America was the very one that developed independently of the Jews. Often enough, when I have asserted that modern capitalism is nothing more or less than an expression of the Jewish spirit, I have been told that the history of the United States proves the contrary. The Yankees themselves boast of the fact that they throve without the Jews. It was an American writer—Mark Twain, if I mistake not—who once considered at some length why the Jews played no great part in the States, giving as his reason that the Americans were as " smart " as the Jews, if not smarter. (The Scotch, by the way, think the same of themselves.) Now, it is true that we come across no very large number of Jewish names to-day among the big captains of industry, the well-known speculators, or the Trust magnates in the country. Nevertheless, I uphold my assertion that the United States (perhaps more than any other land) are filled to the brim with the Jewish spirit. This is recognized in many quarters, above all in those best capable of forming a judgment on the subject. Thus, a few years ago, at the magnificent celebration of the 250th anniversary of the first settlement of the Jews in the United States, President Roosevelt sent a congratulatory letter to the Organizing Committee. In this he said that that was the first time during his tenure of office that he had written a letter of the kind, but that the importance of the occasion warranted him in making an exception. The persecution to which the Jews were then being subjected made it an urgent duty for him to lay stress on the splendid civic qualities which men of the Jewish faith and race had developed ever since they came into the country. In mentioning the services rendered by Jews to the United States he used an expression which goes to the root of the matter—" The Jews participated in the up-building

of this country." [82] On the same occasion ex-President
Cleveland remarked : " I believe that it can be safely
claimed that few, if any, of those contributing nationalities
have directly and indirectly been more influential in
giving shape and direction to the Americanism of
to-day." [83]

Wherein does this Jewish influence manifest itself ?
In the first place, the number of Jews who took part in
American business life was never so small as would appear
at the first glance. It is a mistake to imagine that because
there are no Jews among the half-dozen well-known
multi-millionaires, male and female, who on account of
the noise they make in the world are on all men's lips,
therefore American capitalism necessarily lacks a Jewish
element. To begin with, even among the big Trusts there
are some directed by Jewish hands and brains. Thus,
the Smelters' Trust, which in 1904 represented a combination with a nominal capital of 201,000,000 dollars,
was the creation of Jews—the Guggenheims. Thus,
too, in the Tobacco Trust (500,000,000 dollars), in the
Asphalt Trust, in the Telegraph Trust, to mention but
a few, Jews occupy commanding positions.[84] Again,
very many of the large banking-houses belong to Jews, who
in consequence exercise no small control over American
economic life. Take the Harriman system, which had
for its goal the fusion of all the American railways. It
was backed to a large extent by Kuhn, Loeb & Co., the
well-known banking firm of New York. Especially
influential are the Jews in the West. California is for
the most part their creation. At the foundation of the
State Jews obtained distinction as Judges, Congressmen,
Governors, Mayors, and so on, and last but not least,
as business men. The brothers Seligman—William,
Henry, Jesse and James—of San Francisco ; Louis Sloss
and Lewis Gerstle of Sacramento (where they established

the Alaska Commercial Company), Hellman and New-mark of Los Angelos, are some of the more prominent business houses in this part of the world. During the gold-mining period Jews were the intermediaries between California and the Eastern States and Europe. The important transactions of those days were undertaken by such men as Benjamin Davidson, the agent of the Roth-schilds ; Albert Priest, of Rhode Island ; Albert Dyer, of Baltimore ; the three brothers Lazard, who established the international banking-house of Lazard Frères of Paris, London and San Francisco ; the Seligmans, the Glaziers and the Wormsers. Moritz Friedlaender was one of the chief " Wheat kings." Adolph Sutro exploited the Comstock Lodes. Even to-day the majority of the banking businesses, no less than the general industries, are in the hands of Jews. Thus, we may mention the London, Paris and American Bank (Sigmund Greenbaum and Richard Altschul) ; the Anglo-Californian Bank (Philip N. Lilienthal and Ignatz Steinhart) ; the Nevada Bank ; the Union Trust Company ; the Farmers' and Merchants' Bank of Los Angelos ; John Rosenfeld's control of the coalfields ; the Alaska Commercial Company, which succeeded the Hudson Bay Company ; the North American Commercial Company, and many more.[85]

It can scarcely be doubted that the immigration of numerous Jews into all the States during the last few decades must have had a stupendous effect on American economic life everywhere. Consider that there are more than a million Jews in New York to-day, and that the greater number of the immigrants have not yet embarked on a capitalistic career. If the conditions in America continue to develop along the same lines as in the last generation, if the immigration statistics and the proportion of births among all the nationalities remain the same, our imagination may picture the United States of fifty or a hundred years hence as a land inhabited only by Slavs, Negroes and Jews, wherein the Jews will naturally occupy the position of economic leadership.

But these are dreams of the future which have no place in this connexion, where our main concern is with the past and the present. That Jews have taken a prominent share in American life in the present and in the past may be conceded ; perhaps a more prominent share than would at first sight appear. Nevertheless, the enormous weight which, in common with many others who have the right of forming an opinion on the subject, I attach to their influence, cannot be adequately explained merely from the point of view of their numbers. It is rather the particular kind of influence that I lay stress on, and this can be accounted for by a variety of complex causes.

That is why I am not anxious to overemphasize the fact, momentous enough in itself, that the Jews in America practically control a number of important branches of commerce ; indeed, it is not too much to say that they monopolize them, or at least did so for a considerable length of time. Take the wheat trade, especially in the West ; take tobacco ; take cotton. We see at once that they who rule supreme in three such mighty industries must perforce take a leading part in the economic activities of the nation as a whole. For all that I do not labour this fact, for to my mind the significance of the Jews for the economic development of the United States lies rooted in causes far deeper than these.

As the golden thread in the tapestry, so are the Jews interwoven as a distinct thread throughout the fabric of America's economic history ; through the intricacy of their fantastic design it received from the very beginning a pattern all its own.

Since the first quickening of the capitalistic spirit on the coastlands of the ocean and in the forests and prairies of the New World, Jews have not been absent ; 1655 is usually given as the date of their first appearance.[86] In that year a vessel with Jewish emigrants from Brazil, which had become a Portuguese possession, anchored in the Hudson River, and the passengers craved permission to land in the colony which the Dutch West India Company had founded there. But they were no humble petitioners asking for a favour. They came as members of a race which had participated to a large extent in the new foundation, and the governors of the colony were forced to recognize their claims. When the ship arrived, New Amsterdam was under the rule of Stuyvesant, who was no friend to the Jews and who, had he followed his own inclination, would have closed the door in the face of the newcomers. But a letter dated March 26, 1665, reached him from the Court of the Company in Amsterdam, containing the order to let the Jews settle and trade in the colonies under the control of the Company, " also because of the large amount of capital which they have invested in shares of this Company." [87] It was not long before they found their way to Long Island, Albany, Rhode Island and Philadelphia.

Then their manifold activities began, and it was due to them that the colonies were able to maintain their existence. The entity of the United States to-day is only possible, as we know, because the English colonies of North America, thanks to a chain of propitious circumstances, acquired a degree of power and strength such as ultimately led to their complete independence. In the building up of this position of supremacy the Jews were among the first and the keenest workers.

I am not thinking of the obvious fact that the colonies were only able to achieve their independence by the help of a few wealthy Jewish firms who laid the economic foundations for the existence of the New Republic. The

United States would never have won complete independence had not the Jews supplied the needs of their armies and furnished them with the indispensable sinews of war. But what the Jews accomplished in this direction did not arise out of specifically American conditions. It was a general phenomenon, met with throughout the history of the modern capitalistic States, and we shall do justice to instances of it when dealing with wider issues.

No. What I have in mind is the special service which the Jews rendered the North American colonies, one peculiar to the American Continent—a service which indeed gave America birth. I refer to the simple fact that during the 17th and 18th centuries the trade of the Jews was the source from which the economic system of the colonies drew its life-blood. As is well known, England forced her colonies to purchase all the manufactured articles they needed in the Mother-country. Hence the balance of trade of the colonies was always an adverse one, and by constantly having to send money out of the country they would have been drained dry. But there was a stream which carried the precious metals into the country, a stream diverted in this direction by the trade of the Jews with South and Central America. The Jews in the English colonies maintained active business relations with the West Indian Islands and with Brazil, resulting in a favourable balance of trade for the land of their sojourn. The gold mined in South America was thus brought to North America and helped to keep the economic system in a healthy condition.[88]

In the face of this fact, is there not some justification for the opinion that the United States owe their very existence to the Jews? And if this be so, how much more can it be asserted that Jewish influence made the United States just what they are—that is, American?

For what we call Americanism is nothing else, if we may say so, than the Jewish spirit distilled.

But how comes it that American culture is so steeped in Jewishness ?   The answer is simple—through the early and universal admixture of Jewish elements among the first settlers.   We may picture the process of colonizing somewhat after this fashion.   A band of determined men and women—let us say twenty families—went forth into the wilds to begin their life anew.   Nineteen were equipped with plough and scythe, ready to clear the forests and till the soil in order to earn their livelihood as husbandmen.   The twentieth family opened a store to provide their companions with such necessaries of life as could not be obtained from the soil, often no doubt hawking them at the very doors.   Soon this twentieth family made it its business to arrange for the distribution of the products which the other nineteen won from the soil.   It was they, too, who were most likely in possession of ready cash, and in case of need could therefore be useful to the others by lending them money.   Very often the store had a kind of agricultural loan-bank as its adjunct, perhaps also an office for the buying and selling of land. So through the activity of the twentieth family the farmer in North America was from the first kept in touch with the money and credit system of the Old World.   Hence the whole process of production and exchange was from its inception along modern lines.   Town methods made their way at once into even the most distant villages. Accordingly, it may be said that American economic life was from its very start impregnated with capitalism.   And who was responsible for this ?   The twentieth family in each village.   Need we add that this twentieth family was always a Jewish one, which joined a party of settlers or soon sought them out in their homesteads ?

Such in outline is the mental picture I have conceived

of the economic development of the United States. Subsequent writers dealing with this subject will be able to fill in more ample details ; I myself have only come across a few. But these are so similar in character that they can hardly be taken as isolated instances. The conclusion is forced upon us that they are typical. Nor do I alone hold this view. Governor Pardel of California, for example, remarked in 1905 : " He (the Jew) has been the leading financier of thousands of prosperous communities. He has been enterprising and aggressive." [89]

Let me quote some of the illustrations I have met with. In 1785 Abraham Mordecai settled in Alabama. " He established a trading-post two miles west of Line Creek, carrying on an extensive trade with the Indians, and exchanging his goods for pinkroot, hickory, nut oil and peltries of all kinds." [90] Similarly in Albany : " As early as 1661, when Albany was but a small trading post, a Jewish trader named Asser Levi (or Leevi) became the owner of real estate there." [91] Chicago has the same story. The first brick house was built by a Jew, Benedict Schubert, who became the first merchant tailor in Chicago, while another Jew, Philip Newburg, was the first to introduce the tobacco business. [92] In Kentucky we hear of a Jewish settler as early as 1816. When in that year the Bank of the United States opened a branch in Lexington, a Mr. Solomon, who had arrived in 1808, was made cashier. [93] In Maryland, [94] Michigan, [95] Ohio [96] and Pennsylvania [97] it is on record that Jewish traders were among the earliest settlers, though nothing is known of their activity.

On the other hand, a great deal is known of Jews in Texas, where they were among the pioneers of capitalism. Thus, for example, Jacob de Cordova " was by far the most extensive land locator in the State until 1856." The Cordova's Land Agency soon became famous not only in

Texas but in New York, Philadelphia and Baltimore, where the owners of large tracts of Texas land resided. Again, Morris Koppore in 1863 became President of the National Bank of Texas. Henry Castro was an immigration agent ; " between the years 1843–6 Castro introduced into Texas over 5000 immigrants . . . transporting them in 27 ships, chiefly from the Rhenish provinces. . . . He fed his colonists for a year, furnished them with cows, farming implements, seeds, medicine, and in short with everything they needed." [98]

Sometimes branches of one and the same family distributed themselves in different States, and were thereby enabled to carry on business most successfully. Perhaps the best instance is the history of the Seligman family. There were eight brothers (the sons of David Seligman, of Bayersdorf, in Bavaria) who started a concern which now has branches in all the most important centres in the States. Their story began with the arrival in America in the year 1837 of Joseph Seligman. Two other brothers followed in 1839 ; a third came two years later. The four began business as clothiers in Lancaster, moving shortly after to Selma Ala. From here they opened three branches in three other towns. By 1848 two more brothers had arrived from Germany and the six moved North. In 1850, Jesse Seligman opened a shop in San Francisco—in the first brick house in that city. Seven years later a banking business was added to the clothing shop, and in 1862 the house of Seligman Brothers was established in New York, San Francisco, London, Paris and Frankfort.[99]

In the Southern States likewise the Jew played the part of the trader in the midst of agricultural settlers.[100] Here also (as in Southern and Central America) we find him quite early as the owner of vast plantations. In South Carolina indeed, " Jew's Land " is synonymous

with "Large Plantations."[101]   It was in the South that
Moses Lindo became famous as one of the first undertakers in the production of indigo.

These examples must suffice. We believe they tend
to illustrate our general statement, which is supported
also by the fact that there was a constant stream of Jewish
emigration to the United States from their earliest
foundation. It is true that there are no actual figures
to show the proportion of the Jewish population to the
total body of settlers. But the numerous indications of
a general nature that we do find make it pretty certain
that there must always have been a large number of Jews
in America.

It must not be forgotten that in the earliest years the
population was thinly scattered and very sparse. New
Amsterdam had less than 1000 inhabitants.[102] That
being so, a shipful of Jews who came from Brazil to
settle there made a great difference, and in assessing
Jewish influence on the whole district we shall have to
rate it highly.[103] Or take another instance. When
the first settlement in Georgia was established, forty
Jews were among the settlers. The number may seem
insignificant, but when we consider the meagre population of the colony, Jewish influence must be accounted
strong. So, too, in Savannah, where in 1733 there were
already twelve Jewish families in what was then a tiny
commercial centre.[104]

That America early became the goal of German and
Polish Jewish emigrants is well known. Thus we are
told : " Among the poorer Jewish families of Posen there
was seldom one which in the second quarter of the
19th century did not have at least one son (and in most
cases the ablest and not least enterprising) who sailed
away across the ocean to flee from the narrowness and
the oppression of his native land."[105] We are not

surprised, therefore, at the comparatively large number of Jewish soldiers (7243) [106] who took part in the Civil War, and we should be inclined to say that the estimate which puts the Jewish population of the United States about the middle of the 19th century at 300,000 (of whom 30,000 lived in New York) [107] was if anything too moderate.

CHAPTER V

THE FOUNDATION OF THE MODERN STATE

THE development of the modern colonial system and the establishment of the modern State are two phenomena dependent on one another. The one is inconceivable without the other, and the genesis of modern capitalism is bound up with both. Hence, in order to discover the importance of any historic factor in the growth of capitalism it will be necessary to find out what, and how great a part that factor played in both the colonial system and the foundation of the modern State. In the last chapter we considered the Jews in relation to the colonial system ; in the present we shall do the same for the modern State.

A cursory glance would make it appear that in no direction could the Jews, the "Stateless" people, have had less influence than in the establishment of modern States. Not one of the statesmen of whom we think in this connexion was a Jew—neither Charles the Fifth, nor Louis the Eleventh, neither Richelieu, Mazarin, Colbert, Cromwell, Frederick William of Prussia nor Frederick the Great.[107A] However, when speaking of these modern statesmen and rulers, we can hardly do so without perforce thinking of the Jews : it would be like Faust without Mephistopheles. Arm in arm the Jew and the ruler stride through the age which historians call modern. To me this union is symbolic of the rise of capitalism, and consequently of the modern State. In most countries

the ruler assumed the role of protector of the persecuted
Jews against the Estates of the Realm and the Gilds—
both pre-capitalistic forces. And why? Their interests
and their sympathies coincided. The Jew embodied
modern capitalism, and the ruler allied himself with this
force in order to establish, or maintain, his own position.
When, therefore, I speak of the part played by the Jews
in the foundation of modern States, it is not so much their
direct influence as organizers that I have in mind, as
rather their indirect co-operation in the process. I am
thinking of the fact that the Jews furnished the rising
States with the material means necessary to maintain
themselves and to develop ; that the Jews supported the
army in each country in two ways, and the armies were
the bulwarks on which the new States rested. In two
ways : on the one hand, the Jews supplied the army
in time of war with weapons, and munition and food ;
on the other hand, they provided money not only for
military purposes but also for the general needs of courts
and governments. The Jews throughout the 16th, 17th
and 18th centuries were most influential as army-
purveyors and as the moneyed men to whom the princes
looked for financial backing. This position of the Jews
was of the greatest consequence for the development of
the modern State. It is not necessary to expatiate on this
statement ; all that we shall do is to adduce instances in
proof of it. Here, too, we cannot attempt to mention
every possible example. We can only point the way ;
it will be for subsequent research to follow.

I. The Jews as Purveyors.

Although there are numerous cases on record of Jews
acting in the capacity of army-contractors in Spain
previous to 1492, I shall not refer to this period, because
it lies outside the scope of our present considerations.

We shall confine ourselves to the centuries that followed and begin with England.

In the 17th and 18th centuries the Jews had already achieved renown as army-purveyors. Under the Commonwealth the most famous army-contractor was Antonio Fernandez Carvajal, " the great Jew," who came to London some time between 1630 and 1635, and was very soon accounted among the most prominent traders in the land. In 1649 he was one of the five London merchants entrusted by the Council of State with the army contract for corn.[108] It is said that he annually imported into England silver to the value of £100,000. In the period that ensued, especially in the wars of William III, Sir Solomon Medina (" the Jew Medina ") was " the great contractor," and for his services he was knighted, being the first professing Jew to receive that honour.[109]

It was the same in the wars of the Spanish Succession ; here, too, Jews were the principal army-contractors.[110] In 1716 the Jews of Strassburg recall the services they rendered the armies of Louis XIV by furnishing information and supplying provisions.[111] Indeed, Louis XIV's army-contractor-in-chief was a Jew, Jacob Worms by name ; [112] and in the 18th century Jews gradually took a more and more prominent part in this work. In 1727 the Jews of Metz brought into the city in the space of six weeks 2000 horses for food and more than 5000 for remounts.[113] Field-Marshal Maurice of Saxony, the victor of Fontenoy, expressed the opinion that his armies were never better served with supplies than when the Jews were the contractors.[114] One of the best known of the Jewish army-contractors in the time of the last two Louis was Cerf Beer, in whose patent of naturalization it is recorded that " . . . in the wars which raged in Alsace in 1770 and 1771 he found the opportunity of proving his zeal in our service and in that of the State."[115]

Similarly, the house of the Gradis, of Bordeaux, was an establishment of international repute in the 18th century. Abraham Gradis set up large storehouses in Quebec to supply the needs of the French troops there.[116] Under the Revolutionary Government, under the Directory, in the Napoleonic Wars it was always Jews who acted as purveyors.[117] In this connexion a public notice displayed in the streets of Paris in 1795 is significant. There was a famine in the city and the Jews were called upon to show their gratitude for the rights bestowed upon them by the Revolution by bringing in corn. " They alone," says the author of the notice, " can successfully accomplish this enterprise, thanks to their business relations, of which their fellow citizens ought to have full benefit."[118] A parallel story comes from Dresden. In 1720 the Court Jew, Jonas Meyer, saved the town from starvation by supplying it with large quantities of corn. (The Chronicler mentions 40,000 bushels.)[119]

All over Germany the Jews from an early date were found in the ranks of army-contractors. Let us enumerate a few of them. There was Isaac Meyer in the 16th century, who, when Cardinal Albrecht admitted him a resident of Halberstadt in 1537, was enjoined by him, in view of the dangerous times, "to supply our monastery with good weapons and armour." There was Joselman von Rosheim, who in 1548 received an imperial letter of protection because he had supplied both money and provisions for the army. In 1546 there is a record of Bohemian Jews who provided great-coats and blankets for the army.[120] In the next century (1633) another Bohemian Jew, Lazarus by name, received an official declaration that he " obtained either in person, or at his own expense, valuable information for the Imperial troops, and that he made it his business to see that the army had a good supply of ammunition and clothing."[121] The Great Elector also had recourse to Jews for his military needs. Leimann Gompertz and Solomon Elias were his contractors for cannon, powder and so forth.[122] There are numerous others : Samuel Julius, remount contractor under the Elector Frederick Augustus of Saxony ; the Model family, court-pur-veyors and army-contractors in the Duchy of Ansbach in the 17th and 18th centuries are well known.[123] In short, as one writer of the time pithily expresses it, " all the contractors are Jews and all the Jews are contractors." [124]

Austria does not differ in this respect from Germany, France and England. The wealthy Jews, who in the reign of the Emperor Leopold received permission to re-settle in Vienna (1670)—the Oppenheimers, Wert-heimers, Mayer Herschel and the rest—were all army-contractors.[125] And we find the same thing in all the countries under the Austrian Crown.[126] Lastly, we must mention the Jewish army-contractors who provisioned the American troops in the Revolutionary and Civil Wars.[127]

II. The Jews as Financiers.

This has been a theme on which many historians have written, and we are tolerably well informed concerning this aspect of Jewish history in all ages. It will not be necessary for me, therefore, to enter into this question in great detail ; the enumeration of a few well-known facts will suffice.

Already in the Middle Ages we find that everywhere taxes, salt-mines and royal domains were farmed out to

Jews ; that Jews were royal treasurers and money-lenders,
most frequently, of course, in the Pyrenean Peninsula,
where the Almoxarife and the Rendeiros were chosen
preferably from among the ranks of the rich Jews.   But
as this period does not specially concern us here, I will
not mention any names but refer the reader to the general
literature on the subject.[128]

It was, however, in modern times, when the State as
we know it to-day first originated, that the activity of the
Jews as financial advisers of princes was fraught with
mighty influence.   Take Holland, where although
officially deterred from being servants of the Crown,
they very quickly occupied positions of authority.   We
recall Moses Machado, the favourite of William III ;
Belmonte, a family of ambassadors (Lords of Schoonen-
berg) ; the wealthy Suasso, who in 1688 lent William
two million gulden, and others.[129]

The effects of the Jewish *haute finance* in Holland
made themselves felt beyond the borders of the Netherlands, because that country in the 17th and 18th centuries
was the reservoir from which all the needy princes of
Europe drew their money.   Men like the Pintos,
Delmontes, Bueno de Mesquita, Francis Mels and many
others may in truth be regarded as the leading financiers
of Northern Europe during that period.[130]

Next, English finance was at this time also very
extensively controlled by Jews.[131]   The monetary
needs of the Long Parliament gave the first impetus to
the settlement of rich Jews in England.   Long before
their admission by Cromwell, wealthy crypto-Jews,
especially from Spain and Portugal, migrated thither *via*
Amsterdam : the year 1643 brought an exceptionally
large contingent.   Their rallying-point was the house of
the Portuguese Ambassador in London, Antonio de
Souza, himself a Maranno.   Prominent among them

was Antonio Fernandez Carvajal, who has already been mentioned, and who was as great a financier as he was an army-contractor. It was he who supplied the Commonwealth with funds. The little colony was further increased under the later Stuarts, notably under Charles the Second. In the retinue of his Portuguese bride, Catherine of Braganza, were quite a number of moneyed Jews, among them the brothers Da Sylva, Portuguese bankers of Amsterdam, who were entrusted with the transmission and administration of the Queen's dowry,[132] Contemporaneously with them came the Mendes and the Da Costas from Spain and Portugal, who united their families under the name of Mendes da Costa.

About the same period the Ashkenazi (German) Jews began to arrive in the country. On the whole, these could hardly compare for wealth with their Sephardi (Spanish) brethren, yet they also had their capitalistic magnates, such as Benjamin Levy for example.

Under William III their numbers were still further increased, and the links between the court and the rich Jews were strengthened. Sir Solomon Medina, who has also been already mentioned, followed the King from Holland as his banker, and with him came the Suasso, another of the plutocratic families. Under Queen Anne one of the most prominent financiers in England was Menasseh Lopez, and by the time the South Sea Bubble burst, the Jews as a body were the greatest financial power in the country. They had kept clear of the wild speculations which had preceded the disaster and so retained their fortunes unimpaired. Accordingly, when the Government issued a loan on the Land Tax, the Jews were in a position to take up one quarter of it. During this critical period the chief family was that of the Gideons, whose representative, Sampson Gideon (1699–1762), was the "trusted adviser of the Government," the friend of Walpole, the "pillar of the State credit." In 1745, the year of panics, Sampson raised a loan of £1,700,000 for the assistance of the Government. On his death his influence passed to the firm of Francis and Joseph Salvador, who retained it till the beginning of the 19th century, when the Rothschilds succeeded to the financial leadership.

It is the same story in France, and the powerful position held by Samuel Bernard in the latter part of the reign of Louis XIV and in the whole of that of Louis XV may serve as one example among many. We find Louis XIV walking in his garden with this wealthy Jew, "whose sole merit," in the opinion of one cynical writer,[133] "was that he supported the State as the rope does the hanged man." He financed the Wars of the Spanish Succession; he aided the French candidate for the throne of Poland; he advised the Regent in all money matters. It was probably no exaggeration when the Marquis de Dangeau spoke of him in one of his letters [134] as "the greatest banker in Europe at the present time." In France also the Jews participated to a large extent in the re-consolidation of the French East India Company after the bursting of the South Sea Bubble.[135] It was not, however, until the 19th century that they won a really leading position in financial circles in France, and the important names here are the Rothschilds, the Helphens, the Foulds, the Cerfbeers, the Duponts, the Godchaux, the Dalemberts, the Pereires and others. It is possible that in the 17th and 18th centuries also a great many more Jews than those already mentioned were active as financiers in France, but that owing to the rigorous exclusion of Jews they became crypto-Jews, and so we have no full information about them.

It is easier to trace Jewish influence in finance in

Germany and Austria through that clever invention—the status of " Court Jew." Though the law in these countries forbade Jews to settle in their boundaries, yet the princes and rulers kept a number of "privileged " Jews at their courts. According to Graetz,[136] the status of " Court Jew " was introduced by the Emperors of Germany during the Thirty Years' War. Be that as it may, it is an undoubted fact that pretty well every State in Germany throughout the 17th and 18th centuries had its Court Jew or Jews, upon whose support the finances of the land depended.

A few examples by way of illustration. In the 17th century [137] we find at the Imperial Court Joseph Pinkherle, of Goerz, Moses and Jacob Marburger, of Gradisca, Ventura Parente of Trieste, Jacob Bassewi Batscheba Schmieles in Prague, the last of whom the Emperor Ferdinand raised to the ranks of the nobility under the title von Treuenburg on account of his faithful services. In the reign of the Emperor Leopold I we meet with the respected family of the Oppenheimers, of whom the Staatskanzler Ludewig wrote in the following terms.[138] After saying that the Jews were the arbiters of the most important events, he continues : " In the year 1690 the Jew Oppenheimer was well known among merchants and bankers not only in Europe but throughout the world." No less famous in the same reign was Wolf Schlesinger, purveyor to the court, who in company with Lewel Sinzheim raised more than one large loan for the State. Maria Theresa utilized the services of Schlesinger and others, notably the Wertheimers, Arnsteins and Eskeles. Indeed, for more than a century the court bankers in Vienna were Jews.[139] We can gauge their economic influence from the fact that when an anti-Jewish riot broke out in Frankfort-on-the-Main, the local authorities thought it wise in the

interest of credit to call upon the Imperial Office to
interfere and protect the Frankfort Jews, who had very
close trade relations with their brethren in Vienna.[140]

It was not otherwise at the smaller German courts.
" The continually increasing needs of the various courts,
each vying with the other in luxury, rendered it im-
perative, seeing that communication was by no means
easy, to have skilful agents in the commercial centres."
Accordingly the Dukes of Mecklenburg had such agents
in Hamburg ; Bishop John Philip of Würzburg was
in 1700 served by Moses Elkan in Frankfort. This
activity opened new channels for the Jews ; the enterprising dealer who provided jewels for her ladyship,
liveries for the court chamberlain and dainties for the
head cook was also quite willing to negotiate a loan.[141]
Frankfort and Hamburg, with their large Jewish population, had many such financial agents, who acted for ruling
princes living at a distance. Besides those already
mentioned we may recall the Portuguese Jew, Daniel
Abensur, who died in Hamburg in 1711. He was
Minister-resident of the King of Poland in that city,
and the Polish Crown was indebted to him for many a
loan.[142] Some of these agents often moved to the
court which borrowed from them, and became " Court
Jews." Frederick Augustus, who became Elector of
Saxony in 1694, had a number of them : Leffmann
Berentz, of Hanover, J. Meyer, of Hamburg, Berend
Lehmann, of Halberstadt (who advanced money for
the election of the King of Poland) and others.[143]
Again, in Hanover the Behrends were Chief Court
Purveyors and Agents to the Treasury ;[144] the Models,
the Fraenkels and the Nathans acted in a similar
capacity to the Duchy of Ansbach. In the Palatinate we
come across Lemte Moyses and Michel May, who in
1719 paid the debt of 2½ million gulden which the

Elector owed the Emperor,[145] and lastly, in the Marggravate of Bayreuth, there were the Baiersdorfs.[146]

Better known perhaps are the Court Jews of the Brandenburg-Prussian rulers—Lippold, under Joachim II; Gomperz and Joost Liebmann, under Frederick III; Veit, under Frederick William I; and Ephraim, Moses, Isaac and Daniel Itzig, under Frederick II. Most famous of all the German Court Jews, the man who may be taken as their archetype, was Suess-Oppenheimer, who was at the court of Charles Alexander of Würtemberg.[147]

Finally, we must not leave unmentioned that during the 18th century, more especially in the Revolutionary Wars, the Jews played no small role as financiers in the United States of America. Haym Salomon [148] ranks side by side with the Minis and the Cohens in Georgia,[149] but the most prominent of them all was Robert Morris, the financier *par excellence* of the American Revolution.[150]

And now comes an extraordinary thing. Whilst for centuries (especially during the 17th and the 18th—the two so momentous in the growth of the modern State) the Jews had personal financial dealings with the rulers, in the century that followed (but even during the two already mentioned) the system of public credit gradually took a new form. This forced the big capitalist from his dominating position more and more into the background, and allowed an ever-increasing number of miscellaneous creditors to take his place. Through the evolution of the modern method of floating loans the public credit was, so to speak, " democratized," and, in consequence, the Court Jew became superfluous. But the Jews themselves were not the least who aided the growth of this new system of borrowing, and thus they contributed to the removal of their own monopoly as financiers. In so doing they participated to a greater degree than ever before in the work of building up the great States of the present.

The transformation in the public credit system was but a part of a much vaster change which crept over economic life as a whole, a metamorphosis in which also the Jews took a very great share. Let us consider this change in its entirety.

CHAPTER VI

THE PREDOMINANCE OF COMMERCE IN ECONOMIC LIFE

It is a matter of common knowledge that the Stock Exchange in modern times is becoming more and more the heart of all economic activities. With the fuller development of capitalism this was only to be expected, and there were three clear stages in the process. The first was the evolution of credit from being a personal matter into one of an impersonal relationship. It took shape and form in securities. Stage two : these securities were made mobile—that is, bought and sold in a market. The last stage was the formation of undertakings for the purpose of creating such securities.

In all the stages the Jew was ever present with his creative genius. We may even go further and say that it was due specifically to the Jewish spirit that these characteristics of modern economic life came into being.

I. The Origin of Securities.[151]

Securities represent the standardization of personal indebtedness.[152] We may speak of "standardization" in this sense when a relationship which was originally personal becomes impersonal ; where before human beings directly acted and reacted on each other, now a system obtains. An instance or two will make our meaning clear. Where before work was done by man, it is now done by a machine. That is the standardization of work.

In olden times a battle was won by the superior personal initiative of the general in command ; nowadays victory falls to the leader who can most skilfully utilize the body of experience gathered in the course of years and can best apply the complicated methods of tactics and strategy ; who has at his disposal the best guns and who has the most effective organization for provisioning his men. We may speak in this instance of the " standardization " of war. A business becomes standardized when the head of the firm who came into personal contact with his employees on the one hand and with his customers on the other, is succeeded by a board of directors, under whom is an army of officials, all working on an organized plan, and consequently business is more or less of an automatic process.

Now, at a particular stage in the growth of capitalism credit became standardized. That is to say, that whereas before indebtedness arose as the result of an agreement between two people who knew each other, it was now rearranged on a systematic basis, and the people concerned might be entire strangers. The new relationship is expressed by negotiable instruments, whether bill of exchange or security or banknote or mortgage deed, and a careful analysis of each of them will prove this conclusively.

Of the three persons mentioned in a bill of exchange, the specified party in whose favour the document is made out (the payee) or, if no name is mentioned, the bearer of the document may be quite unknown to the other two ; he may have had no direct business relation with the party making out the bill (the drawer), yet this document establishes a claim of the former on the latter—general and impersonal.[153]

The security gives the owner the right to participate in the capital and the profit of a concern with which he has no direct personal contact. He may never even have seen the building in which the undertaking in question is housed, and when he parts with his security to another person he transfers his right of participation.

Similarly with a banknote. The holder has a claim on the bank of issue despite the fact that he personally may never have deposited a penny with it.

So, in short, with all credit instruments : an impersonal relationship is established between either an individual or a corporation on the one hand (the receiver of moneys), and an unknown body of people (we speak of " the public ") on the other—the lender of moneys.

What share did the Jews take in the creation of this credit machinery ? It would be difficult, perhaps impossible, to show what that share was by reference to documentary evidence, even if we had a very full account of the position of the Jews in the early economic history of most lands. But unfortunately that aspect of economic development which would have been invaluable for the solution of the problem in hand has been sadly neglected. I refer to the history of money and of banking in the Pyrenean Peninsula during the last centuries of the Middle Ages. But even if such a history were at our disposal, the question would still be difficult to answer. We must remember that the origins of economic organization can no more be discovered by referring to documentary evidence than the origins of legal institutions. No form of organization or tendency in economic life can be traced to a particular day or even a particular year. It is all a matter of growth, and the most that the economic historian can do is to show that in any given period this or that characteristic is found in business life, this or that organization dominates all economic activities. Even for this the ludicrously inadequate sources at our disposal are hardly sufficient. The historian will have to turn to the general history of the period, or to that of the particular group in which he happens to be interested.

To take an instance. The history of bills of exchange can scarcely be written merely by referring to the few mediæval bills which chance has left to us. Such documents are certainly useful to supplement or correct general theories. But we must formulate the general theories first. Let us take a case in point. The bill which for a long time was held to be the oldest, extant was drawn by a Jew, Simon Rubens, in the year 1207. That is hardly sufficient evidence on which to base the assertion that the Jews were the inventors of this form of credit instrument.154 Earlier bills have come to light recently, drawn by non-Jews, but they do not render testimony strong enough for the statement that the Jews were *not* the inventors of bills. Do we know how many thousands of bills circulated in Florence or Bruges, and how can we be sure which section of the population issued them? We do know, however, that the Jews were occupied throughout the Middle Ages in money-dealing, that they were settled in various parts of Europe and that they carried on a continuous intercourse with each other. From these facts we may draw the tolerably certain conclusion that "the Jews, the intermediaries in international trade, utilized on a large scale the machinery of foreign exchanges, then traditionally current in the Mediterranean lands, and extended it." 155

That this method of reasoning requires great caution is self-evident. Yet it may lead to useful conclusions for all that. There are cases, as we shall see, where the share of the Jews in the extension of some economic policy or machinery may be proved by a fund of documentary evidence. In other instances, and they are numerous, we must content ourselves if it can be shown that, at any particular time and in any given place, there must have been some special reason for the utilization by Jews of a form of economic organization then current.

Bearing this in mind, let us enquire into the genesis of one or two types of credit instruments.

1. *The Bill of Exchange.*

Not merely the early history of the bill of exchange but rather that of the modern endorsable bill is what we are concerned with most of all. It is generally accepted that the endorsing of bills of exchange had been fully developed prior to the 17th century, and the first complete legal recognition of such endorsement was found in Holland (Proclamation in Amsterdam of January 24, 1651).[156] Now, as we shall see presently, all developments in the money and credit systems of Holland in the 17th century were due more or less to Jewish influence. Some authorities trace the origin of endorsable bills of exchange·to Venice, where they were made illegal by a law of December 14, 1593.[157] It is fairly certain that the use of circulating endorsable bills in Venice must have been first commenced by Jews, seeing that we know that nearly all bill-broking in the Adriatic city in the 16th century was in their hands. In the petition of the Christian merchants of Venice of the year 1550 (to which reference has already been made) the passage relating to the bill business of Jews reads as follows [158]:—

"We carry on the same commerce with them also in matters of exchange, because they continually remit to us their money . . . sending cash, in order that we may change it for them for Lyons, Flanders and other parts of the world on our Exchange, or indeed that we may buy for them silken cloths and other merchandise according to their convenience, gaining our usual commission.

"That which we say of the inhabitants of Florence holds good also of the other merchants of the same Spanish and Portuguese nation, who dwell in Flanders, Lyons, Rome, Naples, Sicily and other countries, who lay themselves out to do business with us, not only in exchanges but in sending hither merchandise of Flanders, selling corn from Sicily and buying other merchandise to transport to other countries."

A further development in the endorsing of bills appears to have taken place at the fairs of Genoa in the 16th century. Who, we may ask, were the "Genoese," met with everywhere throughout that century, but especially at the famous fairs of Besançon, dominating the money market, and who all of a sudden showed a remarkable genius for business and gave an impetus to the growth of new methods, hitherto unknown, for cancelling international indebtedness? It is true that the ancient wealthy families of Genoa were the principal creditors of the Spanish Crown as well as of other needy princes. But to imagine that the descendants of the Grimaldis, the Spinolas, the Lercaras exhibited that extraordinary commercial ability which gave a special character to the activity of the Genoese in the 16th century ; to think that the old nobility gadded about the fairs at Besançon or elsewhere, or even sent their agents with never-failing regularity— this appears to me an assumption hardly warranted without some very good reason. Can the explanation be that the Jews brought new blood into the decrepit economic body of Genoa ? We know [159] that fugitives from Spain landed at Genoa, that some of the settlers became Christians, that the rest were admitted into Novi, a small town near Genoa, and that the Jews of Novi did business with the capital ; we know, too, that the newcomers were "for the most part intelligent Jewish craftsmen, capitalists, physicians," and that in the short space of time between their arrival and 1550 they

had become so unpopular in Genoa that they had aroused
the hatred of the citizens ; we know, finally, that there
were constant communications between the Genoese
bankers and the Jewish, or rather Maranno, banking
houses of the Spanish cities, *e.g.*, with the Espinosas,
the leading bankers in Seville.[160]

2. *Securities (Stocks and Shares).*

If we should wish to speak of securities in those cases
where the capital of a business concern is split up into
many parts, and where the liability of the capitalists is
limited, we have ample justification for so doing in
the case of the Genoa Maones, in the 14th century,[161]
the Casa di San Giorgio (1407) and the important
trading companies of the 17th century. But if stress
is laid on the standardization of the credit-relationship,
it will not be before the 18th century that we shall find
instances of joint-stock enterprise and of securities. For
the early contributions to a joint-stock never lost their
personal character. The Italian Montes were impregnated through and through with the personality of their
founders. In the case of the Maones, the personal factor
was no less important than the financial ; while at the
Bank of St. George in Genoa, the families concerned
jealously guarded the principle that each one should
obtain its proper share in the directing of the work
of the bank. The trading companies too had a strong
personal element. In the English East India Company,
for instance, it was not until 1650 that shares could
be transferred to strangers, but they had to become
members of the Company.

In all early instances the security was for unequal and
varying sums. The personal relationship thus showed
itself plainly enough. In some companies shares could
not be transferred at all except by consent of all the other

members.   In fact, the security was just a certificate of membership, and throughout the 18th century such securities as were made out in the name of a specified person predominated.[162]   Even where there was freedom of transfer from one person to another (as in the case of the Dutch East India Company) the process was beset with innumerable obstacles and difficulties.[163]

The modern form of security can therefore not be found before the 18th century.   If now it be asked what share did the Jews have in the extension of this form of credit in modern times, the reply is obvious enough.   During the last hundred and fifty or two hundred years, Jews have been largely instrumental in bringing about the standardization of what was before a purely personal relationship between the holder of stock and the company in which he participated.   I am bound to admit, however, that I cannot adduce direct proofs in support of my thesis.   But indirectly the evidence is fairly conclusive.   Jews were great speculators, and speculation must of necessity tend to substitute for the security wherein the holder is specified one which has no such limitation.   A little reflection will show therefore that Jews must have had no small influence on the standardization of securities.   In some cases it may even be demonstrated that speculation was responsible for the change from securities of differing amounts to those of equal value.   The Dutch East India Company is a case in point.   Originally its shares were of all values ; later only 3000 florin shares were issued.[164]

3. *Banknotes.*

Many opinions prevail as to the precise occasion when banknotes first came into use.   For my own part I lay stress on the standardization here also.   The first time any banker issued a note without reference to some specific deposit a new type of credit instrument, the modern banknote, came into being. There were bank-notes in existence long before that.[165]   But they bore the depositor's name and referred to his money.[166]   I believe that in all probability the personal banknote became a general (impersonal) one in Venice about the beginning of the 15th century. There are on record instances dating from that time of banks making written promises to pay over and above the sums deposited with them. An edict of the Venetian Senate as early as 1421 made it an offence to deal in such documents.[167] The first permission to establish a bank was granted to two Jews in 1400, and their success was so great that the *nobili* made haste to follow their example.[168]   The question arises, may these two Jews be regarded as the fathers of the modern (impersonal) banknote?

But perhaps no particular firm introduced the new paper money. It may have come into existence in order to satisfy the needs of some locality. Nevertheless, if we take as the place of its origin the town where the earliest banks reached a high degree of perfection, we shall surely be on the safe side. From this point of view Venice is admirably qualified. Now Venice was a city of Jews, and that is wherein its interest for us lies in this connexion. According to a list dating from the year 1152, there were no fewer than 1300 Jews in Venice.[169]   In the 16th century their number was estimated at 6000 ; and Jewish manufacturers employed 4000 Christian workmen.[170]   These figures, to be sure, have no scientific value, but they do show that the Jews must have been pretty numerous in Venice. From other sources we are acquainted with some of their activities. Thus, we find Jews among the leading bankers—one of the most influential families were the Lipmans ; and in 1550, as we have already noted, the

Christian merchants of Venice stated that they might as well emigrate if trade with the Marannos were forbidden them.

It is possible that the Marannos may have founded the business of banking even while they were yet in Spain. We have, however, no satisfactory information, though many writers have dealt with the subject.[171] There is a strong probability that at the time when measures were taken against them (16th century) the Jews were the leading bankers in the Pyrenean Peninsula. If this be so, is not the presumption justifiable that before then, too, the Jews engaged in banking?

Furthermore, Jews were prominent and active figures wherever in the 17th century banks were established. They participated in the foundation of the three great banks of that period—the Bank of Amsterdam, the Bank of England and the Bank of Hamburg. But as none of these owed its origin to purely commercial causes, I shall not emphasize their importance in connexion with the Jews. The facts, nevertheless, are interesting, and I would therefore state that the experience which the Jews gathered when the Bank of Amsterdam was founded served them in good stead when in 1619 the Hamburg Bank came into being. No less than forty Jewish families took shares in the new concern. As for the Bank of England, the latest authorities [171A] on its history are agreed that the suggestion for the Bank came from Jewish immigrants from Holland.

4. *Public Debt Bonds.*[174-176]

The earliest bonds issued for public loans were addressed to some individual lender, and it was long before they changed their character and became " general " instruments. In Austria, to take one example, it was not until the Debt of 1761 was contracted that the bonds had coupons attached which gave the bearer the right to receive interest.[173] Previous to that, the bond was of the nature of a private agreement ; the Crown or the Treasury was the debtor of some specific lender.[172]

To what extent the Jews were responsible for the "standardization" of public credit it is difficult to estimate. So much is certain, that William III's advisers were Jews ; that public borrowing in the German States was commenced on the model of Holland, most probably through the influence of Dutch Jews who, as we have already seen, were the chief financiers in German and Austrian lands. Speaking generally, Dutch Jews were most intimately concerned in European finance in the 18th century.[176A]

As for private loan-bonds or mortgage-deeds, we know very little of their history, and it is almost impossible to compute the direct influence of the Jews here. But indirectly the Jews were, in all likelihood, the originators of this species of credit instrument, more especially of mortgage deeds. We have it on record that Dutch bankers, from about the middle of the 18th century onward, advanced money to colonial planters on the security of their plantations. Mortgage-deeds of this kind were bought and sold on the Stock Exchange, just like Public Debt bonds. The bankers who dealt in them were called " correspondentie " or " Directeurs van de negotiatie," and the instruments themselves " obligatie." Documents to the value of no less than 100,000,000 gulden were in circulation before the crash of the 1770's.[177]

I must confess that nowhere have I found any mention of Jewish bankers participating in these speculations. Yet even the most superficial acquaintance with the Dutch money-market in the 18th century can scarcely leave room for doubt that Jews must have been largely interested in this business. It is a well-known fact (as I hope to show) that in those days anything in Holland connected with money-lending, but especially with stocks and shares and speculation, was characteristically Jewish. We are strengthened in this conclusion through knowing that most of the business in mortgage-banking was carried on with the colony of Surinam. Of the 100,000,000 gulden of mortgage-deeds already mentioned, 60,000,000 worth was from Surinam. Now Surinam, as we noted above, was the Jewish colony *par excellence*. The possibility that the credit relationship at that time between Surinam and the Motherland was maintained by other than Jewish houses is well-nigh excluded.

So much for the "sources" regarding the Jewish share in the development of modern credit instruments. The sum-total is not much; it is for subsequent research to fill in the details and to add to them. Yet I believe the evidence sufficient for the general conclusion that in the standardization of modern credit the Jews took no inconsiderable share. This impression will only be deepened if we think for a moment of the means by which the standardization was brought about or, at any rate, facilitated. I mean the legal form of the credit instruments, which in all probability was of Jewish origin.

There is no complete agreement among authorities on the history of legal documents as to the origin of credit instruments.[178-187] But in my opinion the suggestion that they owe their modern form to Jewish influence has much to be said for it. Let it be remembered that such documents first came into use among merchants, in whose ranks the Jewish element was not insignificant. The form that became current received recognition in judicial decisions, and eventually was admitted into the body of statute law, first of all presumably in Holland.

The only question is, Can we possibly deduce modern credit instruments from Rabbinic law ? I believe we can.

In the first place, the Bible and the Talmud are both acquainted with credit instruments. The Biblical passage is in the Book of Tobit, iv. 20 ; v. 1, 2, 3; ix. 1, 5.

The best known passage in the Talmud is as follows (*Baba Bathra*, 172) :—

" In the court of R. Huna a document was once produced to this effect : 'I, A. B., son of C. D., have borrowed a sum of money from you.' R. Huna decided that ' from you' might mean ' from the Exilarch or even from the King himself.' "

Secondly, in later Jewish law, as well as in Jewish commercial practice, the credit instrument is quite common. As regards practice, special proof is hardly necessary ; and as for theory, let me mention some Rabbis who dealt with the problem.[188]

First in importance was Rabbenu Asher (1250–1327), who speaks of negotiable instruments in his Responsa (lxviii. 6, 8). " If A sends money to B and C, and notes in his bill ' payable to bearer by B and C,' payment must be made accordingly." So also R. Joseph Caro in his *Choshen Mishpat* : " If in any bill no name is mentioned but the direction is to ' pay bearer,' then whoever presents the bill receives payment " (lxi. 10 ; cf. also l.; lxi. 4, 10 ; lxxi. 23). R. Shabbatai Cohen in his *Shach*. (l. 7 ; lxxi. 54) is of the same opinion.

Thirdly, it is very likely that the Jews, in the course of business, independently of Rabbinic law, developed a form of credit instrument which was quite impersonal and general in its wording. I refer to the *Mamre* (*Mamram, Mamran*).[189] It is claimed that this document first appeared among the Polish Jews in the 16th century, or even earlier. Its form was fixed, but a space was left for the name of the surety, sometimes, too, for the amount in question. There is no doubt that such documents were in circulation during three centuries and were very popular, circulating even between Christians and Jews. Their value as evidence consists in that they already had all the characteristics of modern instruments : (1) the holder put the document in circulation by endorsement; (2) there is no mention of the personal relationship of the debtor and the creditor ; (3) the debtor may not demand proof of endorsement or transfer ; (4) if the debtor pays his debt without the presentation of the *Mamre* having been made to him, it is considered that he has not really discharged his obligation ; and lastly (5) the cancellation of the document is almost the same as it is to-day—if it is lost or stolen the holder of the document informs the debtor ; public notice is given by a declaration posted up for four weeks in the synagogue, wherein the bearer of the instrument is requested to come forward ; at the end of four weeks, if nothing happens, the creditor demands payment of the debtor.

In the fourth place, it would appear that Jewish influences were potent in the development of many weighty points of legal practice. Let me mention some.

(1) During the 16th century there circulated in different parts of Europe credit instruments with blanks for filling in names. What was their origin ? Is there not a possibility that they emanated from Jewish commercial circles, having been modelled on the pattern of the *Mamre* ? They are met with in the Netherlands,[190] in France [191] and in Italy.[192] In the Netherlands they appeared towards the beginning of the 16th century at the Antwerp fairs, just when the Jews began to take a prominent part in them. An Ordinance of the year 1536 states explicitly that " at the Antwerp fairs payment for commodities was made by

promissory notes, which might be passed on to third persons without special permission." It would seem from the wording that the practice of accepting notes in payment for goods was a new one. What sort of documents were these notes ? Can they have been Christian *Mamrem* ? Even more Jewish were the documents in vogue in Italy a century later. I mean the first known " open " note, issued by the Jewish bill-brokers, Giudetti, in Milan. The note was for 500 scudi, payable through John Baptist Germanus at the next market day in Novi to the personal order of Marcus Studendolus in Venice for value received. Studendolus sent the bill to de Zagnoni Brothers in Bologna "with his signature, leaving a sufficient blank space at the end for filling in the amount, and the name of the person in whose favour the de Zagnonis preferred payment to be made." The recorder of this instance remarks[192] that " Italian financial intercourse could hardly have thought of a facility of this kind, had there not been a model somewhere to imitate. Such a model is found in France, where from the 17th century onward bearer bonds were in general circulation." The question at once suggests itself, how did this document arise in France ? Will the example of Holland account for it ? Even in Italy it may be a case of Maranno influence—Studendolo (?) in Venice, Giudetti in Milan !

(2) Of very great significance in the development of modern credit instruments is the Antwerp Custom of 1582, wherein it is for the first time admitted that the holder of a note has the right of suing in a court of law.[193] This conception spread rapidly from Antwerp to Holland—as rapidly, indeed, as the Jewish refugees from Belgium settled down among the Dutch.[194]

(3) In Germany the first State to adopt credit instruments was Saxony. In the year 1747 an adventurer of the name of Bischopfield suggested to the Minister of

Finance the plan of a Public Loan, and it seems that
Bischopfield was in communication with Dutch Jews at
the time.[195] Further, an ordinance of 20th September 1757 forbade Dutch Jews to speculate in Saxon
Government Stock. All of which points to Jewish
influence—on the one side of the Dutch Jews, and on the
other of Polish Jews, owing to the connexion of the
royal houses of Saxony and Poland. So great was this
influence that one authority comes to the definite conclusion that the *Mamre* became the model for credit
instruments.[196]

(4) Among the instruments wherein the name of the
holder was inserted we must include marine insurance
policies. It is recorded that the Jewish merchants of
Alexandria were the first to use the formulæ "*o qual si
voglia altera persona*," "*et quævis alia persona*" and
"*sive quamlibet aliam personam*" (" or to any other person
desired ").[197]

Now why did the Jewish merchants of Alexandria
adopt this legal form? The answer to this question
is of the gravest import, more especially as I believe
that the causes for which we are seeking were inherent in
the conditions of Jewish life.

(5) That leads me to my fifth consideration. It was
to the interest of the Jews to a very large degree—in some
respects even it was to the interest of the Jews alone—to
have a proper legal form for credit instruments. For
what was it that impelled the Jewish merchants of
Alexandria to make out their policies to bearer? Anxiety
as to the fate of their goods. Jewish ships ran the risk of
capture by Christian pirates and the fleets of His Catholic
Majesty, who accounted the wares of Jews and Turks as
legitimate booty. Hence the Jewish merchants of Alexandria inserted in their policies some fictitious Christian
name, Paul or Scipio, or what you will, and when

the goods arrived, received them in virtue of the "bearer" formula in their policies.

How often must the same cause have actuated Jews throughout the Middle Ages ! How often must they have endeavoured to adopt some device which concealed the fact that they were the recipients either of money or of commodities sent from a distance. What more natural than that they should welcome the legal form which gave "the bearer" the right of claiming what the document he held entitled him to. This formula made it possible for fortunes to vanish if the Jews in any locality passed through a storm of persecution. It enabled Jews to deposit their money wherever they wanted, and if at any time it became endangered, to remove it through the agency of some fictitious person or to transfer their rights in such a way as not to leave a trace of their former possessions.[198] It may seem inexplicable that while throughout the Middle Ages the Jews were deprived of their "all" at very short intervals, they managed to become rich again very quickly. But regarded in the light of our suggestion, this problem is easily explained. The fact was that the Jews were never mulcted of their "all"; a goodly portion of their wealth was transferred to a fictitious owner whenever the kings squeezed too tight.

Later, when the Jews commenced to speculate in securities and commodities (as we shall see in due course) it was only to be expected that they would extend the use of this form of bond, more particularly in the case of securities.[199] It is obvious that if a big loan is subscribed by a large number of comparatively small contributors bearer bonds offer facilities of various kinds.[200]

The remark of a Rabbi here and there demonstrates this conclusively. One passage in the commentaries of

R. Sabbatai Cohen is distinctly typical. " The purchaser
of a bond," he says, " may claim damages against the
debtor if he pays the debt without obtaining a receipt,
the reason being that as there is no publicity in the
transaction this practice is detrimental to dealings in such
instruments. It is true that Rabbenu Asher and his
school expressed no view concerning *Shetarot* (instruments)
of all kinds, which the Rabbis introduced in order to
extend commerce. That is because dealings in such
instruments were not very common, owing to the difficulty of transfer. But the authorities were thinking
only of personal bonds. In the case of bearer bonds, the
circulation of which at the present time (*i.e.*, the 17th
century) is greater far than that of commodities, all ordinances laid down by the Rabbis for the extension of
commerce are to be observed."

(6) Here again we touch a vital question. I believe
that if we were to examine the whole Jewish law concerning bearer bonds and similar instruments we should
find—and this is my sixth point—that such documents
spring naturally from the innermost spirit of Jewish
law, just as they are alien to the spirit of German and
Roman law.

It is a well-known fact that the specifically Roman conception of indebtedness was a strictly personal one.[200A]
The *obligatio* was a bond between certain persons. Hence
the creditor could not transfer his claim to another, except
under exceedingly difficult conditions. True, in later
Roman law the theory of delegation and transmission
was interpreted somewhat liberally, yet the root of the
matter, the personal relationship, remained unchanged.

In German law a contract was in the same way personal ;
nay, to a certain extent it was even more so than in
Roman law. The German principle on the point was
clear enough. The debtor was not obliged to render

payment to any one but the original creditor to whom he had pledged his word. There could in no wise be transference of claim—as was the case in English law until 1873. It was only when Roman law obtained a strong hold on Germany that the transfer of claims first came into vogue. The form it took was that of "bearer bonds"—the embodiment of an impersonal credit relationship.

It is admitted that the legal notion underlying all "bearer" instruments—that the document represents a valid claim for each successive holder—was not fully developed either in the ancient world or in the Middle Ages.[201] But the admission holds good only if Jewish law be left out of account. Jewish law was certainly acquainted with the impersonal credit relationship.[202] Its underlying principle is that obligations may be towards unnamed parties, that you may carry on business with Messrs. Everybody. Let us examine this principle a little more closely.

Jewish law has no term for obligation : it knows only debt (" Chov ") and demand (" Tvia "). Each of these was regarded as distinct from the other. That a demand and a promise were necessarily bound up with some tangible object is proved by the symbolic act of acquisition. Consequently there could be no legal obstacles to the transfer of demands or to the making of agreements through agents. There was no necessity therefore for the person against whom there was a claim to be defined, the person in question became known by the acquisition of certain commodities. In reality claims were against things and not against persons. It was only to maintain a personal relationship that the possessor of the things was made responsible. Hence the conception that just as an obligation may refer to some specified individual, so also it may refer to mankind as a whole.

Therefore a transference of obligations is effected merely by the transference of documents.

So much would appear from the view held by Auerbach. Jewish law is more abstract in this respect than either Roman or German law. Jewish law can conceive of an impersonal, "standardized" legal relationship. It is not too much to assume that a credit instrument such as the modern bearer bond should have grown out of such a legal system as the Jewish. Accordingly, all the external reasons which I have adduced in favour of my hypothesis are supported by what may be termed an "inner" reason.

And what is this hypothesis? That instruments such as modern bearer bonds owe their origin chiefly to Jewish influences.

II. Buying and Selling Securities.

1. *The Evolution of a Legal Coae Regulating Exchange.*

In modern securities we see the plainest expression of the commercial aspect of our economic life. Securities are intended to be circulated, and they have not served their true purpose if they have not been bought and sold. Of course it may be urged that many a security rests peacefully in a safe, yielding an income to its owner, for whom it is a means to an end rather than a commodity for trading in. The objection has a good deal in it. A security that does not circulate is in reality not a security at all; a promissory note might replace it equally well. The characteristic mark of a security is the ease with which it may be bought and sold.

Now if to pass easily from hand to hand is the real *raison d'être* of the security, everything which facilitates that movement matters, and therefore a suitable legal code most of all. But when is it suitable? When it renders possible speedy changes in the relationship between two people, or between a person and a commodity.

In a society where every commodity continues as a rule in the possession of one and the same person, the law will strive all it can to fix every relationship between persons and things. On the other hand, if a body of people depends for its existence on the continued acquisition of commodities, its legal system will safeguard intercourse and exchange.

In modern times our highly organized system of inter-communication, and especially dealings in securities and credit instruments of all kinds, has facilitated the removal of old and the rise of new legal relationships. But this is contrary to the spirit of Roman and German law, both of which placed obstacles in the way of commodities changing hands. Indeed, under these systems any one who has been deprived of a possession not strictly in accordance with law may demand its return from the present owner, without the need of any compensation, even though his *bona-fides* be established. In modern law, on the other hand, the return of the possession can be made only if the claimant pays the present owner the price he gave for it—to say nothing of the possibility that the original owner has no claim whatever against the present holder.

If this be so, whence did the principle, so alien to the older systems, enter into modern law? The answer is that in all probability it was from the Jewish legal code, in which laws favouring exchange were an integral part from of old.

Already in the Talmud we see how the present owner of any object is protected against the previous owners. "If any one," we read in the "Mishna" (*Baba Kama*, 114*b* and 115*a*), "after it has become known that a burglary took place at his house finds his books and utensils in the possession of another, this other must declare on oath how much he paid for the goods, and on his receiving the amount returns them to the original owner. But if no burglary has taken place, there is no need for this procedure, for it is then assumed that the owner sold the goods to a second person and that the present owner bought them." In every case, therefore, the present owner obtains compensation, and in certain given circumstances he retains the objects without any further ado. The "Gamara," it is true, wavers somewhat in the discussion of the passage, but in general it comes to the same conclusion. The present owner must receive "market protection," and the previous owner must pay him the price he gave.

The attitude of the Talmud, then, is a friendly one towards exchange, and the Jews adopted it throughout the Middle Ages. But more than that—and this is the important point—they succeeded quite early in getting the principle recognized by Christian law-courts in cases where Jews were concerned. For centuries there was a special enactment regulating the acquisition of moveables by Jews; it received official recognition for the first time in the "Privileges" issued by King Henry IV to the Jews of Speyers in 1090. "If a commodity that has been stolen," we read therein, "is found in the possession of a Jew who declares that he bought it, let him swear according to his law how much he paid for it, and if the original owner pays him the price, the Jew may restore the commodity to him." Not only in Germany, but in other lands too [203] (in France already about the middle of the 12th century), is this special ordinance for Jews to be met with. [204]

2. *The Stock Exchange.*

But when all is said, the principal thing was to establish a suitable market for credit instruments. The Stock

Exchange answered the purpose. And just as the commodities there to be bought and sold were impersonal embodiments of claims, so, too, was the dealing divested of its personal character. Indeed, this is a feature of the Stock Exchange which differentiates it from other markets. It is no longer the trustworthiness that a merchant enjoys in the estimation of his fellow-merchants, based upon personal experience, that underlies business activities, but the general, abstract valuation of credit, the *ditta di Borsa*. Prices are no longer formed by the higgling of two or more traders talking over their transactions, but rather by a mechanical process, representing the average of a thousand and one units.[205–206]

As for the history of the Stock Exchange (in the broadest connotation of the term), it may be divided into two periods—(1) from its beginning in the 16th to the end of the 18th century, an epoch of growth and development, and (2) from the 19th century to the present day, when the Stock Exchange dominates all economic activities.

It is now generally agreed that the origin of Stock Exchange dealing most likely began with the associating of bill-brokers.[207] The centres where the famous exchanges first arose in the 16th and 17th centuries were previously well known for a brisk trade in bills.

The important thing for us is that just when the Stock Exchanges came into being the Jews almost entirely monopolized bill-broking. In many towns, indeed, this business was regarded as a Jewish speciality. That such was the case in Venice we have already seen.[208] It was also true of Amsterdam, though we must add that the first mention of Jews in that capacity was not until the end of the 17th century.[209] Despite this, however, I believe we shall be safe in assuming that previous to that date also they were influential bill-brokers.

In Frankfort-on-the-Main we hear the same story. Already in the 16th century a contemporary [210] says of the Jews who came to the fairs that their presence was " hardly ornamental but certainly very useful, especially in the bill-discounting business." Again, in 1685, the Christian merchants of Frankfort complained that the Jews had captured the whole of the business of bill-broking.[211]   Lastly, Glückel von Hameln states in her *Memoirs* that friends of her family dealt in bills, " as was customary among Jews." [212]

As for Hamburg, Jews certainly introduced the business of bill-broking there.   A hundred years after the event (1733) a document in the Archives of the Senate expressed the opinion that "Jews were almost masters of the situation in bill-broking and had quite beaten our people at it." [213]   And even as late as the end of the 18th century the Jews were almost the only purchasers of bills in Hamburg.   Among other German towns, it is recorded that in Fürth bill-broking (in the 18th century) was almost entirely in Jewish hands.[214]

The position in Vienna was no different.   The Austrian capital, as is well known, became a notable centre as a stock market at the end of the 18th century, and the State Chancellor Ludewig remarks concerning the activities of the Jews under Leopold I, [215] " chiefly in Vienna by the influence and credit of the Jews business of the greatest importance is often transacted. Especially exchanges and negotiations of the first import in the market."

So in Bordeaux, where we are told [216] " the chief business activity is buying bills and introducing gold and silver into the realm."   Even from so far north as Stockholm the same story reaches us.[217]   There also the Jews dominated the bill-broking market in the early 19th century (1815).

As the principal bill-brokers of the period, the Jews must have had much to do with the establishment of the Stock Market. But more than that. They gave the Stock Exchange and its dealings their peculiar features in that they became the " originators of speculation in futures," and, indeed, of speculation generally.

When speculation in stocks first arose is as yet difficult to determine. Some have held [218] that the Italian cities furnish examples of this kind of dealing as early as the 15th century.[220-221] But to my mind this has not yet been conclusively proved.[219]

Not in Italy in the 15th, but in Amsterdam in the 17th century will the beginnings of modern speculation have to be more correctly placed. It is almost certain that the Dutch East India Company's shares called stock-jobbing into existence. The large number of shares of equal value that were suddenly put into circulation at that time, the strong speculative temper of the age, the great interest taken in the Company ever since its foundation, the changing rates of profit that its activities produced—all these must surely have given an impetus to stock and share dealing on the Amsterdam Exchange,[222] then already a highly developed institution. In the space of only eight years dealing in stock became so general and so reckless that it was regarded as an evil by the authorities, who tried to abolish it. A proclamation by the Government of the 26th February, 1610, forbade merchants to sell more shares than they actually possessed. Similar prohibitions were issued in 1621, 1623, 1677, 1700 and so on, all equally without effect.

Who were the speculators? The answer is, all those irrespective of religion who had sufficient money to enable them to participate. Nevertheless the assumption will not be too bold that the Jews were more prominent than others in this activity. Their contribution to the growth of Stock Exchange business was their specialization in stockbroking and the device of dealing in futures. We are not without evidence on both points. Towards the end of the 18th century it was a generally accepted fact that Jews had "discovered" the stock and share business.[223]   This belief does not necessarily prove anything; yet that it was without any foundation is hardly likely, especially as there are witnesses to give it support.   Nicolas Muys van Holy, who has already been mentioned, says that Jews were the principal stockholders—already in the second half of the 17th century. Later they are found as large investors in both the Dutch India Companies.   De Pinto [224] is the authority as regards the Dutch East India Company, and for the West India Company there is the letter of the Directors to Stuyvesant,[225] the Governor of New Amsterdam, requesting him to allow the Jews to settle in the Company's colony, "also because of the large amount of capital which they have invested in shares of the Company." Referring to both companies, Manasseh ben Israel [226] reported to Cromwell "that the Jews were enjoying a good part of the Dutch East and West India Company."

Most significant of all, however, the book which for the first time exhaustively treated of Stock Exchange business in all its branches was written by a Portuguese Jew in Amsterdam, towards the end of the 17th century. I refer to Don Joseph de la Vega's *Confusion de confusiones*, etc., which appeared in 1688,[227] and which a Stock Exchange specialist has described as "being still the best description, both in form and substance, of stock and share dealing even to-day." The book bears witness to the fact that a Jew was the first "theorist" in the sphere of speculations in futures. De la Vega was himself engaged in commerce and his treatise clearly reflects the atmosphere in which he lived.

De la Vega's book in conjunction with the other evidence quoted cannot but lead to the conclusion that if the Jews were not actually the " fathers " of Stock Exchange business they were certainly primarily concerned in its genesis.

Should this view nevertheless be sceptically received by some, I have a trump card in the way of direct proof in support of it.

We possess a report, probably of the French Ambassador in The Hague, written for his Government in the year 1698, wherein he distinctly states that the Jews held the Stock Exchange business in their hands, and shaped its development as they willed. The most salient passages [228] here follow in full :—

"In this State (Holland) the Jews have a good deal of power and according to the prognostications of these pretended political speculators, themselves often unreliable, the prices of these stocks vary so considerably that they cause transactions to take place several times a day, transactions which merit the term wager or bet rather than business ; the more so, as the Jews who dominate this kind of activity are up to all manner of tricks which take in people, even if they be ever so skilled." . . . "Their Jewish brokers and agents, the cleverest of their kind in all the world." . . . "Bonds and shares, of all of which they hold large amounts."

The author, acquainted as he is with all the secrets of Stock Exchange activity, describes at length how the Jews succeeded in obtaining the influential position they held on the Amsterdam Stock Exchange. I shall refer to this in due course.

Much light is thrown on the conditions of the Stock Exchange in the Dutch capital when compared with those in other centres. Let us take London first, which from the 18th century onward succeeded Amsterdam as the chief financial centre in Europe. The predominance of Jews in the Stock Exchange in London is perhaps more apparent even than in the case of Amsterdam. The growing activity in the London Stock market towards the end of the 17th century may be traced to the exertions of Amsterdam Jews, who at that time began to settle in England. If this be so, it is proof positive that the Jews were in large measure responsible for the expansion of Stock Exchange dealing in Amsterdam. Else how could they have been so influential in the London Exchange, highly developed as it then already was ?

One or two particulars in the story of the accession to power of the Jews in the London Exchange may be noted.

In 1657 Solomon Dormido applied for admission as a member of the Exchange, from which Jews were officially excluded. The law which ordered this exclusion seems to have been conveniently forgotten. Anyhow, towards the end of the 17th century the Exchange (which since 1698 had become known as 'Change Alley) was full of Jews. So numerous did they become that a special corner of the building was designated the " Jews' Walk." " The Alley throngs with Jews," wrote a contemporary.[229]

Whence these throngs ? [230] The answer is obvious. They came in the train of William III from Amsterdam, and brought with them the machinery of Stock Exchange dealings in vogue there. The events, as related by John Francis, are regarded as a true presentation by many authorities, even on the Jewish side.

The Stock Exchange was like Minerva : it appeared on the scene ready armed. The principal participants in the first English loan were Jews : they assisted William III with their advice, and one of them, the wealthy Medina, was Marlborough's banker, giving the General an annual grant of £6,000 and receiving in return the advantage of being first in the field with news of the wars. The victories of the English troops were as profitable to Medina as they were honourable for England. All the tricks bound up with rising and falling prices, lying reports from the seat of war, the pretended arrival of couriers, the formation of financial cliques and cabals behind the scenes, the whole system of Mammon's wheels—they knew them all, the early fathers of the Stock Exchange, and utilized them to the full to their own advantage.

By the side of Sir Solomon Medina ("the Jew Medina," as he was called), who may be regarded as having originated speculation in the public funds in England, we may place a number of other wealthy Jews of the reign of Anne, all of whom speculated on the Stock Exchange. Manasseh Lopez was one. He amassed a fortune in the panic which followed the false news that the Queen was dead, buying up all Government Stock which had fallen in price in consequence. A similar story is told of Sampson Gideon, known among the Gentiles as "the great Jew broker." [231] A notion of the financial strength of the Jews in the London of those days may be obtained when it is recalled that at the beginning of the 18th century the number of Jewish families with an annual income between £1000 and £2000 was put by Picciotto at 100 ; those with an annual income of £300 at £1000 ; whilst some individual Jews, such as Mendes da Costa, Moses Hart, Aaron Frank, Baron d'Aguilar, Moses Lopez Pereira, Moses or Anthony da Costa (who towards the end of the 17th century was a Director of the Bank of England) and others were among the wealthiest merchants in London.

It is evident then that the wealth of the Jews brought about Stock Exchange speculation on a large scale. But more striking still, the business of stock-jobbing as a specialized profession was introduced into the London Exchange by Jews, probably in the first half of the 18th century. As far as I am aware this fact has hitherto passed unnoticed. But there is abundant proof in support of it.

Postlethwayt, who is pretty reliable in matters of this kind, asserts [232] that " Stock-jobbing . . . was at first only the simple occasional transferring of interest and shares from one to another as persons alienated their estates ; but by the industry of the stockbrokers, who got the business into their hands, it became a trade ; and one, perhaps, which has been managed with the greatest intrigue, artifice, and trick that ever anything which appeared with a face of honesty could be handled with ; for, while the brokers held the box, they made the whole exchange the gamesters, and raised and lowered the prices of stocks as they pleased and always had both buyers and sellers, who stood ready, innocently to commit their money to the mercy of their mercenary tongues."

That Jews formed a considerable proportion of brokers is well-known. As early as 1697, out of one hundred sworn brokers on the London Exchange, no fewer than twenty were Jews and aliens. Doubtless their number increased in the centuries that followed. " The Hebrews flocked to 'Change Alley from every quarter under heaven," wrote Francis. Indeed, a reliable observer of the 1730's (that is to say, a generation after their first appearance on the London Exchange) remarks [233] that there were too many Jewish brokers for them all to do business, consequently this " has occasioned almost one half of the Jew brokers to run into stock-jobbing." The same authority puts the number of Jews then in London at 6000.

This process, by which stock-jobbing was in a sense the outcome of stockbroking, was not limited to London. The same tendencies showed themselves in Frankfort. Towards the end of the 17th century the Jews there were in possession of the entire broking business,[234] and gradually no doubt worked their way into stock-jobbing. In Hamburg[235] the Portuguese Jews had four brokers in 1617, whilst a little later there were twenty.

Taking these facts into consideration, taking into consideration also that public opinion regarded the Jews as responsible for the growth of arbitrage business on the London Exchange,[236] and that Jews participated to a great degree in the big speculations in Government Stock towards the end of the 18th century, we shall be forced to agree with the view that has been expressed by a first-rate authority,[237] that if to-day London is the chief financial centre of the world, it owes this position in large measure to the Jews.

In the period of early capitalism, the Stock Exchanges of other towns lagged far behind those of Amsterdam and London. Even in Paris it was not until towards the end of the 18th century that business became at all brisk. The beginnings of stock speculation (or *Agiotage*, as it is called in France) can be traced to the early 18th century ; Ranke[238] discovered the term *Agioteur* in a letter of Elisabeth Charlotte, dated 18th January, 1711. The writer is of opinion that the term had some connexion with the *billets de monnaye* (bills) but that it was unknown before. It would seem, therefore, that the Law period left no lasting impression. For even in the 1730's the economic pre-eminence of England and Holland, both more capitalistically advanced than their neighbour, was felt in France. One writer of the time[239] makes this clear. "The circulation of stock is one of the sources of great wealth to our neighbours ; they have a bank, dividends are paid, and stocks and shares are sold." Apparently then such was not the case in France. Even in 1785, an edict (7th August) proclaimed that "the King is informed that for some time past a new kind of commodity has been introduced into the capital"—viz., stocks and shares.

The condition of comparative unimportance which Stock Exchange activities occupied in France during the 18th century is a direct indication that the Jews had little influence on the economic life of France (and especially of Paris) in that period. The cities in which they resided, such as Lyons or Bordeaux, were hardly favourable to the development of stockbroking. In Lyons, however, there was for a short space, in the 16th century, a fairly brisk trade in what would to-day be called securities, but no satisfactory reasons have as yet been offered to explain it.[240] Anyhow, it had no after-effects.

But to return to Paris. What stockbroking it had it probably owed to the Jews. The centre of this business was in the Rue Quincampoix, which later became notorious through the swindles connected with the name of Law. Now in this particular street there lived, in the words of a reliable authority,[241] "many Jews." Be that as it may, the man with whom the first stock speculations in France were connected, one who was a greater master of the art of manipulation than even Law, was Samuel Bernard, the well-known financier of Louis XIV. No wonder then that the *billets de monnaye*, when they became merely bits of valueless paper, were nicknamed *Bernardines*.[242] And as for John Law, his knowledge of the mechanism of the Stock Exchange had been acquired in Amsterdam.[243] Whether he was himself a Jew (it has been held [244] that Law = Levy) I have been unable to discover. It is, however, quite possible. Was not

his father a " goldsmith " (and banker) ? He was, it is
true, a Christian, but that is not necessarily a proof of
his non-Jewishness. The Jewish appearance of the man
in portraits (for example, in the German edition (1720) of
his *Money and Trade Considered*) rather supports the thesis
that he was a Jew. On the other hand, the peculiar mixture of the lordling and the adventurer which characterized
his nature is against the assumption.

In Germany the Exchanges of Frankfort and Hamburg,
the two Jewish towns *par excellence*, alone reached a position of any importance. Illustrations of the Jewish influence have already been dealt with.

As for Berlin, it may be said that the Stock Exchange
there was a Jewish institution from its very inception. At
the beginning of the last century, even before 1812, when
they were emancipated, the Jews predominated numerically
on the Exchange. Of the four Presidents, two were
Jews ; and the whole Stock Exchange Committee was
made up as follows :—4 Presidents, 10 Wardens of the
two Gilds, 1 of the Elbe Seamen's Gild, and 8 " of the
merchants of the Jewish nation, elected thereto." Out of
a total of 23, therefore, 10 were Jews. That is to say,
professing Jews : it is impossible to determine whether,
and how many, baptized Jews and crypto-Jews were in
the committee.

As it is, their number shows plainly enough that stockbroking had its large quota of Jews. Of six sworn bill-
brokers three were Jews. Further, of the two sworn
brokers in cotton and silk, one was a Jew, and his substitute was also a Jew. That is to say, of a total of
three, two were Jews.[245]

Stockbroking so far as Germany in the 18th century
was concerned was carried on only in Hamburg and
Frankfort. Already at the beginning of that century
trading in securities was forbidden. A proclamation of

the Hamburg Council, dated 19th July, 1720, expresses itself as follows :—" The Council has heard to its abhorrence and great disgust, that certain private citizens, under the pretext of founding an assurance company, have on their own authority commenced business as dealers in shares. The Council fears that harmful consequences may ensue therefrom as well to the public at large, as also to the said private citizens." [245A] It seems that the powers that be were only voicing the general feeling in the matter ; " the dangerous and wickedly ruinous trade in stocks and shares" a writer of the time [245B] indignantly called it.

Were Jews here also the originators ? So much at least is certain, that the impetus to stock-dealing came from the circles of the assurers, as is apparent from the above-mentioned proclamation of 1720. Now, as a matter of fact, it is known that Jews actively stimulated the growth of marine insurance in Hamburg.[246] Any further evidence as to Stock Exchange influences is only indirect. The same applies to Frankfort. The first certain trace dates from 1817, and refers to Augsburg. There is on record the decision of a court of law in a bill case of the 14th February in the year mentioned. A motion to enforce payment of the difference in the price of a credit-instrument which rose owing to the rise of the market-rate was dismissed, on the ground that it was of the nature of a game of hazard. The sum in question was 17,630 florins, and the original contract was for delivery of 90,000 florins' worth of lottery tickets in the Bavarian State Lottery. The plaintiff's name was Heymann, the defendant's H. E. Ullmann ! This is the first attested case of speculation in bonds in Germany.[247]

But with the year 1817 we reach a period which differed from the preceding one, and which I consider as opening a new epoch in the history of Stock Exchange transactions. Why new? What were its special features that it should be described by that dreadful word " modern " ?

Judgments on the Stock Exchange by contemporaries then and now show how widely different a position it occupies to-day from what it did even a hundred years ago.

Until well on in the 18th century, even in capitalistic circles, speculation in the public funds was looked at askance. The standard commercial handbooks and dictionaries in English, French, Italian and German, which have come down to us from the 18th century, either make no mention at all of dealings in stocks (especially in the economically "backward" countries), or if, like Postlethwayt, they do treat of the subject, they cannot sufficiently express their contempt for it. The view concerning the Stock Exchange which is to-day held by the petty trader, the small shopkeeper or the farmer was in the 18th century that of the rich merchant. When in 1733 Sir John Barnard's Bill (to prevent the "infamous practice of stock-jobbing ") was being discussed in the House of Commons, all the speakers were unanimous in their condemnation of the business. Half a generation later the same harsh terms are to be found in the pages of Postlethwayt, who refers to "those mountebanks we very properly call stockbrokers." Stock-jobbing he regards as a " public grievance," which has become " scandalous to the nation." [248] No wonder that the legislation of the period completely forbade the business.

But the dislike of the Stock Exchange went deeper still. It was bound up with an aversion for what the Exchange rested on—securities in general. Naturally the interests of the State coincided with those who defended the trade in securities, so that Ruler and Jobber were ranged as a lonely couple on one side, while everybody else was on the other—save only those who indulged in the purchase of securities. In truth, the National Debt was looked upon as something of which States had need to be ashamed, and the best men of their generation were agreed that its growth was an evil which should be combated by all possible means. Thinkers and practical men were united on this point. In commercial circles the question was seriously discussed how the public debt could be paid off, and it was even suggested that the State should disavow its responsibilities in connexion with the debt, and so wipe it out. And this in England in the second half of the 18th century ! 249 Nor were the theorists of the time differently minded. The system of public borrowing is called by David Hume " a practice . . . ruinous beyond all controversy ; " 250 Adam Smith writes of " the ruinous practice of funding," " the ruinous expedient of perpetual funding . . . has gradually enfeebled every State which has adopted it " . . . " the progress of the enormous debts, which at present oppress and will in the long run probably ruin all the great nations of Europe." 251 In these opinions, as always, Adam Smith is the mirror of the economic conditions of his age, a period of early capitalistic development, and nothing distinguishes it from our own so well as the fact that in the complete system of Adam Smith there is no niche available for the study of securities, or of the Stock Exchange and its business.

About the same time, however, a book appeared which dealt only with credit and its blessings, with the Stock Exchange and its significance ; a book which may be justly termed the " Song of Songs " of Public Debts and share-dealing ; a book which looked to the Future, as the *Wealth of Nations* looked to the Past. I refer to the *Traité du crédit et de la circulation*, published in 1771 from the pen of Joseph de Pinto. Now Pinto was a

Portuguese Jew ; hence my special reference to him in this connexion. In his pages may be found the very arguments which have been put forward in the 19th century in defence of public credit, of dealings in securities and of speculation in the public funds. If Adam Smith in his system be said to stand at the end of the period in which the Stock Exchange was in its infancy, Pinto may be regarded as standing at the beginning of the modern era with its theory of credit, in which stock and share speculation have become the centre of economic activity, and the Stock Exchange the heart of the body economic.

Silently, but none the less surely, public opinion veered round in favour of dealings in securities and of the recognition of the Stock Exchange as a necessity. Public opinion grew as these grew, and, step by step, hostile legislation was removed, so that when the Napoleonic wars were over and peace reigned once more, the Stock Exchange began to take on enormous dimensions.

We see, then, that there is some justification for speaking of a new period in the history of the Stock Exchange. What were the actual changes ? And to what extent were the Jews concerned in bringing about the new state of affairs ?

There was not much modification in the mechanism of the Stock Exchange ; that was complete as early as 1688, when de la Vega published his book. Naturally, subsidiary kinds of business activities cropped up here and there, and of these, too, Jews were generally the originators. Thus I have discovered [252] that the business of insurance was established (in Germany) by W. Z. Wertheimer in Frankfort, and that of the peculiar form of ship chartering known as "*Heuergeschäft*" Jews were the founders.

But the rise of subsidiary businesses was not the salient

point in the development of Stock Exchange activities.
It was rather the extensive and intensive growth of the
volume of business.

The enormous increase in the number of securities
which have appeared in the market since the beginning
of the 19th century, and the rapidity with which they
came before the public, are facts too well known to need
repetition. But with this increase came also an extension
of speculation. Until about the middle of the 18th
century, speculation in London and Amsterdam may
be compared to little ripples on the face of the water.
It was not till 1763, as a reliable informant tells us,
that the first private loan was floated in Amsterdam.
Previously what speculation there was was limited to
public bonds, " but during the last war a vast ocean
of annuities flooded the market." [253] Even so,
there were only forty-four different kinds of securities
on the Amsterdam Exchange about the middle of the
century. Of these, twenty-five were bonds of internal,
and six of German loans. When the century closed, the
first category of bonds numbered eighty, and the second
thirty.[254] Then came a sudden upward movement,
especially after the defeat of Napoleon. From the first
establishment of the Amsterdam Exchange until the year
1770, a total debt of 250,000,000 Gulden had been dealt
in ; whereas in fourteen years (1808-22) one London firm
alone issued a greater sum—22,000,000 pounds. All
this is common knowledge ; and the identity of that one
London firm, which in a decade floated so vast a sum on
the market, does not need further indication.

With the mention of this firm, and of its four branches,
we have touched on the connexion between the extensive
growth of Stock Exchange activities and the Jewish
influence upon it. For the expansion of the share market
between 1800 and 1850 was also the expansion of the

house of Rothschild and its appendages. The name
Rothschild refers to more than the firm : it stands for
the whole of Jewish influence on the Stock Exchange.
By the aid of that influence the Rothschilds were enabled
to attain to their powerful position—it may even be said
to their unique position—in the market for Government
securities. It was no exaggeration to assert that in many
a land the minister of finance who could not come to an
agreement with this firm might as well close the doors
of his exchequer. "There is only one power in Europe,"
was a dictum well-known about the middle of the 19th
century, "and that is Rothschild : a dozen other banks
are his underlings, his soldiers are all honest merchants
and workmen, and speculation is his sword" (A. Weil).
Heine's wit, in passages that are surely too well-known
to need quoting, has demonstrated the importance of
the family better far than any table of figures.

I have not the least intention of writing here a history
of the Rothschilds, even in outline. The reader will find
ample material [255] at his disposal should he wish to
acquaint himself with the fortunes of this remarkable
family. All I shall do will be to point out one or two
characteristics which the modern Stock Exchange owes to
them, in order to make clear that not only quantitatively,
but also qualitatively, the Stock Exchange bears the
impress of the Rothschilds (and therefore of the Jew).

The first feature to be observed is that, since the
appearance of the Rothschilds, the stock market has
become international. This was only to be expected,
considering the enormous extension of Stock Exchange
activities, which necessitated the flow of vast sums from
all parts of the inhabited world to the borrowing centres.
To-day the internationalization of the stock market is an
accepted fact ; at the commencement of the 19th century
it was regarded with nothing short of amazement. When

in 1808, during the Peninsular War, Nathan Rothschild undertook in London to attend to the pay of the English army in Spain, his action was regarded as a stupendous achievement, and, indeed, laid the foundation of all his influence. Until 1798 only the Frankfort firm had been in existence ; in that year one of the sons of Mayer Amschel established a branch in London, another son settled in Paris in 1812, a third in Vienna in 1816, and a fourth in Naples in 1820. The conditions were thus given whereby a foreign loan might be treated as though it were an internal loan, and gradually the public·became accustomed to investing their capital in foreign securities, seeing that the interest could be paid at home in coins of the realm. Writers of the early 19th century describe it as a marvellous thing that "every holder of Government stock . . . can receive his dividends in various places at his convenience without any difficulty. The Rothschilds in Frankfort pay interest for many Governments ; the Paris house pays the dividends on the Austrian Métalliques, the Neapolitan Rentes, the Anglo-Neapolitan Loan either in London, Naples or Paris." [256]

The circle of possible investors was thus enlarged. But the Rothschilds were also alive to the importance of obtaining every available penny that could be borrowed, and for this purpose they skilfully utilized the machinery of the Stock Exchange for floating loans.

As far as can be judged from contemporary records,[257] the issue by the Rothschilds of the Austrian bonds in 1820–1 was an epoch-making event, both in public borrowing and in Stock Exchange business. For the first time all the ropes were pulled to create a demand for the shares, and speculations in Government stocks may be stated to have begun on this occasion, at least on the Continent.

"To create a demand" was henceforth the watchword

of the Stock Exchange. "To create a demand" was the object in view when, by means of systematic buying and selling, changes were brought about in price; and the Rothschilds devoted themselves to the business from the first.[258] In a sense, they carried on what the French called *agiotage*, and this was something quite new for a great banking firm to do. In reality the Rothschilds only adopted the methods of the Amsterdam Jews for artificially influencing the market, but they applied them to a new purpose—the placing of fresh securities before the public.

The changed relation of the banker to the Stock Exchange on the one hand, and to the public on the other, will become more apparent when we have glanced at the new activities which loomed on the horizon at this period—the age of the Rothschilds—and began to play an independent rôle. I mean the business of bringing out loans.

III. THE CREATION OF SECURITIES.

The business of bringing out loans is an attempt to obtain profit by means of the creation of securities. It is important because it represents a capitalistic force of exceedingly great power. Henceforth, stocks and shares come into being not because of the needs of those who require money and depend on credit, but quite independently, as a form of capitalistic enterprise. Hitherto the possible investor was waited for until he came; now he is sought out. The loan-floater becomes, as it were, aggressive; he gives the impetus to the borrowing movement. But this is hardly ever noticeable. We see how it works, however, when small States require loans; we may imagine a kind of "commercial traveller in loans." "Now we have wealthy firms with large machinery, whose time and staff are devoted to hunting about the world for Powers for whom to bring out loans." [259]

Naturally, the loan-floater's relation to the Stock Exchange and the public changes. He must be aggressive and pushful, now that his main work is to get people to take up shares.

There is as yet no satisfactory history of the business of bringing out loans. We do not know, therefore, when it first began ; its origins, however, no doubt reach back into the 18th century, and probably there were three well marked stages in its growth.

In the first of these, either a bank or a wealthy individual (who, in the pre-Stock Exchange period himself made the loan) was entrusted with the placing of the debt in return for a commission. Such was the method adopted in Austria throughout the whole of the 18th century : " Loans of fairly large sums, especially those contracted abroad, were usually obtained through the intervention of a bank or a group of financiers. The firm in question arranged, by means of public subscription, for the supply of the amount needed ; handed over the sum to the borrower or his agent ; undertook the payment of interest and portions of the principal to the individual lenders—out of their own funds if need be ; all, of course, for a consideration." [260]

But about the middle of the 18th century there were already " dealers in loans." In 1769 there were Italian and Dutch firms who would willingly undertake the floating of loans.[261] Adam Smith's description of this business makes the matter plainer still. " In England . . . the merchants are generally the people who advance money to Government. But by advancing it they do not mean to diminish, but, on the contrary, to increase their mercantile capitals ; and unless they expected to sell with some profit their share in the subscription for a new loan, they never would subscribe." In France, on the other hand, those concerned in the finances were people of private means, who advanced their own money.[262]

Where did the specialists in this business come from? Not from among the bankers, who in the 18th century floated loans, but in all probability from among the dealers in stocks and shares. Towards the end of the 18th century the charmed circle of London bankers who had the monopoly of bringing out Government loans was broken through by competition from the ranks of the stockbrokers. Here, too, it was a Jewish firm that took the initiative, and brought the emission of loans into connexion with the Stock Exchange. I refer to the " Rothschilds of the 18th century," the men who predominated in 'Change Alley in those days—Abraham and Benjamin Goldsmid. In 1792 they came forward as the first members of the Stock Exchange [263] to compete with the bankers of London in the bringing out of the new loan, and from that date until the death of the second brother, Abraham, which occurred in 1810, this firm controlled the money market. Perhaps we may account them as the first " loan specialists," whom the Rothschilds succeeded. But even if there is some doubt about the Goldsmids' claim, there can be no possible doubt about the Rothschilds', who were thus certainly the first in the field.

But it is obvious that only a few wealthy firms could subsist by the business of issuing public loans. After all, the demand was comparatively limited. But as soon as opportunities offered themselves for the creation of securities for private needs, a very wide field of activity was ready for ploughing. All that was necessary was to create a big demand artificially, and this tendency gave birth to company-promoting and mortgage business.

Company-promoting is carried on by firms " whose business it professedly is to make money by manufacturing stocks and shares wholesale and forcing them upon the public " (Crump). The strength of the motive power that thus began to actuate economic activities need scarcely be described. It was now to the interest of undertakers, some of no small importance, to create fresh capital by the issue of new stock or by extending the old, without any reference at all to the question as to whether there was a demand for the stock or not.

Who first started this form of business ? It will not be difficult to show that even if the Jews did not actually establish it, they certainly helped forward its development.

The first ray of light on this matter, as far as we can make out, is once again the activity of the Rothschilds. The railway boom of the 1830's made it possible to carry on company-promoting on a large scale. The Rothschilds, as well as other Jewish houses (the d'Eichthals, the Foulds, etc.), were the first in the field, and brought this branch of business to a flourishing condition.

The extent of the participation may be gathered in some degree from the length of the lines built, or the amount of capital subscribed. But the actual share of the individual firms cannot be estimated. Nevertheless, we know that the Rothschilds " built " the Northern Railway in France, the Northern Railway in Austria, the Austro-Italian Railway, and many more.

Further, judging from the views of contemporaries, it would appear that the Rothschilds were really the first

" Railway Kings." In 1843 the *Augsburger Allgemeine Zeitung* wrote as follows : " When in the last few years speculation became rife in industrial undertakings, and railways grew to be a necessity for the Continent, the Rothschilds took the plunge and placed themselves at the head of the new movement." The house of Rothschild set the fashion in railway building as it had done before in public loans. " Scarcely a company that was started in Germany but looked to the goodwill of Rothschild. Those in which he had no say were not very successful, and little could be made out of them." [264] Statements such as these, in which friend and foe agree, are significant enough.

Ever since those days the activity of floating companies has become a speciality of Jewish undertakers. In the first place, the very biggest men, such as Baron Hirsch or Dr. Strousberg, were Jews. But the rank and file, too, have many Jews among them. A glance at the figures on the next page concerning the promotion of companies in Germany in the two years 1871–3 suffices to show that an astoundingly large number of Jews participated in the work.[265] But these figures do not tell the whole story. In the first place, they form only a selection of the whole, and refer (of set purpose) to the "shaky" companies, from which the Jews will probably have kept away ; and secondly, in many cases, the Jews were behind the scenes as controlling influences, and those in the foreground were merely puppets. Even so the figures will serve a useful purpose.

The tendency is perhaps best seen where private banking is still important, as it is in England. Here, as I am told on the best authority, of the 63 banks in the *Bankers' Almanack* for 1904, 33 were Jewish firms, or at least with a strong Jewish interest, and of these 33, 13 were first-class concerns.

Nature of Establishment.	Total Number of Founders.	Number of Jews.
Twenty-five firms of first-rate importance that floated companies ...	25	16
Two of the biggest mining syndicates...	13	5
Continental Railway Company (capital 1½ million sterling)...	6	4
Twelve Land-purchase Companies in Berlin	80	27
Building Society, "Unter den Linden"	8	4
Nine Building Banks	104	37
Nine Berlin Breweries	54	27
Twenty North German Machine Building Companies	148	47
Ten North German Gasworks ...	49	18
Twenty Paper Factories	89	22
Twelve North German Chemical Works	67	22
Twelve North German Textile Factories	65	27

It is more difficult to determine the proportion of Jews in this calling in countries (*e.g.*, Germany) where the private banker has been displaced by the joint-stock bank. But everything points to Jewish influence in the tendency of the joint-stock banks to act as company promoters.

None of the decades of company-flotation, neither the fifties nor the seventies, nor still less the nineties, would have been conceivable without the co-operation of the speculative bank. The stupendous undertakings in railway construction owe their very existence to the banks, which advanced capital to limited companies of their own creation. Private firms, it is true, did no little in the same direction, but their means did not allow of rivalry with the great banks. In France, between 1842 and 1847, no less than 144 million francs were spent in railway building ; in the following four years 130 millions, while from 1852 to 1854 the sum had reached 250 millions ; in 1855 alone it was 500 millions, and in 1856 520 millions.[266] It was the same in Germany. " The entire work of building our net of railways in this period (1848-70) . . . was carried through . . . with the assistance of banks." [267]

The reason for this is not far to seek. On the one hand, the increase of available capital, which was due to the rise of new joint-stock banks, paved the way for pro-portionately larger undertakings. On the other hand, since the joint-stock company in trying to obtain greater profits strove harder than a private firm to add to its activities, all possible opportunities that presented them-selves were utilized to the full. [268]

How did this special banking activity originate ? [269] I believe it may be traced to 1852, when the *crédits mobiliers* [270] were first established.

The history of the *crédit mobilier* is well known.[271] What interests us specially is that it owes its inception to two Portuguese Jews, Isaac and Emil Pereire, and that other Jews participated in it. The list of subscribers showed that the two Pereires together held 11,446 shares, and Fould-Oppenheim 11,445, that among the other large shareholders were Mallet Frères, Benjamin Fould, Torlonia (of Rome), Solomon Heine (of Hamburg), Oppenheim (of Cologne)—in other words, the chief representatives of European Jewry. The Rothschilds were not found in the list, for the *crédit mobilier* was directed against them.

The French *crédit mobilier* produced in the years that followed a number of offshoots, legitimate and ille-gitimate, all of Jewish blood. In Austria there was the " Kaiserlich-Koenigliche privilegierte oesterreichische Kreditanstalt," established in 1855 by S. M. Rothschild. In Germany the first institution modelled on the new principle was the Bank für Handel und Industrie (Darm-städter Bank), founded in 1853, on the initiative of the Oppenheims of Cologne.[272] One of the first directors of this bank was Hess, who had been a high official in the *crédit mobilier*. The Berliner Discontogesellschaft was the second institution of the same kind. Its origin was Christian, but its transformation into what it is to-day is the work of David Hausemann. It was the same with the third German instance—the Berliner Handelsgesellschaft, which was called into being by the Cologne firms already mentioned in connexion with the Darmstädter Bank, and by the best known Berlin bankers, such as Mendelssohn & Co., S. Bleichröder, Robert Warschauer & Co., Schickler Brothers, and others. Finally, in the case of the Deutsche Bank (1870) the Jewish element again predominated.

IV. The Commercialization of Industry.

With the speculative banks capitalistic development reached its zenith, at any rate, for the time being. They pushed the process of the commercialization of economic life as far forward as it could go. Themselves children of the Stock Exchange, the speculative banks brought Stock Exchange activities (*i.e.*, speculation) to their fullest bloom.[273] Trade in securities was extended to undreamt-of proportions. So much so, that the opinion has been expressed that, in Germany at any rate, the speculative joint-stock banks will replace the Stock Exchange.[274] There may be a grain of truth in this, provided the terms be properly understood. That the Stock Exchange may cease to be an open market and be dominated by *la haute finance* is possible ; but as an economic organization it is bound to gain, if anything, by modern developments, seeing that its sphere is continuously being widened.

That is what I mean by the commercialization of industry. The Stock Exchange activities of the joint-stock banks are becoming more and more the controlling force in every department of economic life. Indeed, all undertakings in the field of industry are now determined by the power of finance. Whether a new industrial concern shall be established or an old one enlarged, whether a "universal provider" shall receive an increase of capital in order to extend his business—all this is now decided in the private offices of banks or bankers. In the same way the distribution of commodities is becoming more and more a financial problem. It is not too much to say that our chief industries are as much financial as industrial concerns. The Stock Exchange determines the price of most international manufactured articles and raw materials, and he who hopes to survive the competitive strain must be able to command the Stock Exchange. In a word, it may be safely asserted that all economic activities nowadays are tending to become commercial dealings.

The electrical industry is the best example. From its first foundations it represented a new type. Hitherto the great capitalistic industries regarded their work as finished when they had obtained and carried out their orders. A particular factory would appoint an agent in every big town, who in most cases represented other factories as well, and whose search for customers could not be marked by any very striking initiative. In the electrical industry all this was changed. Its organizers were the first to see that one of the primary duties of an industry was to create a market for itself. What did they do? They endeavoured to capture the customer. On the one hand, they attempted to control buyers. For example, by purchasing shares either in tram companies about to be turned into electric tramways, or in entirely new undertakings, they could obtain a dominating influence over the body which gave orders for the commodities they were manufacturing.   In case of need, the directors of electrical undertakings would themselves call into being limited companies for such activities as would create a demand for their goods.   The most successful electrical works have to-day become in an increasing degree similar to banks for floating companies.

Nor is this all.   Another policy they adopted was to establish branches in all parts in order to seize upon as much of the market as they could.   Whereas formerly reliance was placed on general agents, now the work of extending the connexion is delegated by each firm to a special representative of its own.   What is the result ?   The customer is seen at closer quarters ; his needs are better understood and, therefore, better supplied ; his wishes more easily met, and so forth.

It is well known that such was the system adopted by the Allgemeine Elektrizitäts-Gesellschaft and that Felix Deutsch was foremost in its extension.   The older companies have but slowly followed suit.   Siemens and Halske long thought themselves " too grand to run after customers," until Berliner, one of their directors, accepted the new plan to such good effect, that his company soon regained the lost ground from its rival.

This instance is typical, and we may say generally that the commercialization of industry was the gap in the hedge through which the Jews could penetrate into the field of the production and transportation of commodities, as they had done earlier in commerce and finance.

By this we are not asserting that the history of the Jews as industrialists commences here.   Far from it.   As soon as modern capitalism differentiated between the technical and commercial aspects of all economic processes, so soon was the Jew found engaged in both.   It is true that commerce attracted him more, but already in the early capitalistic period Jews were among the first undertakers in one industry or another.

Here they established the tobacco industry (Mecklenberg, Austria); there, whisky distilling (Poland, Bohemia); in some countries they were leather manufacturers (France, Austria), in others silk manufacturers (Prussia, Italy and Austria); they made stockings in Hamburg; looking-glasses in Fürth; starch in France; cotton in Moravia. And almost everywhere they were pioneers in the tailoring trade. I could show by reference to the materials I have collected that in the 18th and early 19th centuries there were many other instances of Jews as capitalistic industrialists.[275] But I hold that an account of this aspect of Jewish economic history is useless, seeing that it contains nothing specifically Jewish. Jews were driven into an industry by mere chance, and in all probability it would have thriven without them equally well. Let us take an instance or two. In Poland and Austria the position of the Jews as the stewards of the nobility brought it about that they became whisky distillers. In other countries their enterprise in the tobacco industry was a direct result of their status as Court Jews, in connexion with which they very often held the tobacco monopoly. In the majority of instances their commercial activities led to their stocking manufactured articles, and eventually to their making of them, as in the case of textiles. But the process is a common one, and non-Jews passed through it equally with Jews. There was, however, an exception in the case of old clo' dealing. That was an essentially Jewish business, and led first to the sale of new clothes, and eventually to tailoring.

But when all is said, Jewish influence on industrial undertakings was not very great until their commerciali-

zation came about ; that is, until in almost every modern
industry the work of directing and organizing has become
common to all, and a man may pass from one industry
to another without thereby diminishing his skill. The
technical side is now in all cases a subdivision by itself.
It is no uncommon thing therefore to find that a man
who started in the leather industry ends up as an iron-
master, after having been in turn (shall we say ?) a
manufacturer of alcoholic liquors and of sulphuric acid.
The capitalistic undertaker of old bore a technical
impress, the modern undertaker is quite colourless.   Can
you imagine Alfred Krupp manufacturing anything but
guns, Borsig anything but machines, Werner von Siemens
anything but electrical apparatus ?   Can you picture
H. H. Myer at the head of any other concern but the
Nord-deutscher Lloyd ?   On the other hand, if Rathenau,
Deutsch, Berliner, Arnold, Friedländer, Ballin changed
positions to-morrow they would be no less successful
than in their present capacities.   And what is the reason ?
They are all men of commerce, and the particular sphere
of their activity matters not in the least.

It has been put thus : the Christian makes his way up,
starting as technician ; the Jew as commercial traveller
or clerk.

The extent of Jewish participation in industrial undertakings to-day would be very useful to know, but there
is little material to go upon.   We shall have to be
content with an approximate estimate, based on the
numbers of Jews who are directors of industrial concerns.
The method is unsatisfactory—naturally so.   How is it
possible to say with certainty who is a Jew and who is
not ?   How many people are aware, for example, that
Hagen of Cologne, who holds more directorships than
any other man in Germany, was originally called Levy ?
But apart from this, mere numbers are no criterion of

the extent of influence. Moreover, in some companies business ability alone does not determine the membership of the Board of Directors ; in others there is an unwritten law to exclude Jews from positions of trust. In any case, therefore, the figures that have been obtained relate only to a small portion of the Jewish influence.

MANAGING DIRECTORS.

Industry.	Total.	Number of Jews.	Percentage of Jews.
Leather and rubber	19	6	31·5
Metal	52	13	25·0
Electrical	95	22	23·1
Brewing...	71	11	15·7
Textiles...	59	8	13·5
Chemicals	46	6	13·0
Mining	183	23	12·8
Machinery	90	11	12·2
Potash	36	4	11·1
Cement, timber, glass, china	57	4	7·0
Total	808	108	13·3

BOARD OF DIRECTORS.

Industry.	Total.	Number of Jews.	Percentage of Jews.
Brewing	165	52	31·5
Metal	130	40	30·7
Cement, timber, glass, china	137	41	29·9
Potash	156	46	29·4
Leather and rubber	42	12	28·6
Electrical	339	91	26·8
Mining	640	153	23·9
Chemicals	127	29	22·8
Machinery	215	48	21·4
Textiles	141	19	13·5
Total	2092	511	24·4

For all that I quote them ; they have been compiled for me from the last edition of the *Handbook of
German Joint-Stock Companies*.   In the case of the
electrical industries, only those with a capital of 6 million
mark have been noted ; in the chemical industries those
with 5 millions ; machinery and textiles with 4 millions,
and the remainder with 3 millions.

What do these figures suggest ?   Is the Jewish influence in the industries named great or small ?   I think
it is very large, at any rate quantitatively.   Bear in mind
that the social group which occupies almost a seventh part
of all directorships, and nearly a quarter of all the boards
of directors, forms exactly only a hundredth part of the
entire population of the German Empire.

CHAPTER VII

THE GROWTH OF A CAPITALISTIC POINT OF VIEW IN ECONOMIC LIFE

IT is evident from the survey in the previous chapters that Jewish influence extended far beyond the commercial institutions which it called into being. In other words, the Stock Exchange is not merely a piece of machinery in economic life, it is the embodiment of a certain spirit. Indeed, all the newest forms of industrial organization are the products of this spirit, and it is to this that I wish specially to call the reader's attention.

The outer structure of the economic life of our day has been built up largely by Jewish hands. But the principles underlying economic life—that which may be termed the modern economic spirit, or the economic point of view— may also be traced to a Jewish origin.

Proofs for the statement will have to be sought in directions other than those hitherto followed. Documentary evidence is obviously of little avail here. But what will certainly be a valuable guide is the feeling that prevailed in those circles which first became alive to the fact that the Jewish attitude of mind was something alien. Non-Jewish merchants or their spokesmen expressed opinions which, though one-sided and often harsh, are nevertheless of immense help, because they naïvely set forth the dislike of the Jewish spirit, reflecting it, as it were, as in a mirror (though often enough, to be sure, it was a convex mirror). The people who voiced the

opinions to which we are about to refer looked on
the Jews as their worst enemies, and therefore we must
try to read between the lines, and deduce the truth from
statements which were meant to convey something very
different.   The task is made the more easy because of the
uniformity in the opinions formulated—a uniformity due
by no means to thoughtless imitation, but rather to similarity of conditions.   Their very similarity adds to their
forcefulness as proofs.

In the first place, it must be noted that wherever Jews
appeared as business competitors, complaints were heard
that Christian traders suffered in consequence : their livelihood, we are told, was endangered, the Jews deprived
them of their profits, their chances of existence were
lessened because their customers went to Jews, and so
forth.

A few extracts from documents of the 17th and 18th
centuries, the period which concerns us most, will illustrate
what has been mentioned.   Let us turn first to Germany.
In 1672 the Estates of Brandenburg complain that the
Jews " take the bread out of the mouths of the other
inhabitants." [276]   Almost the same phrase is found
in the petition of the merchants of Danzig, of
March 19th, 1717.[277]   In 1712 and 1717 the good
citizens of the old town of Magdeburg object to the
admission of Jews into their midst, " because the welfare
of the city, and the success of traders, depends upon
the fact that . . . no Jewish dealing is permitted
here." [278]

In 1740 Ettenheim made a communication to its
Bishop, wherein it was stated that " as is well-known,
the Jews' low ways make only for loss and undoing."
The same idea is voiced in the proverb, " All in that
city doth decay, where Jews are plentiful as hay." [279]
In the preamble to the Prussian Edict of 1750, mention is

made that " the big merchants of our town complain . . . that the Jews who deal in the same commodities as they do, lessen their business considerably." It was the same in the South of Germany. In Nuremberg, for example, the Christian traders had to sit by and see their customers make purchases of Jews. In 1469 the Jews were expelled from Nuremberg ; a very large number of them settled in the neighbouring town of Fürth, and their customers from the first-named city, seeking the best advantage for themselves as buyers, journeyed to Fürth to do their shopping.* No wonder that the City Fathers of Nuremberg showered ordinances on the town throughout the 17th and 18th centuries, forbidding dealings with Jews from Fürth.[280]

That Jews all through the 18th century were refused admission to the merchant-gilds, no less than to the craft-gilds, is too well-known to need further emphasis.[281]

Was it different in England ? By no means. Says Josiah Child, " The Jews are a subtil people . . . depriving the English merchant of that profit he would otherwise gain " ; they carry on their business " to the prejudice of the English merchants." [282] When in 1753 the Jews' Naturalization Bill became law, the ill-will of the populace against the hated race was so great that the Act had to be repealed the very next year. One great fear was that if the Jews became English citizens they would " oust the natives from their employment." [283]

From Marseilles to Nantes the same tones were heard in France. The merchants of the latter city in 1752 bewailed their fate in the following terms : " The prohibited trade carried on by these strangers . . . has

[* The first German railway was built between Nuremberg and Fürth (1835). Whether the Jewish influence mentioned in the text had anything to do with it is difficult to say. But it is a curious fact.]

caused considerable loss to the merchants of this town, so much so, that if they are not favoured by the good-will of these gentry, they are in the predicament of being able neither to provide for their families nor to pay their taxes." [284]   Seven years earlier, in 1745, the Christian traders of Toulouse regretfully declared that " everybody runs to the Jewish traders." [285]   " We beseech you to bar the onward march of this nation, which otherwise will assuredly destroy the entire trade of Languedoc "—such was the request of the Montpelier Chamber of Commerce. [286]   Their colleagues in Paris compared the Jews to wasps who make their way into the hive only to kill the bees, rip open their bodies and extract the honey stored in their entrails. [287]

In Sweden, [289] in Poland, [290] the same cry resounded. [288]   In 1619 the civic authorities of Posen complained, in an address to King Sigismund, that " difficulties and stumbling-blocks are put in the way of merchants and craftsmen by the competition of Jews."

But all this does not suffice.   We want to know more than that the Jews endangered the livelihood of the others.   We want to find out the reason for this.   Why were they able to become such keen competitors of the Christian traders ?   Only when this question has been answered will we understand the peculiar nature of Jewish business methods, " les secrets du négoce," as Savary calls them.

Let us refer to contemporary opinion, to the men who were sufficiently in touch with everyday life to know the reason.   Here again the answer is pretty well unanimous. And what is it ?   The Jews were more successful because of their dishonest dealing.   " Jews . . . have one law and custom whenever it pays them : it is called lying and cheating," you may read in the pages of Philander von Sittewald.[291] Equally complimentary is the *Comic Lexicon of Cheating*, compiled by George Paul Hönn,[292] where under " Jews," the only interpolation in the whole book is made as follows : " Jews are cheats, collectively and individually. . . ." The article " Jews," in the *General Treasury for Merchants*, is of the same calibre,[293] while an anonymous writer on manners and morals declares that the Jews of Berlin " make their living by robbing and cheating, which, in their opinion, are no crimes." [294]

Similar views were current in France. " The Jews," says Savary, " have the reputation of being good at business, but they are supposed not to be able to carry it on with strict honesty and trustworthiness." [295]

Now what do these accusations amount to ? Even if the term " cheating " be given a very wide connotation, the commercial practices of many Jews hardly came within its scope. When it was asserted that Jews were cheats, that was only an epithet to describe the fact that Jews in their commercial dealings did not always pay regard to the existing laws or customs of trade. Jewish merchants offended in neglecting certain traditions of their Christian compeers, in (now and again) breaking the law, but above all, in paying no heed to commercial etiquette. Look closely into the specific accusations hurled against Jewish traders, examine their innermost nature, and you shall find that the conflict between Jewish and Christian merchants was a struggle between two outlooks, between two radically differing—nay, opposite—views on economic life.

To understand this conflict in its entirety, it will be necessary to obtain some idea of the spirit that dominated economic activities, activities in which from the 16th century onwards the Jews were obtaining a surer footing from day to day. So much did they seem to be out of harmony with that spirit that everywhere they were looked upon as a disturbing element.

During the whole of the period which I have described as the " early capitalistic age," and in which the Jews began to make their influence felt, the same fundamental notions generally prevailed in regard to economic life as characterized the Middle Ages—feudal relationships, manual labour, three estates of the realm, and so forth.

The centre of this whole was the individual man. Whether as producer or as consumer, his interests determined the attitude of the community as of its units, determined the law regulating economic activities and the practices of commercial life. Every such law was personal in its intent; and all who contributed to the life of the nation had a personal outlook. Not that each person could do as he liked. On the contrary, a code of restrictions hedged about his activities in every direction. But the point is that the restrictions were born of the individualistic spirit. Commodities were produced and bought and sold in order that consumers might have their wants sufficiently satisfied. On the other hand, producers and traders were to receive fair wages and fair profits. What was fair, and what sufficient for your need, tradition and custom determined.

And so, producer and trader should receive as much as was demanded by the standard of comfort in their station in life. That was the mediæval view; it was also the view current in the early capitalistic age, even where business was carried on along more or less modern lines. We find its expression in the industrial codes of the day, and its justification in the commercial literature.[296]

Hence, to make profit was looked upon by most people

throughout the period as improper, as "unchristian"; the old economic teaching of Thomas Aquinas was observed,[297] at least officially. The religious or ethical rule was still supreme; [298] there was as yet no sign of the liberation of economic life from its religious and ethical bonds. Every action, no matter in what sphere, was done with a view to the Highest Tribunal— the will of God. Need it be pointed out that the attitude of Mammon was as opposed to this as pole is to pole?

Producer and trader should receive sufficient for their need. One outstanding result of this principle was strictly to circumscribe each man's activity in his locality. Competition was therefore quite out of the question. In his own sphere a man might work as he willed—when, how, where—in accordance with tradition and custom. But to cast a look at his neighbour's sphere—that he was forbidden to do. Just as the peasant received his holding—so much field, with pasture and woodland, as would keep him and his family, just as he never even dreamt of adding to his possessions, so, too, the craftsman and the merchant were to rest content with their portions and never covet their neighbour's. The peasant had his land, the town-dweller his customers : in either case they were the source whence sprang his livelihood; in either case they were of a size sufficient for the purpose. Hence, the trader had to be assured of his custom, and many were the ordinances which guarded him against competition. Besides, it was commercial etiquette. You did not run after your customers. You waited until they came, "and then" (in the words of De Foe's sermon), "with God's blessing and his own care, he may expect his share of trade with his neighbours." [299] The merchant who attended fairs did not do otherwise; "day and night he waits at his stall." [300]

To take away your neighbour's customers was contemptible, unchristian, and immoral.[301] A rule for "Merchants who trade in commodities" was : "Turn no man's customers away from him, either by word of mouth or by letter, and do not to another what you would not have another do to you." [302] It was, however, more than a rule ; it became an ordinance, and is met with over and over again. In Mayence its wording was as follows : [303] "No one shall prevent another from buying, or by offering a higher price make a commodity dearer, on pain of losing his purchase ; no one shall interfere in another's business undertaking, or carry on his own on so large a scale as to ruin other traders." In Saxony it was much the same.[304] "No shopkeeper shall call away the customers from another's shop, nor shall he by signs or motions keep them from buying."

But to attract customers even without interfering with your neighbour's business was regarded as unworthy. As late as the early 18th century in London itself it was not considered proper for a shopkeeper to dress his window tastefully, and so lure purchasers. De Foe, no less than his later editors, did not mince words in expressing his contempt for such a course, of which, as he mentions apparently with some satisfaction, only a few bakers and toymen were guilty.[305]

To the things that were not permitted belonged also advertising your business and praising your wares. The gentle art of advertising first appeared in Holland sometime about the middle of the 17th century, in England towards its end, in France much later. The *Ghentsche Post-Tijdingen*, founded in 1667, contained the first business advertisement in its issue of October 3rd of that year.[306] At this time none of the London news-sheets published advertisements ; even after the

Great Fire not one business thought of advertising its new address. It was not until 1682, when John Houghton established *The Collection for the Improvement of Husbandry and Trade*, that the merchant community of London became accustomed to utilizing the Press as a medium for advertising.[307] This had been preceded by the practice, in a small way, of distributing bills in the streets to passers-by.

Two generations later Postlethwayt [308] gave currency to the then existing views. " Advertising in the newspapers, in regard to matters of trade and business, is now grown a pretty universal practice all over the kingdoms of England, Scotland and Ireland; . . . and however mean and disgraceful it was looked upon a few years since, by people of reputation in trade, to apply to the public by advertisements in the papers ; at present (1751) it seems to be esteemed quite otherwise ; persons of great credit in trade experiencing it to be the best, the easiest and the cheapest method of conveying whatever they have to offer to the knowledge of the whole kingdom."

They were not quite so far advanced in France at that time. In his Dictionary (1726) Savary [309] says nothing of the economic aspect of the term *réclame*. Not until six years later—in 1732, when his supplement was published—does he add : " A poster exhibited in public thoroughfares to make something generally known." And what does he instance? The sale of ships ; the time of sailing ; the announcement by the big trading companies of the arrival of goods from distant parts, but only in cases where they are to be publicly sold ; the establishment of new factories ; change of address. The business advertisement in its most elementary form is lacking. It is lacking also in the newspapers of the period until the second half of the

18th century. Surprising as it may seem, the first issue of the famous advertisement sheet, *Les Petites Affiches*, which appeared on May 13, 1751, contained no real business advertisement.[310]   In other words, the simple announcement " I sell such-and-such wares at such-and-such a place " did not become general in England until the 18th century, and in France not till much later.   In Germany only one or two towns were to the fore in this respect.   Berlin and Hamburg may be instanced, but even there the innovations are isolated, the only exception being books, which were originally much advertised.

To praise your goods or to point out wherein your business was superior to others was equally nefarious. But the last word in commercial impropriety was to announce that your prices were lower than those of the man opposite.   "To undersell" was most ungentlemanly : " No blessing will come from harming your neighbour by underselling and cutting prices." [311]

Bad as underselling itself was in the eyes of the people of those days, it was beneath contempt to advertise it. "Since the death of our author," say the editors of the fifth edition (1745) of De Foe's *Complete English Tradesman*,[312] " this underselling practice is grown to such a shameful height that particular persons publickly advertise that they undersell the rest of the trade."   It may be asked, Why were the editors so concerned about the matter ?   The reason is manifest in a subsequent passage.   " We have had grocers advertising their underselling one another at a rate a fair trader cannot sell for and live."   It is the old cry : fixed profits, a fixed livelihood, a fixed production and fixed prices.

We possess a French instance which shows even more strikingly how heinous this offence was thought to be, even in Paris. An Ordinance of 1761 [313] proclaimed to all and sundry in the French capital that to advertise that you are selling your goods at a price below the customary one must be regarded as the last resource of a merchant in difficulties, and that such action deserved severe condemnation. The Ordinance proceeded to forbid the traders of Paris and its suburbs "to run after one another trying to find customers, and above all, to distribute hand-bills calling attention to their wares."

Like the producers, the consumers also received attention. In a certain sense the consumer received even more, for the naïve conception that all production was in the interests of consumption had not yet disappeared. Hence the stress laid on *good* wares, on the principle that commodities should really be what they pretended ; and innumerable were the ordinances that were everywhere promulgated to this intent, more especially in the 17th and 18th centuries.

It was long before the purely capitalistic notion gained acceptance that the value in exchange of any commodity was what influenced the undertaker most. We may see how slow its progress was from the conflicting opinions on the subject in England in the 18th century. Sir Josiah Child appears to have been in the minority on this, as on most other questions, when he formulated the demand that every manufacturer should be allowed to judge for himself as to the kind of commodity, and the quality, that he brought into the market. It is curious enough nowadays to read Child's plea for the right of the manufacturer to make shoddy goods. "If we intend to have the trade of the world," he cries,[314] "we must imitate the Dutch, who make the worst as well as the best of all manufactures, that we may be in a capacity of serving all markets and all humours."

In a world of economic ideas such as these, the theory of "just price" was an organic element. Price was not something in the formation of which the individual had a say. Price was determined for him; it was as subject to religious and ethical principles as everything else in economic life. It was to be such as would make for the common good, as well of the consumer as of the producer. Different ages had their own standard for determining it; in Luther's day, for example, the cost of production was the deciding factor. But as commercial intercourse widened, the doctrine of the just price was found to be more and more impossible, and the view that price must be determined by the factors in the market [315] found general acceptance. But be that as it may, the point to accentuate is that price was based on ethical and not (as was held to be the case later) on natural principles. Then people said that the individual *must* not determine price at his own will; whereas later the view was that he *could* not so determine it.

What manner of world was that in which opinions such as these predominated? If we had to describe it in a word, we should say that it was "slow." Stability was its bulwark and tradition its guide. The individual never lost himself in the noise and whirl of business activity. He still had complete control of himself; he was not yet devoid of that native dignity, which does not make itself cheap for the sake of profit. Trade and commerce were everywhere carried on with a dash of personal pride. And all this to a greater extent in the country than in the large towns, where advancing capitalism made itself soonest felt. "The proud and haughty demeanour of the country merchant" is noted by a keen observer of his time. [316] We can almost see the type, in his knee-breeches and long coat, his head bewigged and his manner somewhat stiff. Business with him was an even process ; he got through it without much thought or worry, serving his circle of customers in the traditional way, knowing nothing of excitement, and never complaining that the day was too short.

To-day one of the best signs of a flourishing trade is a universal hurry and scurry, but towards the end of the 18th century that was regarded as a sure token of idleness. The man of business was deliberately slow of stride. " In Paris people are in one continuous haste—because there is nothing to do there ; here (in Lyons, the centre of the silk industry, and a town of some commercial importance) our walk is slow because every one is busy." Such is the verdict of the observer,[317] already mentioned, in the year of grace 1788.

In this picture the Nonconformist, the Quaker, the Methodist, is a fitting figure, even though we are accustomed to think of him as one of the first to be associated with capitalistic ideas. As his inner life, so was his outward bearing to be. " Walk with a sober pace, not tinkling with your feet," was a canon of the Puritan rule of life.[318] " The believer hath, or at least ought to have, and, if he be like himself, will have, a well-ordered walk, and will be in his carriage stately and princely." [319]

This was the world the Jews stormed. At every step they offended against economic principles and the economic order. That seems clear enough from the unanimous complaints of the Christian traders everywhere.

But were the Jews the only sinners in this respect? Was it fair to single out " Jewish dealing " and to stigmatize it as inclined to be dishonest, as contrary to law and practice, as characterized by lying and deception ? There can be little doubt that the practices

of Christian manufacturers and traders were not always
blameless in the matter of being opposed to custom
and regulation. Human nature being what it is, this
was only to be expected. But apart from that, the
age with which we are concerned could not boast of
a very high standard of commercial morality. Else
why the necessity for the plethora of ordinances and
prohibitions which touched economic activities at every
point ? Contemporary evidence certainly leaves no
doubt on the subject.

We have already mentioned the *Cheating Lexicon*
which was published at the beginning of the 18th century.
It must have been widely read, for in the space of a
few years several editions were issued. Turn to its
pages, and you will ask in amazement whether there
was any honesty left in the world. True, this impression
is created by the concentration within a small space of
very many instances and illustrations of cheating and
swindling. But even making allowance for this fact,
the impression cannot be eradicated that there must
have been a good deal of questionable conduct in those
days. And if any doubt still lurks on this point other
witnesses soon obliterate it. " You can find but few
wares nowadays (1742) that have not been adulterated,"
is the plaint of one German writer.[320] Numerous
are the prohibitions of the evil ; imperial edicts (such
as that of 1497), police regulations (such as that of
Augsburg, of 1548) and rules originating in merchant
circles (such as that of Lübeck, of 1607) all deal with
the practice. But falsification was by no means limited
to the production of commodities ; it was not unknown
in commerce too. Fraudulent bankruptcies must have
occurred very frequently in the 17th and 18th centuries,
and must have formed a problem difficult of solution.
Again and again there were complaints about their

uninterrupted reappearance.[321]   Indeed, the loose commercial morality of English merchants in the 17th century was proverbial.[322]   Cheating and falsifying were said to be "the besetting sin of English tradesmen." "Our merchants," says a 17th-century writer,[323] "by their ·infinite over-asking for commodities proclaim to the world that they would cheat all if it were in their power."

Such being the case, what reason was there for marking out the Jews?   And can we really speak of something specially characteristic in the conduct of Jews over against the established principles of the time?   I believe we can.   I believe that the specifically Jewish characteristic consisted in that it was not an individual here and there who offended against the prevailing economic order, but the whole body of Jews.   Jewish commercial conduct reflected the accepted point of view among Jewish traders.   Hence Jews were never conscious of doing wrong, of being guilty of commercial immorality ; their policy was in accordance with a system, which for them was the proper one.   They were in the right ; it was the other outlook that was wrong and stupid. We are not here speaking of capital delinquencies generally acknowledged to be wrong, and generally condemned.   For a distinction must be drawn between the fundamental regulations of any legal institution (*e.g.*, property), and those which vary with the progress of society.   Stealing will be looked upon as a capital offence as long as property exists ; but there will be much difference of opinion from age to age on the question of taking interest.   The first falls under the former category ; the second under the latter.

No doubt, in their peculiar commercial activity, Jews were guilty of both sorts of misdemeanours.   In early times Jews committed wrongs which were uni-

versally regarded as such.   They were constantly accused,
for example, of receiving and dealing in stolen pro-
perty.324   But Jews, as a body, themselves condemned
practices of this kind ; and for that matter, there were
honest and dishonest Jews as there were honest and
dishonest Christians.   If any Jews were addicted to
systematic cheating, they in so far set themselves up
against the majority of Jews and Christians, both of
whom were agreed that such conduct was not in accord
with the accepted standards of right.   We are not
without records that illustrate this very forcibly.   The
history of the Jews in Hamburg is an instance.   In the
17th century, the Portuguese Jews undertook to a
certain extent to be responsible to the authorities for
the proper commercial conduct of the newly arrived
German Jews.   As soon as the *Tedescos* came into the
city, they had to promise their Portuguese brethren not
to buy stolen property, nor otherwise to carry on shady
business.   On one occasion the Elders of the German
Jews were summoned before the *Mahamad** and warned
because several of them had broken their pledge ; on
another occasion because they had bought stolen goods
from soldiers.325

The point I am emphasizing must be remembered
in considering the accusations hurled against the Jews
in the early capitalistic age, accusations which, on the
whole, were not unfounded.   Universally accepted
offences, such as stealing or receiving stolen property,
must not be included under this heading.   Jews equally
with Christians abhorred such crimes.   The practices,
however, common to all Jews, which overstepped law
and custom, but which Jews did not feel as being wrong,
the practices which may be looked upon as being the

[* The governing body of the Portuguese Jewish congregation.   The
term is still used among the Spanish and Portuguese Jews in London.]

result of a specifically Jewish outlook, these must come within our ken. And what do we find on examining them ?

We find that the Jew rises before us unmistakably as more of a business-man than his neighbour ; he follows business for its own sake ; he recognizes, in the true capitalistic spirit, the supremacy of gain over all other aims.

I know of no better illustration than the *Memoirs of Glückel von Hameln*, a mine of information, by the way, about Jewish life and thought in the early capitalistic age. Glückel, the wife of a merchant in Hamburg, lived between 1645 and 1724, the period when the Jewish communities of Hamburg and Altona shot up to a position of prosperity, and in almost every respect we may regard this remarkable woman as a type of the Jew of that day. Her narrative grips the reader because of its natural simplicity and freshness. As I read these *Memoirs*, in which a complete personality is revealed to us in a life rich in experience, I was again and again reminded of the famous Frau Rat (Goethe's mother).

If I cite just this splendid book in order to show the predominating interest of money among Jews in those days, it is because I believe that this characteristic must have been general, seeing that even in so gifted a woman as Glückel it also stands out. In very truth, money is the be-all and end-all with her, as with all the other people of whom she has anything to say. Accounts of business enterprise occupy but a small space in the book, but on no less than 609 occasions (in 313 pages) does the authoress speak of money, riches, gain and so forth. The characters and their doings are mentioned only in some connexion or other with money. Above all, we are told of good matches—good from the financial point of view. To marry her children is in fact the chief object of Glückel's business activities. " He also saw my son, and they were almost on the point of coming to terms, but they could not close because of a thousand marks." Incidents of this kind abound in the book. Of her second marriage she says, " in the afternoon my husband wedded me with a valuable gold ring an ounce in weight." I cannot help regarding the peculiar conception of marriage-making, which used to be current among Jews, as symptomatic of the way they looked upon money, and especially the tendency among them of appraising even the most precious things in life from a purely business point of view. Children, for example, have their value. That was a matter of course among Jews in those days. " They are all my darling children, and may they all be forgiven, as well those on whom I had to spend a lot of money as those on whom I spent nothing," writes Glückel. It was as marriageable persons that they had a price, which varied with the state of the market. Scholars, or the children of scholars, were much in demand. In one case we are told that a father speculated in his children. The fortunes of Solomon Maimon, as related by Graetz, are well known and frequently cited in this connexion. " At eleven years of age he had so complete a mastery of the Talmud that he . . . became much sought after as a possible husband. His needy father, in a speculating spirit, provided him with two brides at once, without his being able to see . . . either of them." Similar incidents are abundant enough to warrant the conclusion that they must have been typical.

But the objection may be urged that among Christians also money was no less valued, only the fact was not admitted ; people were hypocritical. There is perhaps a certain element of truth in this objection. In that case I should say that what was specifically Jewish was the naïveté with which money was made the pivot of life ; it was a matter of course ; no attempt was made to hide it.

What light does contemporary opinion in the 17th and 18th centuries shed upon the characteristic to which we have called attention ? There appears to be universal agreement on the subject, which lends support to our theory. The Jew in those days of undeveloped capitalism was regarded as the representative of an economic outlook, wherein to obtain profit was the ultimate goal of all commercial activity. Not his " usury " differentiated him from the Christian, not that he sought gain, not that he amassed wealth ; only that he did all this openly, not thinking it wrong, and that he scrupulously and mercilessly looked after his business interests. But more awful things are related of Christian " usurers " who " are worse than Jews." " The Jew wears his soul on his sleeve and is not ashamed, but these carry on their devil's trade with hypocritical Christian countenances." [326]

One or two more contemporary opinions must be quoted. " These people have no other God but the unrighteous Mammon, and no other aim than to get possession of Christian property . . . they . . . look at everything for their profit." [327] Such is the verdict of the Rev. John Megalopolis, who wrote on March 18th, 1655. Another judgment is harsher still. [328] " No trust should be put in the promises made there (in Brazil) by the Jews, a race faithless and pusillanimous, enemies to all the world and especially to all Christians, caring not whose house burns so long as they may warm themselves at the coals, who would rather see a hundred thousand Christians perish than suffer the loss of a hundred crowns." The statement of Savary,[329] who was amicably disposed towards the Jews, is also to the point. " A usurious merchant

or one too keen, who tries to get a mean advantage
and flays those who have dealings with him, is termed
'a real Jew.' People say ' he has fallen into the hands
of Jews ' when those with whom a man does business are
hard, immovable and stingy." It is true that a very
Christian merchant first coined the phrase " Business
is business," but Jews undoubtedly were the first to
mould their policy in accordance with it.

In this connexion we ought to mention also that
the proverbs of all nations have always depicted the
Jew as the gain-seeker, who had a special love of money.
" Even to the Jew our Lady Mary is holy " (Hungarian)
—in reference to the Kremnitzer gold ducats. " Yellow
is the colour that suits the Jew best" (Russian). " Yellow
is the dearest colour for the Jew " (German).

This profit-seeking, which the Jew held to be legitimate, will account for his business principles and
practices, of which complaints were so frequently made.
In the first place, he paid no attention to the strict
delimitation of one calling or of one handicraft from
another, so universally insisted on by law and custom.
Again and again we hear the cry that Jews did not
content themselves with one kind of activity ; they did
whatever they could, and so disturbed the order of
things which the gild system wished to see maintained.
Their aim was to seize upon all commerce and all production ; they had an overpowering desire to expand
in every direction. " The Jews strive to destroy
the English merchants by drawing all trade towards
themselves," is a further complaint of the Rev. John
Megalopolis in 1655.[330] " The Jews are a subtil
people prying into all kinds of trade," said Sir Josiah
Child.[331] And Glückel von Hameln thus describes her
father's business : " He dealt in precious stones, and in
other things—for every Jew is a Jack-of-all-trades."

Innumerable were the occasions when the German gilds complained of this Jewish ubiquitousness in trade, which paid no heed to the demarcation of all economic activities into strictly separate categories. In 1685, the city authorities of Frankfort-on-the-Main were loud in their cry that Jews had a share in all kinds of business—*e.g.*, in linen and silk retailing, in cloth and book selling.[332]   In the other Frankfort (on the Oder) [333] Jews were blamed for selling foreign braid to the detriment of the gold-lace makers, and so forth.

Perhaps the reason for this tendency to universal trading may be found in that a large number of miscellaneous articles, all forfeited pledges, brought together by mere chance, collected in the shops of Jews, and their sale would naturally enough interfere with the special business of all manner of dealers.   The very existence of these second-hand shops—the prototype of the stores in modern times—was a menace to the prevailing order of commerce and industry.   A vivid picture of such a collection of second-hand goods is given in an old Ratisbon song, dating from the 15th century,[334] and the details could not but have become more well-marked as time went on.

> "No handicraft however mean,
> But the Jew would damage it i' the extreme.
> For if any one had need of raiment
> To the Jew he'd hie with payment;
> Whether 'twas silver or linen or tin,
> Or aught his house was lacking in,
> The Jew was ready to serve his need,
> With pledges he held—right many indeed.
> For stolen goods and robbers' plunder
> They and the Jew were seldom asunder.
>
> .   .   .   .
>
> Mantle, hose or damsel's veil,
> The Jew he had them all for sale.
> To the craftsman, then, there came but few,
> For all the world dealt with the Jew."

Here an interesting question presents itself. Is there any connexion between the breach of gild regulations and the stress laid on pure business ends on the part of the Jews, and their hostile attitude to mercantilism? Was it their aim to establish the principle that trade should be untrammelled, regardless of the commercial theory which guided the mercantilist States? It looks like it. "Jewish trade," was the term applied to the commerce of Frankfort in the 18th century, because it was mostly import trade, "which gives useful employment to but few German hands and flourishes only by reason of home consumption." 335 And when in the early 19th century Germany was flooded with the cheap products of England, which were sold for the most part at auctions, Jews were held to be the mainstay of this import trade. The Jew almost monopolized the auctions. "Since dealing in manufactured articles is to a great extent in the hands of Jews, the commerce of England is for the most part with them." The Jew had "his shop full of foreign hats, shoes, stockings, leather gloves, lead and copper ware, lacquer work, utensils, ready-made clothing of all sorts—all brought over by English ships." 336 It was the same story in France. 337 Nor was this all. The Jews were guilty of another deadly sin in the mercantilist calendar: they imported raw materials.337A

We see, then, that the Jews, in following their business interests, gave as little heed to the barriers between States as to those between industries. Still less did they have regard to the prevailing code of etiquette in any industry. We have already seen how custom-chasing was looked upon in the early capitalistic age. Here the Jews were continual offenders. Everywhere they sought out sellers or buyers, instead of waiting for them in their shops, as commercial custom prescribed. Of this we have abundant proof.

A complaint was lodged by the furriers of Königs-berg [338] in 1703 against "the Jews Hirsch and Moses, who with their agents are always first in the field in buying raw material and selling the ready-made furs, whereby they (the supplicants) suffer much loss." In 1685 the jewellers and goldsmiths of Frankfort had a similar experience.[339] They were forced to buy all the old gold and silver they needed from Jews, who, by means of their numerous "spies," snapped it away from under the very noses of the Christians. A few years previously the whole of the trading body of that town had protested against Jews "spying out the business of Christian merchants." Earlier still, in 1647, the tailors of Frankfort petitioned [340] that the Jews should be forbidden to engage in the sale of new cloth-ing. "A source of bitter weeping it is, that the Jews may freely wander up and down the streets, laden with all manner of goods and cloth, like so many camels and asses, running to meet every newcomer to Frankfort, be he of high or low degree, and offering to sell him what he wants ; and so deprive us of our daily bread." [340] Still earlier even than this, in 1635, was the petition of the silk merchants, who bemoaned the fact that the Jews "wait about in the city outside the bounds of the Jewish quarter, in inns and wherever opportunity offers ; they run through many a street, both openly and in secret, to meet the soldiers and their officers, when these come to town. They have arranged with certain master-tailors to give them facilities for exhibiting their wares at their shops when troops march past." [340]

In 1672 a complaint is heard from Brandenburg.[341] "Jews go about as chapmen among the villages and in the towns and force their wares on people." A similar story comes from Frankfort-on-the-Oder, [341] wherein the details are fuller. Jews run after customers—the travellers to their hotels, the nobility to their castles and the students to their lodgings. And in Nikolsburg, in Austria, we are told [342] that " the Jews have drawn to themselves all the trade, all the money, all the goods. They wait outside the city, try to strike up an acquaintance with travellers while they are yet on the road, and endeavour to take away their custom from Christian citizens."

How the Jews were ever on the look-out for new customers is described by a well-informed writer of the early 19th century. [343] It was a practice with them, he says, " to pay frequent visits to all and sundry places of public resort where, by reading the many news-sheets, they sought to obtain knowledge of possibilities for doing business, and especially of noting what strangers were expected to arrive ; and by listening to every conversation, to find out whose houses were in danger in order to make bargains or contracts with them."

The streets in which the Jewish old clo' men lived were the scenes of similar activities, the end in view always being the same. In fact, the dealers sometimes seized the passer-by by the arm and tried to force him to make purchases. This method of carrying on business is not unknown in our modern cities ; it was known in the Paris of the 18th century, where it was associated with the *fripiers*, the old clo' dealers, who, as we are informed, [344] were for the most part Jews. One description of such a scene is too good not to be quoted. [345] " The touts of these disorderly shops call to you uncivilly enough ; and when one of them has invited you, all the other shopkeepers on your road repeat the deafening invitation. The wife, the daughter, the servant, the dog, all howl in your ears. . . . Sometimes these fellows seize an honest man by the arm, or by his shoulder, and force him to enter in spite of himself; they make a pastime of this unseemly game. . . . "

We hear the same tale from a traveller who journeyed in Western Germany about that time. " To walk in the streets of those places where there are many Jews has become a nuisance. You are badgered by them every minute and at every turn. You are constantly being asked, Can I sell you anything? Won't you buy this, that or the other ? " [346]

Or they turn into wandering traders in order to sweep in custom. " The Jew thinks nothing of turning the seats in the porches into a shop counter, often extending them by means of planks ; he places a form or table against the wall of any house he can get at, or even makes the front passage into a shop ; or, he hires a cart which becomes his moving shop, and often enough he has the bad manners to pull up in front of a shop which sells the same wares as he." [347]

" Get hold of the customers "—that was the end and aim. Is it not the guiding principle of the big industries of to-day? Is not the splendid organization of a concern like the Allgemeine Elektricitäts-Gesell-schaft, for example, directed to the same object ?

The policy was first systemized when advertising was resorted to. The " deafening invitation " which, as we have just noted, came from the small *fripier*, is now made by the million-voiced advertisements of our business life. If the Jews are to be considered the originators of the system of " getting hold of the customers," their claim to be the fathers of modern advertising is equally well established. I am, however, unable to adduce conclusive evidence for this. What is needed is a careful study of the files of the earliest newspapers, in order to discover the names of the people who advertised. As a matter of fact, the whole subject of advertising has as yet been dealt with but scantily. The only branch which has received adequate attention is the history of business announcements. Nevertheless, I am able to give one or two instances which show the connexion of Jews with the practice of advertising.

The very earliest advertisement with which I am acquainted is to be found in No. 63 of the *Vossische Zeitung*, of May 28, 1711, which is to this effect : " This is to inform all and sundry that a Dutch (Jewish ?) merchant has arrived at Mr. Boltzen's in the Jews' Street, with all kinds of tea of the finest quality, to be sold cheap. Any one who may care to buy should come early, as the visitor will not stay for more than eight days."

The first known advertisement in the text of the paper dates from 1753, and hails from Holland. The advertiser was an eye-specialist of the name of Laazer. [348] A very old advertisement in the United States—whether the oldest I cannot say—appeared on August 17, 1761, in the *New York Mercury*, as follows [349] :—" To be sold by Hayman Levy, in Bayard Street, Camp Equipages of all sorts, best soldiers' English shoes . . . and everything that goes to make up the pomp and circumstance of glorious war."

Finally, the Jews are the founders of the modern Press, *i.e.*, the machinery for advertising, more especially of the cheap newspapers. [350] Polydore Millaud, who established the *Petit Journal*, was the father of the " halfpenny Press."

But to obtain likely addresses, to intercept travellers on their way, to sing the praises of your wares—that was only one side of the game of catching customers. It was supplemented by another, which consisted in so decking-out the goods for sale as to attract people. In this art the Jews were great adepts. Nay more, there is sufficient evidence that they were the first to stand up for the general principle, that it is the right (and the duty) of every trader to carry on his business in such a way as will obtain for him as much of the available custom as possible, or by creating new demands, will increase the circle of buyers.

Now in a community where quality was regulated, the only effective means of achieving this end was price-cutting. We shall therefore not be surprised to find the Jews availing themselves of this weapon, and we shall see that it was just this that made them so dis-liked among Christian traders, whose economic outlook was all for maintaining prices. The Jew undersells ; the Jew spoils prices ; the Jew tries to attract customers by low prices—that was the burden of the complaints heard in the 17th and 18th centuries wherever Jews did business.

Our pages would be overloaded did we attempt to cite all the proofs on this point. A few, therefore, will have to suffice.

First for England where, in 1753, the storm burst forth against the Jews on the passing of the Naturaliza-tion Bill. One of the principal fears was that if they became recognized citizens, they would oust the natives from their means of livelihood by underselling them.[351]

Next for France. "The stuffs . . which the Jews bring to the fairs . . . are worth more at the price at which they sell them than those in the traders' shops," is the reply [352] of the Intendant of Languedoc to the plaints of the merchants of Montpellier (May 31, 1740). The merchants of Nantes [353] were of opinion that the public, which dealt with Jews under the impression that they were making a good bargain, were generally duped. At the same time, they admit that prices at Jewish shops are lower than elsewhere. The same admission is made by the Paris traders : the Jews sell even more cheaply than the factories.[354] Concerning a Fürth Jew, of the name of Abraham Oulman,[355] the bronze-dealers of Paris reported that "he sells the same bronzes below the price for which they are sold in this country." In Lyons the master silk-weavers passed a resolution (October 22, 1760) in which they ascribed the bad times to the influence of the Jews, who had cut prices, and thereby made themselves masters of the silk industry in all the provinces.[356]

The Swedish Parliament in 1815 debated the question whether the Jews should be allowed entire liberty of trade, and one of the chief reasons which prevailed against the motion was that Jews lowered prices.[357]

From Poland the same strains reach us. Jews tell Christian traders that if they (the latter) sold their goods as cheaply as the Jews, they too would attract customers.[358]

It is no different in Germany. From Brandenburg (1672),[359] from Frankfort (17th century),[360] from Magdeburg (1710)[361] the old story is repeated. A Wallachian traveller in Germany[362] about the same time reports the ubiquity of this accusation. The General Prussian Edict of 1750 takes cognizance of it. "The merchants of our towns . . . complain . . . that the Jewish traders who sell the same goods do them great harm, because they sell at a lower price." Right up to the 19th century it is still met with. In the Supplication of the Augsburg wholesale merchants against the admission of the Jews[363] (1803) we may read that "the Jews understand how to derive advantages from the general depression of trade. They obtain goods from people who need money badly at shameful prices, and then spoil the market by selling them at a cheaper rate."

In many branches of industry Christian manufacturers and merchants even to-day regard the cutting of prices by Jews as a serious endangering of their trade. That this is an open secret and often enough discussed, is well known. I hope to touch upon the matter again in due course.

One more instance from the history of Finance, as showing that the Jews had the reputation of making lower terms. When the Austrian Government early in the 18th century determined on raising another loan, as usual, in Holland, an order was issued (December 9, 1701) to Baron Pechmann, who was negotiating the matter, to make private enquiries whether, in view of the fact that the Hungarian Copper Mines were being pledged to guarantee the loan, a greater sum might not be raised. More especially was he to communicate with the Portuguese Jews in Holland, since the other subjects of the United Provinces asked for an additional guarantee beside the general one.[364] In a report of the Court Chancery of Vienna (May 12, 1762) the view is expressed that "it is advisable to come to terms with the Jews in reference to contracts for the army . . . seeing that they are prepared to quote lower prices than others."

Here, then, was a problem for all the wiseacres to put their heads together and try to solve. They did, asking each other again and again, at their work and in their shops, on Sunday afternoons in their walks outside the city rampart, and in the evenings at the social pint of beer: How is it possible? How on earth is it done? How can the Jew carry through his " dirty trick " of underselling? What was the reason for it?

The answer differed in accordance with the capacity and the prejudice of each enquirer. And so the numberless explanations on record cannot be accepted without testing their value ; unlike the assertion that Jews lowered prices, which, in view of its unanimity, there is no reason to doubt. In any case, for the present only those opinions will be of interest to us which give indication of a special way of carrying on business, or of a special commercial morality.

The commonest explanation is that of dishonesty, and the conclusion was arrived at in some such way as this. Seeing that the Jews have the same expenses, seeing that the cost of production is also the same, if the price is below the current one, everything is not quite above-board. The Jews must have obtained possession of their wares by dishonest means. They were doubtless stolen goods. The bad reputation of the Jews generally must have given probability to this explanation, and the low prices must have lent support to the accusation levelled against them that they were receivers.

I have no intention of citing instances where this line of argument is taken, for in reality it is the least interesting of any. In many cases, no doubt, it was correct. But if that were the only reason forthcoming to account for low prices among Jewish traders, there would be no need to mention the matter at all, for then it would not have the significance which it actually possesses.

As a matter of fact, even the extremists among gild members could not but cast about for other causes to account for the underselling of Jewish traders, and they found them close at hand, not in actual breach of the law, but in practices that were not all they should be. And what were these ? That the Jews dealt in pro-hibited articles (contraband of war, etc.) ; in lapsed pledges ; in goods that had been confiscated (*e.g.*, by customs officials); in goods that had been bought for a mere song from the owners, who were deep in debt and whose necessity, therefore, was great,[365] or from those who needed money badly ;[366] in old goods, bought for next to nothing at auctions ; in bankrupt stock ; [367] in goods the quality of which was not up to the standard of the ordinances of the industrial code ; [369] or, finally, that the Jew cut prices with the intention of going into bankruptcy himself.[368]

To what extent instances such as these—" the miserable methods of the Jews " as they were termed by the traders of Metz [370]—were general or only sporadic, it is difficult to say. Nor does it much matter for our purpose. As to their probability, it is hardly likely that they were all pure inventions. The important thing to note, however, is that shady practices such as those enumerated were laid to the Jews' door. And even if only a minute proportion were in accordance with actual fact, that would be enough to make them symptomatic, and they would be very useful as supporting the result obtained in other ways. I shall return to this question later. Here we will continue the catalogue of reasons which were urged in explanation of the Jews' lower prices.

Side by side with those already mentioned was the accusation that the commodities sold by the Jews were of an inferior quality. So frequently is this statement met with that its correctness can hardly be doubted. An official report from Magdeburg, a petition from Brandenburg, a complaint from Frankfort [371]—all harp on this same string. And the *Traders' Lexicon*, to which I have already more than once referred as a reliable authority, states that Jews sold inferior goods " which they know how to polish up, to colour anew, to show off at their best, to provide with a fresh cover, smell and taste that even the greatest connoisseur is often taken in."

This is repeated almost verbally in the Report of the merchants of Nantes, with which we are by this time so well acquainted. The goods of the Jews are really dear, despite their cheapness. For they sell things that are out of fashion or that cannot be used any longer. Silk stockings they re-dye, pass them through a calender, and then sell them as new. But they cannot be worn more than once. The silk weavers of Lyons tell the same tale : [372] the Jews have ruined the silk industry because, in order to be able to sell at low prices, they order goods of second-rate quality only. So, too, the Governor of Bohemia in 1705 : [373] " The Jews have got hold of all manual occupations and all commerce, but as for the most part they make only poor stuff, there is no chance for a profitable export trade to spring up." The opinion of Wegelin in the Swedish Parliament (1815), likewise referred to already, is only in accord with the preceding. " It is true," he said, " that the Jews alone engaged in calico-printing, but they have completely spoiled this branch of industry because of their low quality goods—the so called " Jews' calico."

This complaint, which started in the early capitalistic period, has not yet ceased. The cry of the Christian manufacturers that the Jews cut prices has been followed by the corollary that, in order to maintain low prices at all costs, Jews lowered the quality of goods.

Summing up all the facts adduced, we shall perceive that the Jews originated the principle of substitution.

What was called inferior quality in the wares of the Jews was not in reality so. It was not as if the articles were of the same sort as those of other traders, except that they were worse in quality. It was rather that they were new articles, intended for similar use as the old, but made of a cheaper material, or by new processes which lessened the cost of production. In other words, the principle of substitution was brought into play, and Jews may thus be regarded as the pioneers in its application. The most frequent cases occurred in textile fabrics ; but other instances are also on record—for example, substitutes for coffee. In one sense, too, dyeing must be mentioned in this connexion. Jewish influence aided its growth. Originally, the inventors of artificial alizarine used expensive chemicals to mix with their red colouring matter ; the Jews introduced cheaper materials, and thus gave an impetus to the dyeing industry.

There is yet one other, though less frequent, accusation levelled against the Jews. It was that the Jews could sell more cheaply than Christians because they gave less weight or short measure.[374] They were taunted with this in Avignon, where woollen articles were mentioned, and in the case of German Jews an actual illustration is given. " The Jew is on the look-out for the least advantage. If he measured 10 ells there were only 9⅞. The Christian (customer) is aware of this, but he says to himself, ' Jews' measure is short, ten ells are never quite ten, but then the Jew sells cheap.' " [375]

In all this the point for us to discover is whether, and if so to what extent, the different courses, which were alleged to have been taken by the Jewish traders in order to reduce prices, may be traced to some general business principle characteristic of the Jews. To my mind, the whole case can be summed up by saying that the Jew to a certain extent held that in business the means justified the end. His consideration for the other traders and his respect for legal enactments and social demands were not very great, while on the other hand, the idea of value in exchange in relation to goods, and the idea that all business activity had reference to wealth and to that only—these became keen. What I have elsewhere described as the inherent tendency in capitalism to obtain profit, regardless of all else, is here seen in its early origin.

But we have not yet done with the inventory of methods adopted by Jews to lower prices. We now turn to those which were of equal fundamental importance with the others already mentioned, but which differed from them materially. While the first brought about only apparent reductions, or actual reductions at other people's expense, these produced lower prices really and absolutely. What were they? Innovations which decreased the total cost of production in some way or other. Either the producer or the dealer was content with less for himself, or the actual expenses of production were reduced in that wages were lowered or the manufacturing and distributing processes made more efficient.

That all these means of cheapening commodities were adopted by Jews, and by them first, is amply evidenced by records in our possession.

First, the Jew could sell more cheaply because he was satisfied with less than the Christian trader. Unprejudiced observers remarked this fact on many occasions, and even the competitors of the Jews admitted its truth. Let us once again quote the Magdeburg official report. The Jews sell cheaply, " whereby the merchants must suffer loss. For they need more than the Jew, and, therefore, must carry on their business in accordance with their requirements." [376] In another document it is also stated that " the Jew is satisfied with a smaller profit than the Christian." [377] And what did the Polish Jews tell the Christian Poles? [378] That if they (the Poles) did not live so extravagantly, they would be able to sell their goods at the same prices as the Jews. A keen-eyed traveller in Germany towards the end of the 18th century came to the same conclusion. " The reason for the complaint (that Jews sell cheaply) is apparent : it lies in the extravagant pride of the haughty shopkeeper, who in his dealings requires so much for mere show, that he cannot possibly charge low prices. The Jew, therefore, deserves the gratitude of the public, to whom he brings gain by his frugal habits, and forces the shopkeeper with his large expenditure either to be more economical, or to go to the wall." [379] The Report of the Vienna Court Chancery (May 12, 1762) was of the same opinion. The Jews can deliver at a lower rate than the Christians " because they are more thrifty and live more cheaply." The tale was repeated in a Hungarian document of January 9, 1756, wherein the proposed reduction by Joseph II of Jewish spirit-licences was discussed. It was there pointed out [380] that Jews were able to pay more for their licences because of their cheap and poor living.

No less explicit on the point is Sir Josiah Child for the England of his age. "They are a penurious people, living miserably," he says, [381] " and therefore can, and do afford to trade for less profit than the English." By the middle of the 18th century this belief was still current, for the cry went up that the Jews by reason of their extreme frugality were able to undersell the natives.[382] The identical view prevailed in France. "It is my firm belief," said the Intendant of Languedoc,[383] in reply to the chronic complaints of the traders of Montpellier, " that Jewish commerce . . . does less harm to the merchants of Montpellier than their own lack of attention to the requirements of the public, and their rigid determination to make as large profits as they can."

But this is not all. There were people who asserted— and they must have been gifted with no little insight— that the Jews had discovered yet another trick, by means of which they succeeded in obtaining as great, or even greater, profits than their Christian neighbours despite their comparatively low prices—they increased their turnover. As late as the early part of the 19th century this was regarded as a specifically " Jewish practice " [384]—

" small profits with a frequent turnover of your capital pay incomparably better than big profits and a slow turnover." This is no isolated opinion ; it occurs very frequently indeed.[385]

Small profits, quick returns—obviously this was a breaking away from the preconceived idea of an economic organization of society, where one of the cardinal doctrines was to produce for subsistence only. And the Jews were the fathers of this new business-principle. Profit was considered as something fixed by tradition ; henceforward it was determined by each individual trader. That was the great novelty, and again it emanated from Jews. It was a Jewish practice to settle the rate of profit as each trader thought fit ; it was a Jewish practice to decide whether to sell at a profit at all, or for a time to do business without making profits in order to earn more afterwards.[386]

Lastly, we have still to mention the taunt levelled against Jews, that they sought to reduce the cost of production, either by employing the cheapest labour, or by utilizing more economical methods.

With regard to the first, numerous plaints abound. The woollen manufacturers of Avignon,[387] the merchants of Montpellier,[388] the civic authorities of Frankfort-on-the-Oder [389] and the Tailors' Craft of the other Frankfort are a few cases in point. But none of these disaffected people could realize that the Jews were the earliest undertakers in industries with capitalistic organizations, and, consequently, utilized new forms of production, just as they had utilized them in commerce.

And here we must not pass over another characteristic of Jewish business methods, one, however, which is not mentioned in the literature of the early capitalistic period, probably because it was developed at a later date. I refer to the conscious endeavour of attracting new customers by some device or other—whether it was the placing of goods for sale in a new juxtaposition, or a new system of payment, or a new combination of departments, or the organization of some new service.   It would be a most fascinating study to compile a list of all the inventions (exclusive, of course, of technical inventions) which trade and commerce owe to the Jews.   Let me refer to a few, about which we are tolerably certain that they are of Jewish origin.   I say nothing as to whether Jews were merely the first to apply them, or whether they were actually created by Jews.

First in order I would mention the trade in old and damaged goods, the trade in remnants and rubbish—the Jews were able " here and there to maintain themselves and make a profit out of the commonest articles, which before had no value whatever, such as rags, rabbit-skins and gall-nuts." [390]   In short, we may term the Jews the originators of the waste-product business.   Thus, in the 18th century in Berlin, Jews were the first feather-cleaners, the first vermin-killers and the inventors of the so-called " white beer." [391]

To what extent the general store owes its existence to the Jew it is impossible to say.   Anyhow, the Jews, in that they held pledges, were the first in whose shops might be found a conglomeration of wares.   And is it not one of the distinguishing marks of a modern store to have for sale articles of various kinds, intended for various uses ?   The result is that the owner of the store is but little concerned with what he sells, so long as he does sell.   His aim is to do business, and this policy is in accordance with the Jewish spirit.   But apart from that, it is well-known that to-day stores in the United States [392] and in Germany [393] are for the most part in the hands of Jews.

An innovation of no little importance in the organization of retail trading at the time of its introduction was the system of payment by instalments when goods to a large amount or very costly goods were sold. In Germany, at any rate, it is possible to say with tolerable certainty, that in this, too, Jews were pioneers. "There is a class of shopkeeper among Jews," we may read in an early 19th-century writer, "indispensable to the ordinary man, and of exceeding great benefit to trade. They are the people who sell clothes or material for clothes to the ordinary customer, and receive payment for it in small instalments." 394

Of Jewish origin also are a number of innovations in the catering business. Thus, the first coffee-house in England (perhaps the first in the world) was opened in Oxford in 1650, or 1651, by a Jew of the name of Jacobs.395 It was not until 1652 that London obtained its first coffee-house. And to come to a later period, everybody knows that a new era dawned in catering when Kempinsky * introduced the standard-ization of consumption and of prices as the guiding principles of the business.

In all these instances it is not so much the inno-vations themselves that interest us, as the tendency to which they bear witness—that a new business ideal had come into existence : the adoption of new tricks. Hence my treatment of this subject in the present chapter, which deals with the Jewish spirit, Jewish commercial morality and the specifically Jewish economic outlook.

Reviewing the ground we have traversed, we see clearly the strong contrast between the Jewish and the non-Jewish outlooks in the early capitalistic period. Tradition, the subsistence ideal, the overpowering in-fluence of status—these were the fundamentals of the latter. And the former—wherein lay its novelty ?

[* Kempinsky is the Lyons of Berlin.]

How may it be characterized? I believe one all-comprehensive word will serve our purpose, and that word is "modern." The Jewish outlook was the "modern" outlook ; the Jew was actuated in his economic activities in the same way as the modern man. Look through the catalogue of "sins" laid at the door of the Jews in the 17th and 18th centuries, and you will find nothing in it that the trader of to-day does not regard as right and proper, nothing that is not taken as a matter of course in every business. Throughout the centuries the Jews championed the cause of individual liberty in economic activities against the dominating views of the time. The individual was not to be hampered by regulations of any sort, neither as to the extent of his production nor as to the strict division between one calling and another : he was to be allowed to carve out a position for himself at will, and be able to defend it against all comers. He should have the right to push forward at the expense of others, if he were so able ; and the weapons in the struggle were to be cleverness, astuteness, artfulness ; in economic competition there should be no other consideration but that of overstepping the law ; finally, all economic activities should be regulated by the individual alone in the way he thinks best to obtain the most efficient results. In other words, the idea of free-trade and of free competition was here to the fore ; the idea of economic rationalism ; in short, the modern economic outlook, in the shaping of which Jews have had a great, if not a decisive influence. And why? It was they who introduced the new ideas into a world organized on a totally different basis.

Here a pertinent question suggests itself. How are we to explain that even before the era of modern capitalism, Jews showed a capacity for adopting its principles? The question must be expanded into a much larger one. What was it that enabled the Jew to exercise so decisive an influence in the process that made modern economic life what it is, an influence such as we have observed in the foregoing enquiry?

PART II

THE APTITUDE OF THE JEWS FOR MODERN CAPITALISM

CHAPTER VIII

THE PROBLEM

BEFORE us lies a great problem. We are to explain why the Jews played just the part they did in the economic life of the last two or three centuries. That this *is* a problem will be admitted with but few exceptions by all. There are a few faddists who deny that the Jews occupied any special position in modern economic life, asserting as they do that there are no Jews. These will object. Then, too, there is that other small category of people who hold that the Jews were economically of such slight import that they were without any influence whatever on modern economic life. But we shall pay little heed to either class in our considerations, which are for all those who think with me that the Jews had a decisive influence on the structure of modern economic life.

I have spoken of the aptitude of the Jews for modern capitalism. If our researches are to be fruitful of results we shall have to make two things absolutely clear : (1) their aptitude—for what ? and (2) their aptitude— how developed ?

Their aptitude for what ? For everything which in the first part of the book we have seen them striving to achieve—founding and promoting international trade, modern finance, the Stock Exchange and the com- mercialization generally of all economic activities ; supporting unrestricted intercourse and free competition, and infusing the modern spirit into all economic life. Now in my superscription of this part of our subject all these activities are summed up in the word " capitalism." In a special chapter (the ninth) we shall show that all the single facts that have been mentioned hang together, and that they are kept together by means of capitalistic organization. The essentials of the latter, at least in their outline, will therefore also have to be dealt with, in order to demonstrate the special functions of the individual in the capitalistic system. This method will give the death-blow to such vague conceptions, usually met with in connexion with the Jewish problem, as " economic capacity," " aptitude for commerce and haggling " or other equally dilettante phrases, which have already done too much mischief.

As for the second point, how, by what means, is it possible to achieve any result ? If any one rescues a drowning man, it may be that it was because he happened to be standing at the water's edge, just where a boat was tied, or on a bridge, where a life-belt was ready to hand. In a word, his accidental presence in a particular spot made it possible for him to do the deed, by rowing out in the boat to the man in danger, or by throwing the life-belt to him. Or he may have done it because he was the only one among the crowd on the shore who had the courage to jump into the water, swim out to the sinking man and bring him safely to land. In the first case we might term the circumstances " objective," in the second " subjective." The same distinction can be applied to the Jews in considering their aptitude for capitalism : it may be due to objective or to subjective circumstances.

My immediate business will be to deal with the first set of causes, and for many reasons. To begin with, every explanation that is put forward must be closely scrutinized, in order to make sure that no unproved hypothesis is its basis, and that what has to be proved is not a dogma. Dangerous in most cases, it is particularly so in the problem before us, in which racial and religious prejudices may work havoc, as, indeed, they have done in the writings of the great majority of my precursors on this question. I shall do my utmost to avoid their error in this respect, and shall be at great pains to see to it that my considerations are above criticism. My aim is to discover the play of cause and effect as it really was, without any preconceived idea influencing my reasoning, and I shall adduce my proofs in such a way, that they may be easily followed by all—by the assimilationist Jew no less than by the Nationalist; by him who pins his faith to the influence of race as by the warmest supporter of the doctrine of environment; by the anti-Semite as by his opponent. Hence my starting-point will always have to be from facts admitted on all hands. That will preclude any appeal to " special race characteristics " or arguments of that ilk.

Any one who does not admit that the Jews have special gifts may demand that the part played by this people in modern economic life should be explained without any reference to national peculiarities, but rather from the external circumstances in which Jews were placed by the accident of history. I shall endeavour to satisfy this demand in the tenth chapter.

Finally, if it becomes apparent that the contribution of the Jews to modern economic life cannot be entirely explained by the conditions of their historic situation, then will be the time for looking to subjective causes, and for considering the Jews' special characteristics. This shall be the purpose of the twelfth chapter.

CHAPTER IX

WHAT IS A CAPITALIST UNDERTAKER?

CAPITALISM [396] is the name given to that economic organization wherein regularly two distinct social groups co-operate—the owners of the means of production, who at the same time do the work of managing and directing, and the great body of workers who possess nothing but their labour. The co-operation is such, that the representatives of capital are the subjective agents, that is, they decide as to the "how" and the "how much" in the process of production, and they undertake all risks.

Now what are the mainsprings of the whole system? The first, and perhaps the chiefest, is the pursuit of gain or profit. This being the case, there is a tendency for undertakings to grow bigger and bigger. Arising from that, all economic activities are strictly logical. Whereas in the pre-capitalistic period *quieta non movere* was the watchword and Tradition the guiding star, now it is constant movement. I characterize the whole as "economic rationalism," and this I would term the second mainspring of the capitalistic system.

Economic rationalism expresses itself in three ways. (1) There is a *plan*, in accordance with which all things are ordered aright. And the plan covers activities in the distant future. (2) *Efficiency* is the test applied in the choice of all the means of production. (3) Seeing that the "cash nexus" regulates all economic activity, and that everywhere and always a surplus is sought for, exact *calculations* become necessary in every undertaking.

Everybody knows that a modern business is not merely, say, the production of rails or cotton or electric motors, or the transport of stones or of people. Everybody knows that these are but parts in the organization of the whole. And the characteristics of the undertaker are not that he arranges for the carrying out of the processes named. They are to be found elsewhere, and for the present we may put it roughly that they are a constant buying and selling of the means of production, of labour or of commodities. To vary the phrase somewhat, the undertaker makes contracts concerning exchanges, wherein money is the measure of value.

When do we speak of having accomplished a successful piece of business? Surely when the contract-making has ended well. But what is meant precisely by "well"? It certainly has no reference to the quality or to the quantity of the goods or services given or received; it refers solely and only to the return of the sum of money expended, and to a surplus over and above it (profit). It is the aim of the undertaker so to manipulate the factors over which he has control as to bring about this surplus.

Our next step must be to consider what functions the capitalistic undertaker (the subjective economic factor) has in the sphere of capitalism, seeing that our purpose is to show the capacity of the Jews in this direction. We shall try to discover what special skill is necessary in order to be successful in the competitive struggle In a word, we shall seek for the type.

To my mind, the best picture of the modern capitalistic undertaker is that which paints him as the combination of two radically different natures in one person. Like Faust, he may say that two souls dwell within his breast ; unlike Faust's, however, the two souls do not wish to be separated, but rather, on the contrary, desire to work harmoniously together. What are these two natures ? The one is the undertaker (not in the more limited sense of capitalistic undertaker, but quite generally), and the other is the trader.

By the undertaker I mean a man who has an object in view to which he devotes his life, an object which requires the co-operation of others for its achievement, seeing that its realization is in the world of men. The undertaker must thus be differentiated from the artist or the prophet. Like them he has a mission ; unlike them he feels that he must bring it to realization. He is a man, therefore, who peers into the distant future, whose every action is planned and done only in so far as it will help the great whole. As an instance of an undertaker in this (non-capitalistic) sense we may mention an African or a North Pole explorer. The undertaker becomes a capitalistic undertaker when he combines his original activities with those of the trader.

And what is a trader ? A man whose whole being is set upon doing profitable business ; who appraises all activities and all conditions with a view to their money value, who turns everything into its gold equivalent. The world to such a man is one great market-place, with its supply and demand, its conjunctures—good and bad—and its profits and losses. The constant question on his lips is, " What does it cost? What can I make out of it ? " His last question would in all probability be, " What is the price of the universe ? " The circle of his thoughts is circumscribed by one piece of business, to the successful issue of which he devotes all his energies.

In the combination I have endeavoured to sketch, the undertaker is the constant factor, the trader the variant one.

Constant the undertaker must be, for, having set his heart upon some far-distant goal, he is of necessity bound to follow some plan in order to reach it. Change in his policy is contrary to his nature. Constancy is the basis of his character. But the trader is changeable, for his conduct wavers with the conditions of the market. He must be able to vary his policy and his aim from one moment to another if the prevailing conjuncture so demands it. " Busy-ness " marks him out above all else.

This theory of the two souls in one body is intended to clarify our conception of the capitalistic undertaker. But we must analyse the conception still further, this time into its actual component parts.

In the undertaker I perceive the following four types :—

(1) The Inventor—not merely in the technical sense, but in that of the organizer introducing new forms which bring greater economies into production, or transport, or marketing.

(2) The Discoverer—of new means of selling his commodities, either intensively or extensively. If he finds a new sphere for his activities—let us say he sells bathing-drawers to Eskimos, or gramophones to negroes—we have a case of extensive discovery ; if he creates new demands in markets where he already has a footing, we may speak of intensive discovery.

(3) The Conqueror. An undertaker of the right kind is always a conqueror, with the determination and will-power to overcome all the difficulties that beset his path. He must also be able to risk much, to stake his all (that is to say, his fortune, his good name, even his life), if need be, to achieve great results for his undertaking. It

may be the adoption of new methods in manufacture, the extension of his business though his credit is unstable, and so on.

(4) The Organizer.   Above all else the undertaker must be an organizer; *i.e.*, he must be able so to dispose of large numbers of individuals as to bring about the most successful result ; must be able to fit the round man into the round hole and the square man into the square ; must be able to give a man just the job for which he is best equipped, so as to obtain the maximum of efficiency.   To do this satisfactorily demands many gifts and much skill.   For example, the organizer must be able to tell at a glance what a man can do best, and which man among many will best suit his purpose.   He must be able to let others do his work—*i.e.*, to place in positions of trust such persons as will be able to relieve him of responsibility.   Finally, he must be able to see to it that the human factors in the work of production are sufficient for the purpose, both quantitatively and qualitatively, and that their relationship to each other is harmonious.   In short, the management of his business must be the most efficient possible.

Now business organization means a good deal more than the skilful choice of men and methods ; it means taking into consideration also geographical, ethnological and accidental circumstances of all sorts.   Let me illustrate my point.   The Westinghouse Electric Company is one of the best organized concerns in the United States.   When the Company decided to capture the English market it set up a branch in this country, the organization of which was modelled exactly on that of the parent concern.   After a few years, what was the result?   The financial break-up of the English branch, chiefly because sufficient allowance had not been made for the difference in English conditions.

This leads us to the activities of the trader. A trader has no definite calling ; he has only certain well-defined functions in the body economic. But they are of a very varied kind. For example : to provision ships and supply them with men and ammunition, to conquer wild lands in distant parts, to drive the natives from hearth and home and seize their goods and chattels, to load the ships with these latter and bring them home in order to sell them at public auctions to the highest bidder—all this is a form of trading.

Or, it may be a different form—as when a dealer obtains a pair of old trousers from a needy man of fashion, to whose house he comes in vain five times in succession, and then palms those same trousers off on a stupid yokel.

Or, again, it may take the form of arbitrage dealing on the Stock Exchange.

Clearly there are differences in these instances, as there were between trading in modern and in mediæval times. In the pre-capitalistic period, to trade meant to trade on a big scale, as the " royal merchants " did in the Italian and German cities, and the trader had to be an undertaker (in the general, and not merely in the capitalistic sense). " Each (of the citizens of Genoa) has a tower in his house ; if civil war breaks out, the battlements of these towers are the scenes of conflict. They are masters of the sea ; they build them ships, called galleys, and roam for plunder in the most distant parts, bringing the spoil back to Genoa. With Pisa they live in continual enmity." " Royal merchants " these, if you like ; but not traders in my sense.

I regard those as traders who set out with the intention of doing good business ; who combine within themselves two activities—calculation and negotiation. In a word, the trader must be (1) a speculating calculator, and (2) a business man, a negotiator.

As a speculating calculator, he must buy in the cheapest market and sell in the dearest. Which means that he must obtain his labour and his raw material at as low a rate as possible, and not waste anything in the process of manufacture. And when the commodity is ready for sale, he must part with it to the man whose credit is sound, and so forth. For all this he must calculate, and he must speculate. By speculation in this sense I mean the drawing of several conclusions from particular instances —let us call it the power of economic diagnosis, the complete survey of the market, the evaluation of all its symptoms, the recognition of future possibilities and the choice of that course which will have the greatest utility in the long run.

To this end the dealer must have a hundred eyes, a hundred ears and a hundred feelers in all directions. Here he may have to search out a needy nobleman, or a State bent on war, in order to offer them a loan at the psychological moment ; there, to put his hand on a labour group that is willing to work a few pence below the prevailing rate of wages ; here he may have to form a right estimate of the chances that a new article is likely to have with the public ; there, to appraise the true effect of a political crisis on the Stock Exchange. In every case the trader expresses the result in terms of money. That is where the calculation comes in. "A wonderfully shrewd calculator" is a term common in the United States for an adept in this direction.

But a discerning eye for a profitable piece of business is not sufficient : the trader must also possess the capacity for doing business. In this, his negotiating powers will come into play, and he will be doing something very much more akin to the work of an arbitrator between two litigants. He will talk to his opponent, urge reasons and counter-reasons in order to induce him to embark on a certain course. To negotiate is to fence with intellectual weapons.

Trading, then, means to negotiate concerning the buying and selling of some commodity, be it a share, a loan, or a concern. Trading must be the term applied to the activity of the hawker at the back-door, trying to sell the cook a " fur " collar, or to that of the Jewish old clo' man, who talks for an hour to the bucolic driver to persuade him to purchase a pair of trousers. But it must be equally applied to the activities of a Nathan Rothschild, who negotiated with the representative of the Prussian Government for a loan of a million. The difference is not one of kind, but of extent, for the essence of all trading is negotiation, which need not necessarily be by word of mouth. The shopkeeper who recommends his goods to the public, be his method what you will, is in reality negotiating. What is all advertisement but " dumb show " negotiation? The end in view is always the same—to convince the possible buyer of the superiority of a particular set of goods. The ideal of the seller is realized when everybody purchases the article he has recommended.

To create interest, to win confidence, to stir up a desire to buy—such is the end and aim of the successful trader. How he achieves it is of little moment. Sufficient that he uses not outward force but inner forces, his customers coming to him of their own free will. He wins by suggestion, and one of the most effective is to arouse in the heart of the buyer the feeling that to buy at once will be most advantageous. " We shall have snow, boys, said the Finns, for they had Aander (a kind of snow-shoe) to sell," we read in the Magnus Barford Saga (1006 A.D.). This is the prototype of all traders, and the suggestion of the Finns the prototype of all advertising—the weapon with which the trader fights. No longer does he dwell in fortified towers, as did his precursor in Genoa in the days of Benjamin of Tudela, nor does he wreck the houses of the natives with his guns if they refuse to " trade " with him, as did the early East India settlers in the 17th century.

CHAPTER X

THE OBJECTIVE CIRCUMSTANCES IN THE JEWISH APTITUDE FOR MODERN CAPITALISM

Now that we know what a capitalist undertaker is our next question must be, What were the outward circumstances that made it possible for the Jews to do so much in shaping the capitalistic system? To formulate an answer we shall have to review the position of the Jews of Western Europe and America from the end of the 15th century until the present time—the period, that is, in which capitalism took form.

How can that position be best characterized?

The Governor of Jamaica in a letter he wrote (December 17, 1671) to the Secretary of State was happy in his phraseology.397 " He was of opinion," he said, " that His Majesty could not have more profitable subjects than the Jews : *they had great stocks and correspondence.*" These two reasons, indeed, will account in large measure for the headway made by Jews. But we must also bear in mind their peculiar status among the peoples with whom they dwelt. They were looked upon as strangers and were treated not as full, but as " semicitizens."

I would therefore assign four causes for the success of the Jews : (1) their dispersion over a wide area, (2) their treatment as strangers, (3) their semi-citizenship, and (4) their wealth.

I. Jewish Dispersion over a wide Area.

The fact of primary significance is that the Jews were scattered all over the world. Scattered they had been from the time of the first Exile ; they were scattered anew after their expulsion from Spain and Portugal, and again when great masses of them left Poland. We have already accompanied them on their wanderings during the last two or three centuries, and have noted how they settled in Germany and France, in Italy and in England, in the Near East and in the Far West, in Holland, in Austria, in South Africa and in Eastern Asia.

One result of these wanderings was that off-shoots of one and the same family took root in different centres of economic life and established great world-famed firms with numerous branches in all parts. Let us instance a few cases.[398]

The Lopez family had its seat in Bordeaux, and branches in Spain, England, Antwerp and Toulouse. The Mendès family, well-known bankers, also hailed from Bordeaux, and were to be found in Portugal, France and Flanders. The Gradis, relatives of the Mendès, were also settled in all directions. So, too, the Carceres in Hamburg, in England, in Austria, in the West Indies, in Barbados and in Surinam. Other famous families with world-wide branches were the Costas (Acostas, D'Acostas), the Coneglianos, the Alhadibs, the Sassoons, the Pereires, the Rothschilds. We might continue the list *ad infinitum ;* suffice it to say that Jewish business concerns that had a footing in at least two places on the face of the globe may be counted in hundreds and in thousands.

What all this means is obvious enough. What Christian business houses obtained only after much effort, and even then only to a much less degree, the

Jews had at the very beginning—scattered centres from which to carry on international commerce and to utilize international credit ; " great correspondence " in short, the first necessity for all international organization.

Let us recall what I observed about the participation of the Jews in Spanish and Portuguese trade, in the trade of the Levant, and in the economic growth of America. It was of great consequence that the great majority of Jews settling in different parts hailed from Spain ; they were thus agents in directing colonial trade, and to an even greater extent the flow of silver, into the new channels represented by Holland, England, France and Germany.

Was it not significant that the Jews directed their footsteps just to these countries, all on the eve of a great economic revival, and were thus the means of allowing them to benefit by Jewish international connexions? It is well known that Jews turned away the flow of trade from the lands that expelled them to those that gave them a hospitable reception.

Was it not significant that they were predominant in Leghorn, which in the 18th century was spoken of as " one of the great depôts in Europe for the trade of the Mediterranean," 399 significant that they forged a commercial chain binding North and South America together, which assured the North American Colonies of their economic existence, significant above all, that by their control of the Stock Exchanges in the great European centres they were the means of internationalizing public credit ?

It was their distribution over a wide area which enabled them to do all this.

An admirable picture of the importance of the Jews from this point of view was drawn by a clever observer who made a study of that people two hundred years ago.   The picture has lost none of its freshness ; it may be found in the *Spectator* of September 27, 1712 [400] :—

"They are so disseminated through all the trading Parts of the World, that they are become the Instruments by which the most distant Nations converse with one another and by which mankind are knit together in a general correspondence.   They are like the pegs and nails in a great building, which though they are but little valued in themselves, are absolutely necessary to keep the whole frame together."

How the Jews utilized for their own advantage the special knowledge that their scattered position gave them, how they regulated their activities on the Stock Exchange, is related in all detail in a Report of the French Ambassador in The Hague, written in the year 1698.[401] Our informant is of opinion that the dominance of the Jews on the Amsterdam Stock Exchange was due in a large degree to their being so well-informed.   This piece of evidence is of such great value that I shall translate the whole of the passage :—

"They carry on a correspondence on both these subjects (news and commerce) with those they call their brotherhoods (congregues). Of these, Venice is considered to be the most important (although neither the richest nor the most populous) because it is the link, by way of the brotherhood of Salonica, between the East and the West as well as the South.   Salonica is the governing centre for their nation in these two parts of the world and is responsible for them to Venice, which together with Amsterdam, rules the northern countries (including the merely tolerated community of London, and the secret brotherhoods of France).   The result of this association is that on the two topics of news and commerce they receive, one might almost say, the best information of all that goes on in the world, and on this they build up their system every week in their assemblies, wisely choosing for this purpose the day after Saturday, *i.e.*, the Sunday, when the Christians of all denominations are engaged in their religious exercises. These systems, which contain the minutest details of news received during the week, are, after having been carefully sifted by their rabbis and the heads of their congregations, handed over on the Sunday afternoon to their Jewish stockbrokers and agents. These are men of great cleverness, who after having arranged a preconcerted plan among themselves, go out separately to spread news which should prove the most useful for their own ends ; ready to start manipulations on the morrow, the Monday morning, according to each individual's disposition : either selling, buying, or exchanging shares. As they always hold a large reserve of these commodities, they can always judge of the most propitious moment, taking advantage of the rise or fall of the securities, or even sometimes of both, in order to carry out their plans."

Equally beneficial was their dispersion for winning the confidence of the great. Indeed, the progress of the Jews to *la haute finance* was almost invariably as follows. In the first instance their linguistic ability enabled them to be of service to crowned heads as interpreters, then they were sent as intermediaries or special negotiators to foreign courts. Soon they were put in charge of their employer's fortunes, at the same time being honoured through his graciousness in allowing them to become his creditors. From this point it was no long step to the control of the State finances, and in later years of the Stock Exchanges.

It is no far-fetched assumption that already in ancient times their knowledge of languages and their acquaintance with foreign civilizations must have made them welcome visitors at the courts of kings and won for them royal confidence. Think of Joseph in Egypt ; of the Alabarch Alexander (of whom Josephus tells), the intimate of King Agrippa and of the mother of the Emperor Claudius ; think of the Jewish Treasurer of Queen Candace of Ethiopia, of whom we may read in the Acts of the Apostles (viii. 27).

As for the Court Jews in the Middle Ages, we have definite information that they won their spurs in the capacity of interpreters or negotiators. We know it of the Jew Isaac, whom Charlemagne sent to the court of the Caliph Haroun al Rashid ; of Kalonymus, the Jewish friend and favourite of the Emperor Otto II ; of the famous Chasdai Ibn Shaprut (915–70), who achieved honour and renown as the diplomatic representative of the Caliph Abdul-Rahman III in his negotiations with the Christian courts of Northern Spain.[402] Similarly when the Christian princes of the Iberian Peninsula required skilful negotiators they sought out Jews. Alphonso VI is a good example. Intent on playing off the petty Mohammedan rulers against each other, he chose Jewish agents, with their linguistic abilities and their insight into foreign ways, to send to the courts of Toledo, Seville and Granada. In the period which followed, Jewish emissaries are met with at all the Spanish courts, including those Jews, learned in ethnography, whom James II commissioned to travel into Asia in order to supply his spies with information and who tried to discover the mythical country of Prester John ; [403] including also the many interpreters and confidential agents associated with the discovery of the New World.[404]

Considering the importance of the Spanish period in Jewish history not only from the general, but also from the special economic point of view, these cases are worthy of note in that they clearly show the reason for the rise of Jews to influential positions. But they are not limited to the Spanish period ; they abound in subsequent epochs also. Thus, Jewish diplomatists were employed by the States-General in their intercourse with the Powers ; and names like Belmonte, Mesquita [405] and others are well-known. Equally famous is the Seigneur Hebræo, as Richelieu called the wealthy Ildefonso Lopez, whom the French statesman sent on a secret mission to Holland, and on his return bestowed upon him the title of " Conseiller d'Etat ordinaire." [406]

Finally, the dispersion of the Jews is noteworthy in another way. Their dispersion internationally was, as we have seen, fruitful enough of results; but their being scattered in every part of some particular country had consequences no less potent. To take one instance —the Jews were army-purveyors (and their activities as such date from the days of antiquity, for do we not read that when Belisarius besieged Naples, the Jewish inhabitants offered to supply the town with provisions?) [407] One reason was surely that they were able to accumulate large quantities of commodities much more easily than the Christians, thanks to their connexions in the different centres. " The Jewish undertaker," says one 18th-century writer, "is free from these difficulties. All he need do is to stir up his brethren in the right place, and at a moment's notice he has all the assistance he requires at his disposal." [408] In truth, the Jew at that time never carried on business "as an isolated individual, but always as a member of the most extended trading company in the world." [409] In the words of a petition of the merchants of Paris in the second half of the 18th century, [410] "they are atoms of molten money which flow and are scattered, but which at the least incline reunite into one principal stream."

II. THE JEWS AS ALIENS.

During the last century or two Jews were almost everywhere strangers in the sense of being new-comers. They were never old-established in the places where their most successful activities were manifest; nor did they arrive in such centres from the vicinity, but rather from, distant lands, differing in manners and customs, and often in climate too, from the countries of their settlements. To Holland, France and England they came from Spain and Portugal and then from Germany ; they journeyed to Hamburg and Frankfort from other German cities ; later on they dispersed all over Germany from Russian Poland.

The Jews, then, were everywhere colonists, and as such learned the lesson of speedy adaptation to their new surroundings. In this they were ahead of the European nations, who did not become masters of this art until the settlements in America were founded.

New-comers must have an observant eye in order to find a niche for themselves amid the new conditions ; they must be very careful of their behaviour, so that they may earn their livelihood without let or hindrance. While the natives are still in their warm beds the new-comers stand without in the sharp morning air of dawn, and their energy is all the keener in consequence. They must concentrate their thoughts to obtain a foot-hold, and all their economic activities will be dictated by this desire. They must of necessity determine how best to regulate their undertakings, and what is the shortest cut to their goal—what branches of manufacture or commerce are likely to prove most profitable, with what persons business connexions should be established, and on what principles business itself should be conducted. What is all this but the substitution of economic rationalism for time-honoured Tradition ? That the Jews did this we have already observed ; why they were forced to do it becomes apparent when we recall that everywhere they were strangers in the land, new-comers, immigrants.

But the Jews were strangers among the nations throughout many centuries in yet another sense, which might be termed psychological and social. They were strangers because of the inward contrast between them and their hosts, because of their almost caste-like separation from the peoples in whose midst they dwelt. They, the Jews, looked upon themselves as a peculiar people : and as a peculiar people the nations regarded them. Hence, there was developed in the Jews that conduct and that mental attitude which is bound to show itself in dealings with "strangers," especially in an age in which the conception of world-citizenship was as yet non-existent. For in all periods of history innocent of humanitarian considerations the mere fact that a "stranger" was being dealt with was sufficient to ease the conscience and loosen the bonds of moral duty. In intercourse with strangers people were never quite so particular. Now the Jews were always brought into contact with strangers, with "others," especially in their economic activities, seeing that everywhere they were a small minority. And whereas the "others" dealt with a stranger, say, once in ten times or even in a hundred, it was just the reverse with the Jews, whose intercourse with strangers was nine out of the ten or ninety-nine out of the hundred times. What was the consequence? The Jew had recourse to the "ethics for strangers" (if I may use this term without being misunderstood) far more frequently than the non-Jew; for the one it was the rule, whilst for the other it was only the exception. Jewish business methods thus came to be based on it.

Closely interwoven with their status as strangers was the special legal position which they occupied everywhere. But this has an importance of its own, and we shall therefore assign an independent section to it.

III. JEWS AS SEMI-CITIZENS.

At first glance the legal position of the Jews would appear to have had an immense influence on their economic activities in that it limited the callings to which they might devote themselves, and generally closed the avenues to a livelihood. But I believe that the effect of these restrictions has been over-estimated. I would even go so far as to say that they were of no moment whatever for the economic growth of Jewry. At least, I am not aware that any of the traces left by Jews on the development of the modern economic system were due to the restraining regulations. That these could not have left a very deep impress is obvious, seeing that during the period which is of most interest to us the laws affecting Jews differed greatly according to locality. For all that we note a remarkable similarity in Jewish influence throughout the whole range of the capitalistic social order.

How varied the laws in restraint of Jews were is not always sufficiently realized. To begin with, there were broad differences between those of one country and of another. Thus, while the Jews in Holland and England were in a position of almost complete equality with their Christian neighbours so far as their economic life was concerned, they laboured under great disabilities in other lands. But even in these last their treatment was not uniform, for in certain towns and districts they enjoyed entire economic freedom, as, for example, in the papal possessions in France. [411] Moreover, even the disabilities varied in number and in kind in each country, and sometimes in different parts of the same country. In most instances they appeared to be quite arbitrary ; nowhere was there any underlying principle visible. In one place Jews might not be hawkers, and in another they were not allowed to be shopkeepers. Here they received permission to be craftsmen ; there this right was denied them. Here they might deal in wool, there they might not. Here they might sell leather, there it was forbidden them. Here the sale of alcoholic liquors was farmed out to them, there such an idea seemed preposterous. Here they were encouraged to start factories, there they were strictly enjoined to desist from all participation in capitalistic undertakings. Such examples might be continued indefinitely.

Perhaps the best is furnished by Prussia's treatment of her Jews in the 18th century. Here in one and the same country the restrictive legislation for one locality was totally opposed to that of another. The revised General Privileges of 1750 (Article 2) forbade Jews the exercise of handicrafts in many places ; yet a royal order of May 21, 1790, permitted the Jews in Breslau " to exercise all manner of mechanical arts," and went on to say that " it would be a source of much pleasure to Us if Christian craftsmen of their own free will took Jewish boys as apprentices and eventually received them into their gilds." A similar enactment was made in the General Reglement for the Jews of South-East Prussia, dated April 17, 1797 (Article 10).

Again, while the Jews of Berlin were forbidden (by Articles 13 and 15 of the General Privileges of 1750) to sell meat, beer and brandy to non-Jews, all the native-born Jews of Silesia had complete freedom of trade in this respect (in accordance with an Order of February 13, 1769).

The list of commodities in which they were allowed or forbidden to trade seems to have been drawn up with an arbitrariness that passes comprehension. Thus, the General Privileges of 1750 allowed the Jews to deal in foreign or home leather prepared though undyed, but not in raw or dyed leather ; in raw calf and sheep skins, but not in raw cow or horse hides ; in all manner of manufactured woollen and cotton wares, but not in raw wool or woollen threads.

The picture becomes still more bewildering when we take into consideration the varying legal status of the different classes of Jews. The Jewish community of Breslau, for instance, was (until the Order of May 21, 1790, changed things) composed of four groups : (1) those with " general privileges," (2) those with " privileges," (3) those who were only tolerated, and (4) temporary residents.

The first class included those Jews who were on an equal footing with Christians so far as trade and commerce were concerned, and whose rights in this respect were hereditary. In the second were comprised such Jews as had "special (limited) privileges" given them, wherein they were allowed to trade in certain kinds of goods specifically mentioned. But their rights did not pass to their children, though the children received preference when privileges of this kind were being granted. The third class was composed of Jews who had the right of living in Breslau, but whose economic activities were even more limited than those in the second class. As for the fourth, it contained the Jews who received permission to dwell in the town for a temporary period only.

But even of such rights as they had they were never sure. In 1769, for example, the Silesian Jews who lived in country districts were allowed to receive in farm the sale of beer, brandy and meat ; in 1780 the permission was withdrawn ; in 1787 it was renewed.

Yet in all this it must not be forgotten that regulations in restraint of industry and commerce during the last two or three centuries were for the most part a dead letter ; as a matter of fact, capitalistic interests found

ways and means of getting round them. The simplest
method was to overstep the law, a course to which
as time went on the bureaucratic State shut its eyes.
But there were lawful means too of circumventing
inconvenient paragraphs : concessions, privileges, patents,
and the whole collection of documents granting exceptional
treatment which princes were always willing to issue
if only an additional source of income accrued therefrom.
The Jews were not slow in obtaining such privileges.
The proviso mentioned in the Prussian Edicts of 1737
and 1750—that all restraints referring to Jews might
be removed by a special royal order—was tacitly held
to apply in all cases. Some way out must have been
possible, else how could the Jews have engaged in
those trades (*e.g.*, leather, tobacco) which the law forbade
them ?

At one point, however, industrial regulations made
themselves felt as very real checks to the progress
of the Jew, and that was wherever economic activities
were organized on a corporate basis. The gilds were
closed to them ; they were kept back by the crucifix
which hung in each gild-hall, and round which members
assembled. Accordingly, if they wished to engage
in any industry or trade monopolized by a gild, they
were forced to do so as "outsiders," interlopers and
free traders.

But a still greater obstacle in their path were the
laws regulating their position in public life. In all
countries there was a remarkable uniformity in these ;
everywhere the Jew was shut out from public offices,
central or local, from the Bar, from Parliament, from
the Army, from the Universities. This applied to
the States of Western Europe—France, Holland,
England—and also to America. But there is no need
to consider with any degree of fullness the legal status

of the Jews in the pre-emancipation era, seeing that it is fairly generally known. Only this we would mention here—that their condition of semi-citizenship continued in most countries right into the 19th century. The United States was the first land in which they obtained civil equality ; the principle was there promulgated in 1783. In France the famous Emancipation Law dates from 27th September 1791 ; in Holland the Batavian National Assembly made the Jews full citizens in 1796. But in England it was not until 1859 that they were granted complete emancipation, while in the German States it took ten years longer. On 3rd July 1869 the North German Confederation finally set the seal on their civil equality ; Austria had already done so in 1867, and Italy followed suit in 1870.

Equally well-known is it that in many cases the emancipation laws have become dead letters. Open any Liberal paper in Germany (to take a good instance) and day by day you will find complaints that Jews are never given commissions in the Army, that they are excluded from appointments to the Bench, and so on.

This set-back which the Jews received in public life was of great use to industry and commerce in that the Jew concentrated all his ability and energy on them. The most gifted minds from other social groups devoted themselves to the service of the State ; among the Jews, in so far as they did not spend themselves in the *Beth Hamidrash* [the Communal House of Study], such spirits were forced into business. Now the more economic life aimed at profit-making and the more the moneyed interests acquired influence, the more were the Jews driven to win for themselves by means of commerce and industry what was denied them by the law—respect and power in the State. It becomes apparent why gold (as we have seen) was appraised so highly among Jews.

But if exclusion from public life was of benefit to the economic position of the Jews in one direction, giving them a pull over their Christian neighbours, it was equally beneficial in another. It freed the Jews from political partisanship. Their attitude towards the State, and the particular Government of the day, was wholly unprejudiced. Thanks to this, their capacity to become the standard-bearers of the international capitalistic system was superior to that of other people. For they supplied the different States with money, and national conflicts were among the chief sources from which Jews derived their profit. Moreover, the political colourlessness of their position made it possible for them to serve successive dynasties or governments in countries which, like France, were subjected to many political changes. The history of the Rothschilds illustrates the point. Thus the Jews, through their inferior civil position, were enabled to facilitate the growth of the indifference of capitalism to all interests but those of gain. Again, therefore, they promoted and strengthened the capitalistic spirit.

IV. The Wealth of the Jews.

Among the objective conditions which made possible the economic mission of the Jews during the last three or four centuries must be reckoned that at all times and in all places where their rôle in economic life was no mean one, they disposed of large sums of money. But this assertion says nothing about the wealth of the whole body of Jews, so that it is idle to urge the objection that at all periods there were poor Jews, and very many of them. Any one who has ever set foot in a Jewish congregation on the Eastern borders of Germany, or is acquainted with the Jewish quarter of New York, knows that well enough. But what I maintain—a more limited proposition—is that much wealth and great fortunes were to be found, and still are to be found, among Jews ever since the 17th century. Put in a slightly different way, there were always many wealthy Jews, and certainly the Jews on an average were richer than the Christians round them. It is beside the mark to say that the richest man in Germany or the three richest in America are not Jews.

A good many of the exiles from the Pyrenean Peninsula must have been very wealthy indeed. We are informed that their flight brought with it an " exodo de capitaes," a flow of capital from the country. However, in many instances they sold their property, receiving foreign bills in exchange. [412] The richest among the fugitives probably made for Holland. At any rate it is recorded that the first settlers in that country—Manuel Lopez Homen, Maria Nunez, Miguel Lopez and others—had great possessions.[413] Whether other wealthy Spaniards followed in the 17th century, or whether those already resident added to their fortunes, it is not easy to discover. But certain it is that the Jews of Holland in the 17th and 18th centuries were famed for their riches. True, there are no statistics to illustrate this, but an abundance of other weighty evidence exists. Travellers could not sufficiently admire the splendour and the luxury of the houses of these refugees who dwelt in what were really palaces. And if you turn to a collection of engravings of that period, do you not very soon discover that the most magnificent mansions in, say, Amsterdam or The Hague were built by Jews or inhabited by them—those of Baron Belmonte, of the noble Lord de Pinto, of the Lord d'Acoste and others ? (At the close of the 17th century de Pinto's fortune was estimated at 8,000,000 florins.) Of the princely luxury at a Jewish wedding in Amsterdam, where one of her daughters married, Glückel von Hameln draws a vivid picture in her *Memoirs*.[414]

It was the same in other lands. For 17th and 18th century France we have the generalization of Savary, who knew most things. "We say," these are his very words, "we say that a tradesman is 'as rich as a Jew' when he has the reputation of having amassed a large fortune." [415]

As for England, actual figures are extant concerning the wealth of the rich Sephardim soon after their arrival. A crowd of rich Jews followed in the train of Catharine of Braganza, Charles II's bride, so that while in 1661 there were only 35 Jewish families in London, two years later no less than 57 new-comers were added to the list. In 1663, as appears from the books of Alderman Blackwell, the following was the half-yearly turnover of the wealthy Jewish merchants : [416] Jacob Aboab, £13,085 ; Samuel de Vega, £18,309 ; Duarte da Sylva, £41,441 ; Francisco da Sylva, £14,646 ; Fernando Mendes da Costa, £30,490 ; Isaac Dazevedo, £13,605 ; George and Domingo Francia, £35,759 ; and Gomez Rodrigues, £13,124.

The centres of Jewish life in Germany in the 17th and 18th centuries were, as we have already observed, Hamburg and Frankfort-on-the-Main. For both cities it is possible to compute the wealth of the resident Jews by the aid of figures.

In Hamburg, too, it was Spanish and Portuguese Jews who were the first settlers. It 1649, 40 of their families participated in the foundation of the Hamburg Bank, which shows that they must have been fairly comfortably off. Very soon complaints were made of the increasing

wealth and influence of the Jews. In 1649 they were
blamed for their ostentatious funerals and for riding in
carriages to take the air ; in 1650 for building houses
like palaces. In the same year sumptuary laws forbade
them too great a show of magnificence.[417] Up to
the end of the 17th century the Sephardic Jews appear
to have possessed all the wealth ; about that time,
however, their Ashkenazi brethren also came quickly to
the fore. Glückel von Hameln states that many German-
Jewish families which in her youth were in comparative
poverty later rose to a state of affluence. And Glückel's
observations are borne out by figures dating from the
first quarter of the 18th century.[418] In 1729 the
Jewish community in Altona was composed of 279
subscribing members, of whom 145 were wealthy,
possessing between them 5,434,300 mark [£271,715],
that is, an average of more than 37,000 mark [£1850]
per head. The Hamburg community had 160 subscribing members, 16 of whom together were worth
501,500 mark [£25,075]. These figures appear to be
below the actual state of things, if we compare them with
the particulars concerning each individual. In 1725 the
following wealthy Jews were resident in Hamburg,
Altona and Wandsbeck : Joel Solomon, 210,000 mark ;
his son-in-law, 50,000 ; Elias Oppenheimer, 300,000 ;
Moses Goldschmidt, 60,000 ; Alex Papenheim, 60,000 ;
Elias Salomon, 200,000 ; Philip Elias, 50,000 ; Samuel
Schiesser, 60,000 ; Berend Heyman, 75,000 ; Samson
Nathan, 100,000 ; Moses Hamm, 75,000 ; Sam Abra-
ham's widow, 60,000 ; Alexander Isaac, 60,000 ; Meyer
Berend, 400,000 ; Salomon Berens, 1,600,000 ; Isaac
Hertz, 150,000 ; Mangelus Heymann, 200,000 ; Nathan
Bendix, 100,000 ; Philip Mangelus, 100,000 ; Jacob
Philip, 50,000 ; Abraham Oppenheimer's widow, 60,000 ;
Zacharias Daniel's widow and widowed daughter,

150,000 ; Simon del Banco, 150,000 ; Marx Casten,
200,000 ; Abraham Lazarus, 150,000 ; Carsten Marx,
60,000 ; Berend Salomon, 600,000 rthlr. ; Meyer Berens,
400,000 ; Abraham von Halle, 150,000 ; Abraham
Nathan, 150,000.

In view of this list it can scarcely be doubted that
there were many rich Jews in Hamburg.

Frankfort presents the same picture ; if anything the
colours are even brighter. The wealth of the Jews
begins to accumulate at the end of the 16th century,
and from then onwards it increases steadily. In 1593
there were 4 Jews and 54 Christians (making 7·4 per
cent.) in Frankfort who paid taxes on a fortune of over
15,000 florins ; in 1607 their number had reached 16
(compared with 90 Christians, *i.e.*, 17·7 per cent.).[419]
In 1618 the poorest Jew paid taxes on 100 florins, the
poorest Christian on 50. Again, 300 Jewish families
paid as garrison and fortification taxes no less than
100,900 florins in the years 1634 to 1650.[420]

The number of taxpayers in the Frankfort Jewish
community rose to 753 by the end of the 18th century,
and together they possessed at least 6,000,000 florins.
More than half of this was in the hands of the
twelve wealthiest families : [421] Speyer, 604,000 florins ;
Reiss-Ellissen, 299,916 ; Haas, Kann, Stern, 256,500 ;
Schuster, Getz, Amschel, 253,075 ; Goldschmidt,
235,000 ; May, 211,000 ; Oppenheimer, 171,500 ;
Wertheimer, 138,600 ; Flörsheim, 166,666 ; Rindskopf,
115,600 ; Rothschild, 109,375 ; Sichel, 107,000.

And in Berlin the Jews in the early 18th century
were not by any means poor beggars. Of the 120
Jewish families resident in the Prussian capital in 1737
only 10 owned less than 1000 thalers, the rest all had
2000 to 20,000 thaler, and over.[422]

That the Jews were among the richest people in the

land is thus attested, and this state of affairs has continued through the last two or three hundred years right down to our own day, except that to-day it is perhaps more general and more widespread. And its consequence? It can scarcely be over-estimated for those countries which offered a refuge to the wanderers. The nations that profited by the Jews' sojourn with them were well equipped to help forward the development of capitalism. Hence it should be specially noticed that the wanderings of the Jews had the effect of shifting the centre where the precious metals had accumulated. Obviously it could not but influence the trend of economic life that Spain and Portugal were emptied of their gold and England and Holland enriched.

Nor is it difficult to prove that Jewish money called into existence all the large undertakings of the 17th century and financed them. Just as the expedition of Columbus would have been impossible had the rich Jews left Spain a generation earlier, so the great India Companies might never have been founded and the great banks which were established in the 17th century might not so quickly have attained their stability had it not been that the wealth of the Spanish exiles came to the aid of England, Holland and Hamburg ; in other words, had the Jews been expelled from Spain a century later than was actually the case.

This in fact was why Jewish wealth was so influential. In enabled capitalistic undertakings to be started, or at least facilitated the process. To establish banks, warehouses, stock and share broking—all this was easier for the Jew than for the others because his pockets were better lined. That, too, was why he became banker to crowned heads. And finally, because he had money he was able to lend it. This activity paved the way for capitalism to a greater degree than anything else did. For modern capitalism is the child of money-lending.

Money-lending contains the root idea of capitalism; from money-lending it received many of its distinguishing features. In money-lending all conception of quality vanishes and only the quantitative aspect matters. In money-lending the contract becomes the principal element of business; the agreement about the *quid pro quo*, the promise for the future, the notion of delivery are its component parts. In money-lending there is no thought of producing only for one's needs. In money-lending there is nothing corporeal (*i.e.*, technical), the whole is a purely intellectual act. In money-lending economic activity as such has no meaning; it is no longer a question of exercising body or mind; it is all a question of success. Success, therefore, is the only thing that has a meaning. In money-lending the possibility is for the first time illustrated that you can earn without sweating; that you may get others to work for you without recourse to force.

In fine, the characteristics of money-lending are the characteristics of all modern capitalistic economic organizations.

But historically, too, modern capitalism owes its being to money-lending. This was the case wherever it was necessary to lay out money for initial expenses, or where a business was started as a limited company. For essentially a limited company is in principle nothing but a matter of money-lending with the prospect of immediate profit.

The money-lending activities of the Jews were thus an objective factor in enabling the Jews to create, to expand and to assist the capitalistic spirit. But our last remarks have already touched upon a further problem, going beyond objective considerations. Is there not already a specific psychological element in the work of the money-lender? But more than this. It may be asked, Can the objective circumstances alone entirely explain the economic rôle of the Jews? Are there not perhaps special Jewish characteristics which must be taken into account in our chain of reasoning? Before proceeding to this chapter, however, we must turn to an influence of extreme importance in this connexion—to the Jewish religion.

CHAPTER XI

THE SIGNIFICANCE OF THE JEWISH RELIGION IN ECONOMIC LIFE

INTRODUCTORY NOTE.

THREE reasons have actuated me in devoting a special chapter to the consideration of the religion of the Jewish people and the demonstration of its enormous influence on Jewish economic activities. First, the Jewish religion can be fully appreciated in all its bearings from the economic standpoint only when it is studied in detail and by itself; secondly, it calls for a special method of treatment; and thirdly, it occupies a position midway between the objective and the subjective factors of Jewish development. For, in so far as any religion is the expression of some particular spiritual outlook, it has a "subjective" aspect; in so far as the individual is born into it, it has an objective aspect.

I. THE IMPORTANCE OF RELIGION FOR THE JEWISH PEOPLE.

That the religion of a people, or of a group within a people, can have far-reaching influences on its economic life will not be disputed. Only recently Max Weber demonstrated the connexion between Puritanism and Capitalism. In fact, Max Weber's researches are responsible for this book. For any one who followed them could not but ask himself whether all that Weber ascribes to Puritanism might not with equal justice be referred to Judaism, and probably in a greater degree ; nay, it might well be suggested that that which is called Puritanism is in reality Judaism. This relationship will be discussed in due course.

Now, if Puritanism has had an economic influence, how much more so has Judaism, seeing that among no other civilized people has religion so impregnated all national life. For the Jews religion was not an affair of Sundays and Holy Days ; it touched everyday life even in its minutest action, it regulated *all* human activities. At every step the Jew asked himself, Will this tend to the glory of God or will it profane His name ? Jewish law defines not merely the relation between man and God, formulates not merely a metaphysical conception ; it lays down rules of conduct for all possible relationships, whether between man and man or between man and nature. Jewish law, in fact, is as much part of the religious system as are Jewish ethics. The Law is from God, and moral law and divine ordinances are inseparable in Judaism.[423] Hence in reality there are no special ethics of Judaism. Jewish ethics are the underlying principles of the Jewish religion. [424]

No other people has been so careful as the Jews in providing for the teaching of religion to even the humblest. As Josephus so well put it : Ask the first Jew you meet concerning his " laws " and he will be able to tell you them better even than his own name. The reason for this may be found in the systematic religious instruction given to every Jewish child, as well as in the fact that divine service partly consists of the reading and explanation of passages from Holy Writ. In the course of the year the Torah is read through from beginning to end. Moreover, it is one of the primary duties of the Jew to study the Torah. "Thou shalt speak of them when thou sittest in thine house and when thou walkest by the way and when thou liest down and when thou risest up" (Deut. vi. 5).[425]

No other people, too, has walked in God's ways so conscientiously as the Jews ; none has striven to carry out its religious behests so thoroughly. It has indeed been asserted that the Jews are the least religious of peoples. I shall not stay to weigh the justice of this remark. But certain it is that they are the most "God-fearing" people that ever were on the face of the earth. They lived always in trembling awe, in awe of God's wrath. "My flesh trembleth for fear of Thee, and I am afraid of Thy judgments," said the Psalmist (Ps. cxix. 120), and the words may be taken as applicable to the Jews in every age. "Happy is the man that feareth alway" (Prov. xxviii. 14). "The pious never put away their fear" (*Tanchuma Chukkath*, 24).[426] One can understand it when one thinks of the Jewish God— fearful, awful, curse-uttering Jehovah. Never in all the world's literature, either before or since, has humanity been threatened with so much evil as Jehovah promises (in the famous 28th chapter of Deuteronomy) to those who will not keep His commandments.

But this mighty influence (the fear of God) did not stand alone. Others combined with it, and together they had the tendency of almost forcing the Jews to obey the behests of their religion most scrupulously. The first of these influences was their national fate. When the Jewish State was destroyed the Pharisees and Scribes—*i.e.*, those who cherished the traditions of Ezra and strove to make obedience to the Law the end and aim of life—the Pharisees and Scribes came to the head of affairs and naturally directed the course of events into channels which they favoured. Without a State, without their sanctuary, the Jews, under the leadership of the Pharisees, flocked around the Law (that " portable Fatherland," as Heine calls it), and became a religious brotherhood, guided by a band of pious Scribes, pretty much as the disciples of Loyola might gather around them the scattered remnants of a modern State. The Pharisees now led the way. Their most distinguished Rabbis looked upon themselves as the successors of the ancient Synhedrium, and were indeed so regarded, becoming the supreme authority in spiritual and temporal affairs for all the Jews in the world.427 The power of the Rabbis originated in this fashion, and the vicissitudes of the Jews in the Middle Ages only helped to strengthen it. So oppressive did it eventually become that the Jews themselves at times complained of the burden. For the more the Jews were shut off, or shut themselves off, from the people among whom they dwelt, the more the authority of the Rabbis increased, and the more easily could the Jews be forced to be faithful to the Law. But the fulfilment of the Law, which was urged upon them by the Rabbis, must have been a necessity for the Jews for inner reasons : it satisfied their heart's desire, it appeared the most precious gift that life had to offer. And why ? Because amid all the persecution and suffering which was meted out to the Jews on all sides, that alone enabled them to retain their dignity, without which life would have been valueless. For a very long period religious teaching was enshrined in the Talmud, and hence Jews through many centuries lived in it, for it and through it. The Talmud was the most precious possession of the Jew ; it was the breath of his nostrils, it was his very soul. The Talmud became a family history for generation after generation, with which each was familiar. "The thinker lived in its thought, the poet in its pure idealism. The outer world, the world of nature and of man, the powerful ones of the earth and the events of the times, were for the Jew during a thousand years accidents, phantoms; his only reality was the Talmud." [428] The Talmud has been well compared (and the comparison to my mind applies equally to all religious literature) to an outer shell with which the Jews of the Diaspora covered themselves; it protected them against all influences from without and kept alive their strength within.[429]

We see, then, what forces were at work to make the Jews right down to modern times a more Godfearing people than any other, to make them religious to their inmost core, or, if the word "religious" be objected to, to keep alive among high and low a general and strict observation of the precepts of their religion. And for our purpose, we must regard this characteristic as applicable to all sorts and conditions of Jews, the Marannos of the 16th, 17th and 18th centuries included. We must look upon these too as orthodox Jews. Says the foremost authority on that period of Jewish history,[430] "The great majority of the Marannos were Jews to a much larger extent than is commonly supposed. They submitted to force of circumstance and were Christians only outwardly. As a matter of fact they lived the Jewish life and observed the tenets of the Jewish religion. . . . This admirable constancy will be appreciated to the full only when the wealth of material in the Archives of Alcalia de Henares, Simancas and other places has been sorted and utilized."

But among professing Jews the wealthiest were often enough excellent Talmudic scholars. Was not a knowledge of the Talmud a highway to honour, riches and favour among Jews ?   The most learned Talmudists were also the cleverest financiers, medical men, jewellers, merchants.   We are told, for example, of some of the Spanish Ministers of Finance, bankers and court physicians that they devoted to the study of the Holy Writ not only the Sabbath day but also two nights of each week.   In modern times old Amschel Rothschild, who died in 1855, did the same.   He lived strictly according to Jewish law and ate no morsel at a stranger's table, even though it were the Emperor's. One who knew the Baron well says of him that " he was looked upon as the most pious Jew in all Frankfort. Never have I seen a man so afflict himself—beating his breast, and crying to Heaven—as Baron Rothschild did in the synagogue on the Day of Atonement.   The continual praying weakens him so that he falls into a faint.   Odorous plants from his garden are held to his nose to revive him." 431 *   His nephew William Charles, who died in 1901 and who was the last of the Frankfort Rothschilds, observed all the religious prescriptions in their minutest detail.   The pious Jew is forbidden to touch any object which under certain circumstances has become unclean by having been already touched by some one else.   And so a servant always walked in front of this Rothschild and wiped the door-handles.   Moreover, he never touched paper money that had been in use before ; the notes had to be fresh from the press.

If this was how a Rothschild lived, it is not surprising to come across Jewish commercial travellers who do not touch meat six months in the year because they are not absolutely certain that the method

[* Sombart in the German text quotes this as an occurrence on the Sabbath.   It is obvious that the description refers to the Day of Atonement.]

of slaughtering has been in accordance with Jewish law.

However, if you want to study orthodox Judaism you must go to Eastern Europe, where it is still without disintegrating elements—you must go there personally or read the books about it. In Western Europe the orthodox Jews are a small minority. But when we speak of the influence of the Jewish religion it is the religion that held sway until a generation ago that we mean, the religion that led the Jews to so many victories.

II. THE SOURCES OF THE JEWISH RELIGION.

Mohammed called the Jews " the people of the Book." He was right. There is no other people that lived so thoroughly according to a book. Their religion in all its stages was generally incorporated in a book, and these books may be looked upon as the sources of the Jewish religion. The following is a list of such books, each originating at a particular time and supplementing some other.

1. The Bible, *i.e.*, the Old Testament, until the destruction of the Second Temple. It was read in Hebrew in Palestine and in Greek (Septuagint) in the Diaspora.
2. The Talmud (more especially the Babylonian Talmud), from the 2nd to the 6th century of the Common Era, the principal depository of Jewish religious teaching.
3. The Code of Maimonides, compiled in the 12th century.
4. The Code (called the *Turim*) of Jacob ben Asher (1248–1340).
5. The Code of Joseph Caro—the *Shulchan Aruch* (16th century).

These " sources " from which the Jewish religion drew its life appear in a different light according as they are regarded by scientific research or with the eyes of the believing Jew. In the first case they are seen as they really are ; in the second, they are idealized.

What are they in reality? The Bible, *i.e.*, the Old Testament, is the foundation upon which the entire structure of Judaism was built up. It was written by many hands at different periods, thus forming, as it were, a piece of literary mosaic.[432] The most important portion of the whole is the Torah, *i.e.*, the Pentateuch. It received its present shape by the commingling of two complete works some time in the period after Ezra. The one was the old and the new (the Deuteronomic) Law Book (650 B.C.) and the other, Ezra's Law Book (440 B.C.).* And its special character the Torah owes to Ezra and Nehemiah, who introduced a strict legal system. With Ezra and the school of *Soferim* (scribes) that he founded, Judaism in the form which it has to-day originated; from that period to the present it has remained unchanged.

Beside the Torah we must mention the so-called Wisdom Literature—the Psalms, Job, Ecclesiastes, Ecclesiasticus and the Proverbs. This section of Jewish literature is wholly post-exilic; only in that period could it have arisen, assuming as it did the existence of the Law, and the prevailing belief that for obeying the Law God gave Life, for transgressing it Death. The Wisdom Literature, unlike the Prophetic Books, was concerned with practical life. Some of the books contain the crystallized wisdom of many generations and are of a comparatively early date. The Book of Proverbs, for example, the most useful for our purpose, dates from the year 180 B.C.[433]

Two streams flow from the Bible. The one, chiefly by way of the Septuagint, ran partly into Hellenistic philosophy and partly into Pauline Christianity. That does not concern us further.

* *I.e.* Deut. v. 45.–xxvi. 69 (about 650 B.C.) and Exod. xii. 25–31, xxxv. to Lev. xv.; Numb. i.–x.; xv.–xix.; xxvii.–xxxvi. (about 445 B.C.).

The other, chiefly by way of the Hebrew Bible current in Palestine, ran into Jewish " Law," and the course of this we shall have to follow.

The specifically Jewish development of the Holy Writ already began as early as Ezra's day ; it was due to the first schools of *Soferim* (scribes), and the later schools of Hillel and Shammai only extended and continued the work. The actual " development " consisted of explanations and amplifications of the Holy Writ, arrived at as the result of disputation, the method in vogue in the Hellenistic World. The development was really a tightening of the legal formalism, with the view of protecting Judaism against the inroads of Hellenistic Philosophy. Here, as always, the Jewish religion was the expression of a reaction against disintegrating forces. The Deuteronomic Law was the reaction against Baal worship ; the Priestly Code against Babylonian influences ; the later Codes of Maimonides and Rabbenu Asher and Caro against Spanish culture ; and the teaching of the *Tannaim* [Tannai —teacher] in the century preceding and that commencing the Common Era against the enervating doctrines of Hellenism.434

The old oral tradition of the " Wise " was codified about the year 200 A.D. by R. Judah Hanassi (the Prince), usually called Rabbi. His work is the *Mishna*. Following on the Mishna are further explanations and additions which were collected and given a fixed form in the 6th century (500–550 A.D.) by the *Saboraim* [Saborai—those who give opinions]. Those portions which had reference to the Mishna alone were termed the *Gemara*, the authors of which were the *Amoraim* [Amorai—speaker]. Mishna and Gemara together form the Talmud, of which there are two versions, the Palestinian and the Babylonian. The latter is the more important.435

The Talmud, as edited by the Saboraim, has become the chief depository of Jewish religious teaching, and its universal authority resulted from the Mohammedan conquests. To begin with, it became the legal and constitutional foundation for Jewish communal life in Babylon, at the head of which stood the "Prince of the Captivity" and the Presidents of the two Talmudic colleges, the *Gaonim* [Gaon—Excellency]. As Islam spread further and further afield the Jewish communities in the lands that it conquered came into closer relation with the Gaonate in Babylon; they asked advice on religious, ethical and common law questions and loyally accepted the decisions, all of which were based on the Talmud. Indeed, Babylonian Jewry came to be regarded as the new centre of Jewish life.

As soon as the Gemara was written down, and so received permanent form, the development of Judaism ceased. Nevertheless we must mention the three codes which in the post-Talmudic period embodied all the substance of the religion, first, because they presented it in a somewhat different garb, and secondly, because in their regulation of the religious life they could not but pay some heed to changed conditions. All the three codes are recognized by Jews as authoritative side by side with the Talmud, and the last, the *Shulchan Aruch*, is looked upon to-day by the orthodox Jew as containing the official version of religious duties. What is of interest to us in the case of all the codes is that they petrified Jewish religious life still more. Of Maimonides even Graetz asserts as much. "A great deal of what in the Talmud is still mutable, he changed into unmodifiable law. . . . By his codification he robbed Judaism of the power of developing. . . . Without considering the age in which the Talmudic regulations arose, he makes them binding for all ages and circumstances." R. Jacob ben Asher went beyond Maimonides, and Joseph Caro beyond Jacob ben Asher, reaching the utmost limit. His work tends to ultra-particularism and is full of hair-splitting casuistry. The religious life of the Jews "was rounded off and unified by the *Shulchan Aruch*, but at the cost of inwardness and unfettered thought. Caro gave Judaism the fixed form which it has retained down to the present day." [436]

This, then, is the main stream of Jewish religious life; these the sources from which Judaism drew its ideas and ideals. There were, of course, tributary streams, as, for instance, that of the Apocalyptic literature of the pre-Christian era, which stood for a heavenly, a universal, an individualistic Judaism ; [437] or that of the Kabbala, which busied itself with symbols and arithmetical figures. But these had small share in the general development of Jewish life, and may be neglected so far as their effect on historic Judaism is concerned. Nor were they ever recognized by "official" Judaism as sources of the Jewish religion.

So much for the realistic conception of these sources. But what of that current in orthodox Jewish circles? In many respects the belief of the pious Jew touching the origin of the Jewish system is of much more consequence than its real origin. We must therefore try and acquaint ourselves with that belief.

The traditional view, which every orthodox Jew still holds, is that the Jewish system has a twofold birth : partly through Revelation and partly in the inspiration of the "Wise." Revelation refers to the written and the oral tradition. The former is contained in the holy books of the Bible—the Canon as it was fixed by the members of the Great Synagogue. It has three parts [438] :— the Torah or Pentateuch, the Prophetical Books and the "Writings" (the remaining books). The Torah was

given to Moses on Sinai and he "gradually instructed
the people in it during their forty years' wandering in the
wilderness. . . . It was not until the end of his life that
he finished the written Torah, the five books of Moses,
and delivered them unto Israel, and we are in duty
bound to consider every letter, every word of the written
Torah as the Revelation of God." 439 The remaining
books were also the outcome of divine revelation, or, at
any rate, were inspired by God. The attitude towards
the Prophetical literature and the Hagiographa, however,
is somewhat freer than that towards the Torah.

The Oral Tradition, or the Oral Torah, is the explanation of the written one. This, too, was revealed
to Moses on Sinai, but for urgent reasons was not
allowed to be written down at once. That took place
at a much later date—only after the destruction of the
second Temple—and was embodied in *Mishna* and
Gemara, which thus contain the only correct explanation of the Torah, seeing that they were divinely revealed. In the Talmud are included also rabbinic
ordinances and the *Haggada*, *i.e.*, the interpretation of
those portions of Holy Writ other than the legal enactments. The interpretation of the latter was called the
Halacha, and *Halacha and Haggada* supplemented each
other. Beside these were placed the collection of decisions, *i.e.*, the three codes already referred to.

What was the significance of all this literature for the
religious life of the Jews? What was it that the Jew
believed, what were the commands he obeyed?

In the first place it must be premised that so far as I
am aware there is no system of dogmas in Judaism.440
Wherever compilation of such a system has been attempted it was invariably the work of non-Jews.440A
The nature of the Jewish religion and more especially
the construction of the Talmud, which is characterized

by its lack of order, is inconsistent with the formulation of any dogmatic system. Nevertheless certain principles may be discovered in Judaism, and its spirit will be found expressed in Jewish practices. Indeed, it will not be difficult to enumerate these principles, since they have remained the same from the very beginning. What has been termed the " spirit of Ezekiel " has been paramount in Judaism from Ezra's day to ours. It was only developed more and more, only taken to its logical conclusions. And so to discover what this "spirit" is we need only refer to the sources of the religion—the Bible, the Talmud and the later Rabbinic literature.

It is a harder task to determine to what extent this or that doctrine still finds acceptance. Does, for example, the Talmudic adage, "Kill even the best of the Gentiles," still hold good? Do the other terrible aphorisms ferreted out in Jewish religious literature by Pfefferkorn, Eisenmenger, Röhling, Dr. Justus and the rest of that fraternity, still find credence, or are they, as the Rabbis of to-day indignantly protest, entirely obsolete? It is obvious, of course, that the single doctrines were differently expressed in different ages, and if the whole literature, but more especially the Talmud, is referred to on particular points, opposite views, the " pros " and the " cons," will be found. In other words, it is possible to "prove" absolutely anything from the Talmud, and hence the thrust and counter-thrust between the anti-Semites and their Jewish and non-Jewish opponents from time immemorial; hence the fact that what the one proved to be black by reference to the Talmud the others proved to be white on the same authority. There is nothing surprising in this when it is remembered that to a great extent the Talmud is nothing else than a collection of controversies of the different Rabbinical scholars.

To discover the religious ordinances which regulated

actual life we must make a distinction which, to my mind, is very real—the distinction between the man who by personal study strives to find out the law for himself, and the one who accepts it on the authority of another. In the case of the first, the thing that matters is that some opinion or other is found expressed. It is of no consequence that its very opposite may also be there. For the pious Jew who obtains edification by the study of his literature the one view was enough. It may have been the spur to a particular course of action ; or it may have provided him with an additional reason for persisting in a course upon which he had already entered. The sanction of the book was sufficient in either event, most of all if it was the Bible or, better still, the Torah. Since all was of divine origin, one passage was as binding as another. This held good whether applied to the Bible, to the Talmud or to the later Rabbinic writings.

The matter assumes a different aspect if the individual does not, or cannot, study the sources himself but relies on the direction of his spiritual adviser or on books recommended by him. Such a one is confronted with only one opinion, arrived at by the proper interpretation of contradictory texts. Obviously these views must have varied from time to time, in accordance with the Rabbinic traditions in each epoch. Hence, to find the laws that in any period were binding we must search for its Rabbinic traditions—no great task since the publication of the Rabbinic law-books. From the 11th to the 14th century we have the *Yad Hachazaka* ["Strong Hand"] of Maimonides, from the 14th to the 16th the *Tur* of R. Jacob ben Asher, and after the 16th the *Shulchan Aruch* of Caro. Each of these gives the accepted teachings of the age, each is the decisive authority. For the last three hundred years the *Shulchan Aruch* has thus laid down the law wherever there were differences of opinion. As the text-book I have already quoted says, "First and foremost the *Shulchan Aruch* of R. Joseph Caro, together with the notes of R. Moses Isserlein and the other glosses, is recognized by all Israel as the Code on which we model our ritual observances." The Law is also summed up in the 613 precepts which Maimonides derived from the Torah and which even to-day are still in force. "According to the tradition of our Teachers (of blessed memory) God gave Israel by the hand of Moses 613 precepts, 248 positive and 365 negative. All these are binding to all eternity ; only those which have reference to the Jewish State and agricultural life in Palestine and to the Temple service in Jerusalem are excepted, as they cannot be carried out by the Jews of the Diaspora. We can obey 369 precepts, 126 positive and 243 negative ; and in addition the seven Rabbinic commands." 441

The lives of Orthodox Jews were governed by these manuals during the last century and still are so to-day, in so far as the guidance of the Rabbinic law was followed and opinions based on a personal study of the sources were not formed. From the manuals we have mentioned, therefore, we must gather the ordinances which were decisive for each individual instance in religious life. Hence Reformed Judaism is of no concern to us, and books trimmed to suit modern ideas, such as the great majority of the latest expositions of the "Ethics of Judaism," are absolutely useless for our purpose—which is to show the connexion between capitalism and genuine Jewish teaching, and its significance in modern economic life.

III. The Fundamental Ideas of the Jewish Religion.

Let me avow it right away : I think that the Jewish religion has the same leading ideas as Capitalism. I see the same spirit in the one as in the other.

In trying to understand the Jewish religion—which, by the way, must not be confused with the religion of Israel (the two are in a sense opposites)—we must never forget that a *Sofer* was its author, a rigidly minded scribe, whose work was completed by a band of scribes after him. Not a prophet, mark you ; not a seer, nor a visionary nor a mighty king ; a *Sofer* it was. Nor must we forget *how* it came into being : not as an irresistible force, not as the expression of the deepest needs of contrite souls, not as the embodiment of the feelings of divinely inspired votaries. No ; it came into being on a deliberate plan, by clever deductions, and diplomatic policy which was based on the cry "Its religion must be preserved for the people." The same calm consideration, the same attention to the ultimate goal were responsible in the centuries that followed for the addition of line to line and precept to precept. That which did not fit in with the scheme of the *Soferim* from before the days of Ezra and that which grew up afterwards, fell away.

The traces of the peculiar circumstances which gave it birth are still visible in the Jewish religion. In all its reasoning it appeals to us as a creation of the intellect, a thing of thought and purpose projected into the world of organisms, mechanically and artfully wrought, destined to destroy and to conquer Nature's realm and to reign itself in her stead. Just so does Capitalism appear on the scene ; like the Jewish religion, an alien element in the midst of the natural, created world ; like it, too, something schemed and planned in the midst of teeming life. This sheaf of salient features is bound together in one word : Rationalism. Rationalism is the characteristic trait of Judaism as of Capitalism ; Rationalism or Intellectualism—both deadly foes alike to irresponsible mysticism and to that creative power which draws its artistic inspiration from the passion world of the senses.

The Jewish religion knows no mysteries, and is perhaps the only religion on the face of the globe that does not know them. It knows not the ecstatic condition wherein the worshipper feels himself at one with the Godhead, the condition which all other religions extol as the highest and holiest. Think of the Soma libation among the Hindoos, think of entranced Indra himself, of the Homa sacrifice of the Persians, of Dionysus, the Oracle of Greece and of the Sibylline books, to which even the staid Romans went for advice, only because they were written by women who in a state of frenzy prophesied the future.

Down to the latest days of the Roman Empire the characteristic of religious life which remained the same in all aspects of heathenism continued to manifest itself— the characteristic which spread far and wide and infected large masses of people, of working yourself up by sheer force to a pitch of bodily or mental excitement, often becoming bacchanalian madness, and then regarding this as the deity's doing and as part of his service. It was a generally accepted belief that certain sudden impulses or bursts of passion or resolutions were roused in the soul of a man by some god or other ; and conduct of which a man was ashamed or which he regretted, was usually ascribed to the influence of a god.[442] " It was the god who drove me to it "—so, in Plautus's comedy, the young man who had seduced a maiden excused himself to his father.

The same thing must have been experienced by Mohammed in his morbid condition when his fits of ecstasy were upon him, and there is a good deal of mysticism in Islam. At least Mohammedanism has its howling dervishes.

And in Christianity, too, so far as it was not Judaism, room was found for emotional feeling—witness the doctrine of the Trinity, the sweet cult of Mariolatry, the use of incense, the communion. But Judaism looks with proud disdain on these fantastic, mystical elements, condemning them all. When the faithful of other religions hold converse with God in blissful convulsions, in the Jewish synagogue, called a *Shool* [*i.e.*, School] not without significance, the Torah is publicly read. So Ezra ordained, and so it is done most punctiliously. " Ever since the destruction of the State, study became the soul of Judaism, and religious observances without knowledge of the ordinances which enjoined them was considered as being of little worth. The central feature of public service on Sabbaths and Holy Days was the lesson read from the Law and the Prophets, the translation of the passages by the *Targumists* [Interpreters] and the homiletic explanation of them by the *Haggadists* [Preachers]."

> " Radix stultitiæ, cui frigida sabbata cordi
>   Sed cor frigidus relligione sua
>   Septima quæque dies turpi damnato veterno
>   Tanquam lassati mollis imago dei."

> [" The Sabbath—monstrous folly !—fills the need
>   Of hearts still icier than their icy creed,
>   Each seventh day in shameful sloth they nod,
>   And ape the languor of their weary God."]

Such was the Roman view.443

Judaism then looked askance at mysteries. With no different eye did it regard the holy enthusiasm for the divine in the world of feeling. Astarte, Daphne, Isis and Osiris, Aphrodite, Fricka and the Holy Virgin— it would have none of them. It banished all pictorial art from its cult. " And the Lord spake unto you out of the midst of the fire : ye heard the sound of words but ye saw no form " (Deut. iv. 12). " Cursed be the man that maketh a graven or molten image, an abomination unto the Lord, the work of the hands of the craftsman. . . ." (Deut. xxvii. 15). The command, "Thou shalt not make unto thee any graven image" finds acceptance to-day, and the pious Jew has no statues made, nor does he set them up in his house.444

The kinship between Judaism and Capitalism is further illustrated by the legally regulated relationship—I had almost said the businesslike connexion, except that the term has a disagreeable connotation—between God and Israel. The whole religious system is in reality nothing but a contract between Jehovah and His chosen people, a contract with all its consequences and all its duties. God promises something and gives something, and the righteous must give Him something in return. Indeed, there was no community of interest between God and man which could not be expressed in these terms—that man performs some duty enjoined by the Torah and receives from God a *quid pro quo*. Accordingly, no man should approach God in prayer without bringing with him something of his own or of his ancestors' by way of return for what he is about to ask.445

The contract usually sets forth that man is rewarded for duties performed and punished for duties neglected ; the rewards and punishments being received partly in this and partly in the next world. Two consequences must of necessity follow : first, a constant weighing up of the loss and gain which any action needs must bring, and secondly, a complicated system of bookkeeping, as it were, for each individual person.

The whole of this conception is excellently well illustrated by the words of Rabbi [164–200 A.D.] : " Which is the right course for a man to choose ?

That which he feels to be honourable to himself and which also brings him honour from mankind. Be heedful of a light precept as of a grave one, for you do not know what reward a precept brings. Reckon the loss incurred by the fulfilment of a precept against the reward secured by its observance, and the gain gotten by a transgression against the loss it involves. Reflect on three things and you will not come within the power of sin. Know what is above thee—a seeing eye, and a hearing ear, and all your deeds written in a book." [446] So that whether one is accounted "righteous" or "wicked" depends on the balance of commands performed against commands neglected. Obviously this necessitates the keeping of accounts, and each man therefore has his own, in which his words and his deeds, even the words spoken in jest, are all carefully registered. According to one authority (*Ruth Rabba*, 33a) the prophet Elijah keeps these accounts ; according to another (*Esther Rabba*, 86a) the duty is assigned to angels.

Every man has thus an account in heaven : Israel a particularly large one (*Sifra*, 44b). And one of the ways of preparing for death is to have your "account" ready (*Kohelet Rabba*, 77c). Sometimes "extracts" from the accounts are forthcoming (by request). When the angels brought an accusation against Ishmael, God asked, "What is his position at present ? Is he a righteous man or a wicked ? " (*i.e.*, do the commands performed outweigh those neglected ?) And the angels replied, " He is a righteous man." When Mar Ukba died, he asked for a statement of his account (of the money he had given to charity). It totalled 7000 zuzim. As he was afraid that this would not suffice for his salvation he gave away half of his fortune in order to be on the safe side (*Kethuboth*, 25 ; *Baba Bathra*, 7). The final decision as to the righteousness or wickedness of any man is made after his death. The account is then closed, and the grand total drawn up. The result is inserted in a document (*Shetar*) which is handed to each individual after it has been read out.447

It is not difficult to perceive that the keeping of these accounts was no easy matter. In Biblical times, so long as rewards and punishments were meted out in the life on earth, the task was no great one. But in the period that followed, when rewards and punishments were granted partly in this life and partly in life everlasting, the question grew to be troublesome, and in the Rabbinic theology an intricate and artistic system of bookkeeping was evolved. This distinguished between the capital sum or the principal, and the fruits or the interest, the former being reserved for the future world, the latter for this. And in order that the reward which is laid up in heaven for the righteous may not be diminished, God does not lessen the stock when He grants him ordinary earthly benefits. Only when he receives extraordinary, *i.e.*, miraculous, benefits on earth does the righteous man suffer a diminution of his heavenly reward. Moreover, the righteous is punished for his sins at once on earth, as the wicked is rewarded for his good deeds, so that the one may have only rewards in heaven and the other only chastisements.448

Another conception is bound up with this of divine bookkeeping and is closely akin to a second fundamental trait of capitalism—the conception of profit. Sin or goodness is regarded as something apart from the sinner. Every sin, according to Rabbinic theology, is considered singly and by itself. " Punishment is according to the object and not the subject of the sin." 449 The quantity of the broken commandments alone counts.

No consideration whatever is had for the personality of the sinner or his ethical state, just as a sum of money is separated from persons, just as it is capable of being added to another abstract sum of money. The ceaseless striving of the righteous after well-being in this and the next world must needs therefore take the form of a constant endeavour to increase his rewards. Now, as he is never able to tell whether at a particular state of his conscience he is worthy of God's goodness or whether in his " account " the rewards or the punishments are more numerous, it must be his aim to add reward after reward to his account by constantly doing good deeds to the end of his days. The limited conception of all personal values thus finds no admission into the world of his religious ideas and its place is taken by the endlessness of a pure quantitative ideal.

Parallel with this tendency there runs through Jewish moral theology another which regards the getting of money as a means to an end. The conception is frequently found in books of religious edification, the authors of which realizing but seldom that in their warnings against the acquisition of too much wealth they are glorifying this very practice. Usually the treatment of the subject is under the heading " covetousness," forbidden by the tenth commandment. " A true Israelite," remarks one of the most popular of modern " helps to faith," [450] " avoids covetousness. He looks upon all his possessions only as a means of doing what is pleasing in the sight of God. For is not the entire purpose of his life to use all his possessions, all enjoyment as the means to this end ? Indeed it is a duty . . . to obtain possessions and to increase one's enjoyments, not as an end in themselves but as a means to do God's will on earth."

But if it is urged that this is no conclusive proof

of the connexion between the religious idea and the principle of getting gain, a glance at the peculiar ordering of divine service will soon be convincing. At one stage in the service there is a veritable public auction. The honorary offices connected with the reading of the law are given to the highest bidder. Before the scrolls are taken from the Ark, the beadle walks round the central platform (the Almemor) and cries out : " Who will buy *Hazoa vehachnosa*? (*i.e.*, the act of taking the scrolls from the Ark and of replacing them). Who will buy *Hagboha*? (the act of raising the scroll in the sight of the people). Who will buy *Gelilah*? " (the act of rolling up the scroll when the reading is finished). These honours are knocked down to the highest bidder, and the money given to the synagogue poor-box. It need hardly be said that to-day this practice has long been eliminated from synagogue worship. In days of long ago it was quite general.451

Again, the words of some of the Talmudic doctors, who at times dispute over the most difficult economic questions with all the skill of experienced merchants, cannot but have a curious connotation, and must needs lead to the conclusion that they preached the getting of gain. It would be fascinating to collect those passages of the Talmud wherein the modern practice of making profit is recommended by this or that Rabbi, in many cases themselves great traders. I will quote an instance or two. " R. Isaac also taught that a man should always have his money in circulation." It was R. Isaac, too, who gave this piece of good advice. A man should divide his fortune into three parts, investing one in landed property, one in moveable goods, and holding the third as ready cash (*Baba Mezia*, 42*a*). " Rav once said to his son, Come let me instruct thee in worldly matters. Sell

your goods even while the dust is yet upon your feet."
(What is this but a recommendation to have a quick
turnover?) "First open your purse and then unloose
the sack of wheat. . . . Have you got dates in the box?
Hasten at once to the brewer" (*Pesachim*, 113*a*).

What is the meaning of this parallelism between the
Jewish religion and capitalism? Is it a mere chance?
A stupid joke perpetrated by Fate? Is the one the
effect of the other, or are both traceable to the
same causes? Questions such as these naturally suggest
themselves to us, and I hope to answer them as we
proceed. Here it will suffice to have called attention
to them. Our next step will be the comparatively
simpler one of showing how individual customs, conceptions, opinions and regulations of the Jewish religion
influenced the economic conduct of Jews, of showing
whether they facilitated the extension of capitalism by
the Jews, and, if so, to what degree. We shall limit
ourselves in this to primary psychological motives,
avoiding all speculative difficulties. Our first problem
will be to discover the goal set up by the Jewish
religion and its influence on economic life, and the
next section is devoted to it.

IV. The Idea of Rewards and Punishments.

The idea of contract, which is part and parcel of the
underlying principles of Judaism, must perforce have
the corollary that whoever carries out the contract
receives reward, whoever breaks it receives punishment. In other words, the legal and ethical assumption
that the good prosper and the evil suffer punishment
was in all ages a concept of the Jewish religion. All
that changed was the interpretation of prosperity and
punishment.

The oldest form of Judaism knows nothing of another

world. So, weal and woe can come only in this world. If God desires to punish or to reward, He must do so during man's lifetime. The righteous therefore is prosperous here, and the wicked here suffer punishment. Obey my precepts, says the Lord, " so that thou mayest live long and prosper in the land which the Lord thy God hath given unto thee." Hence the bitter cry of Job, " Wherefore do the wicked live, become old, yea, wax mighty in power ? . . . But my way He hath fenced up, that I cannot pass . . . He hath broken me down on every side . . . He hath also kindled His wrath against me " [Job xxi. 7 ; xix. 8, 10, 11]. " Why hath all this evil come upon me, seeing that I walked in His path continually ? "

A little after Ezra's time the idea of another world (*Olam Habo*) finds currency in Judaism, the idea, too, of the immortality of the soul and of the resurrection of the body. These beliefs were of foreign origin, coming probably from Persia. But like all other alien elements in Judaism they, too, were given an ethical meaning, in accordance with the genius of the religion. The doctrine grew up that only the righteous and the pious would rise up after death. The belief in eternity was thus made by the *Soferim* to fit in with the old teaching of rewards and punishments, in order to heighten the feeling of moral responsibility, *i.e.*, of the fear of the judgment of God.452

The idea of prosperity on earth is now extended. It is no longer the only reward of a good life, for a reward in the world to come is added to it. Still, God's blessing in this world is no small part of the total reward. Moreover, the very fact that a man is prosperous here was proof positive that his life was pleasing to God, and that therefore he might expect reward in the next world also. Then, too, the idea of a blind fate is no longer troublesome. What appeared as such is now regarded as God's punishment on earth to the righteous for his transgressions, so that his heavenly recompense may suffer no diminution.

The "doctrine of possession" (if the term may be allowed in connexion with the Jewish religion) received some such shape as this, more especially through the Wisdom Literature. The great aim of life is to obey God's commandments. Earthly happiness apart from God has no existence. Hence it is folly to seek to obtain earthly possessions for their own sake. But to obtain them in order to use them for divine ends, so that they become at one and the same time the outward symbols and guarantees of God's pleasure, as signs of His blessing—such a course is wise. Now earthly possessions in this view of them include a well-appointed house and material well-being—in a word, wealth.

Look through Jewish literature, more especially through the Holy Writ and the Talmud, and you will find, it is true, a few passages wherein poverty is lauded as something higher and nobler than riches. But on the other hand you will come across hundreds of passages in which riches are called the blessing of the Lord, and only their misuse or their dangers warned against. Here and there, too, we may read that riches alone do not necessarily bring happiness, other things are essential in addition (such as health, for example), that there are "goods" (in the broadest use of the word) more valuable or as valuable as riches. But in all this nothing is said *against* riches; and never is it stated that they are an abomination to the Lord.

I once gave expression to this view in a public lecture, and it was severely criticized on all sides. Just this point more than any other was controverted—the statement that riches are in the Jewish religion accounted as a valuable good. Many of my critics, among them several distinguished Jewish rabbis, went to the trouble of compiling lists of passages from the Bible and Talmud which confuted my opinion. I admit that there are many places in the Bible and the Talmud which regard wealth as a danger to the righteous, and in which poverty is extolled. There are some half-dozen of them in the Bible ; the Talmud has rather more. But the important thing is that each of these passages may be capped by ten others, which breathe a totally different spirit. In such cases numbers surely count.

I put the question to myself in this way. Let us imagine old Amschel Rothschild on a Friday evening, after having " earned " a million on the Stock Exchange, turning to his Bible for edification. What will he find there touching his earnings and their effect on the refinement of his soul, an effect which the pious old Jew most certainly desired on the eve of the Sabbath ? Will the million burn his conscience ? Or will he not be able to say, and rightly say, " God's blessing rested upon me this week. I thank Thee, Lord, for having graciously granted the light of Thy countenance to Thy servant. In order to find favour in Thy sight I shall give much to charity, and keep Thy commandments even more strictly than hitherto " ? Such would be his words if he knew his Bible, and he did know it.

For his eye would rest complacently on many a passage in the Holy Writ. In his beloved Torah he would be able to read again and again of the blessing of God. " And He will love thee and bless thee and multiply thee, He will also bless the fruit of thy body and the fruit of thy ground, thy corn and thy wine and thine oil . . . thou shalt be blessed above all peoples " (Deut. vii. 13–15). And how moved he would be when he reached the words, " For the Lord, thy God, will bless thee, as He promised thee : and thou shalt lend unto many nations, but thou shalt not borrow ' (Deut. xv. 6). Then suppose he turns to the Psalms, what would he find there ?

"O fear the Lord, ye His saints : for there is no want to them that fear Him" (Psa. xxxiv. 10).

"Blessed is the man that feareth the Lord. . . . Wealth and riches are in his house" (Psa. xc. 1-3).

"Our garners are full, affording all manner of store, our sheep bring forth thousands and ten thousands in our fields" (Psa. cxliv. 13).

He would rejoice with Job when on concluding the story of his trials he found that his latter end was more blessed than his beginning, and that " he had 14,000 sheep, 6000 camels, 1000 yoke of oxen and 1000 she-asses " and the rest. (Happily our friend Amschel knew nothing of modern Biblical criticism, and was not aware therefore that this particular portion of Job is a later interpolation in the story.)

The prophets also promised Israel earthly rewards if he kept to God's way and walked therein. If Amschel turned to the 60th chapter of Isaiah he would find the prophecy that one day the Gentiles should bring their gold and silver to Israel.

But perhaps Amschel's favourite book would be Proverbs, 453 "which expresses in a most pregnant form the ideas of life current in Israel " (as a rabbi wrote to me who quoted this book in proof of my error, Prov. xxii. 1, 2 ; xxiii. 4 ; xxviii. 20, 21 ; xxx. 8). Here he would be warned that riches alone do not bring happiness (xxii. 1, 2), that God must not be denied amid great wealth (xxx. 8), that " he that maketh haste to be rich shall not be unpunished " (xxviii. 20). (Perhaps he will say to himself that he does not " hasten " to be rich.) The only verse that may disquieten him is when he reads

" Weary not thyself to be rich ; cease from thine own wisdom " (xxiii. 4). But only for a moment, for his mind will be eased when he observes the connexion with the preceding passage. Possibly these six little words may not after all trouble him much when he remembers the numerous passages in this very book which commend riches. So numerous indeed that it may be said they give the tone to the whole of Proverbs.454 A few only shall be quoted :—

" Length of days are in her right hand ; in her left are riches and honour " (iii. 16).
" Riches and honour are with me ; yea, durable riches and righteousness " (viii. 18).
" The rich man's wealth is his strong city " (x. 15).
" Their riches are a crown unto the wise " (xiv. 24).
" The reward of humility and the fear of the Lord is riches and honour and life " (xxii. 4).

The Wisdom Literature included Ecclesiastes and the Wisdom of Solomon. The first 455 certainly does not breathe a uniform spirit ; the many accretions of later times make it full of contradictions. Yet even here the pious Jew found never a passage which taught him to despise wealth. On the contrary, wealth is highly valued.

" Every man also to whom God hath given riches and wealth, and hath given him power to eat thereof . . . this is the gift of God " (v. 19).
" A feast is made for laughter and wine maketh glad the life : and money answereth all things " (x. 19).

The Wisdom of Solomon likewise praises riches. No less does the Book of Jesus, the son of Sirach, that fund of wise saws, which old Amschel must have conned with delight. If any Rabbi had told him that Ben Sirach's book regards the wealthy man almost as a sinner and wealth as the source of evil, instancing chapters x.–xiii.

in proof, Amschel would have replied, "My dear Rabbi, you are mistaken. Those passages are a warning against the dangers of wealth. But a rich man who avoids the dangers is thereby the more righteous. 'Blessed is the rich that is found without blemish . . . his goods shall be established and the congregation shall declare his alms' (xxxi. 8, 11). And why, my dear Rabbi" (so Amschel might continue), "do you not mention the passages which speak of the man who has amassed millions, passages like the following?

"'Better is he that laboureth and aboundeth in all things, than he that boasteth himself and wanteth bread' (x. 27).
"'The poor man is honoured for his skill, and the rich man is honoured for his riches' (x. 30).
"'Prosperity and adversity, life and death, poverty and riches come of the Lord' (xi. 14).
"'Gold and silver make the foot stand sure' (xl. 25).
"'Riches and strength lift up the heart' (xl. 26).
"'Better it is to die than to beg' (xl. 28).

"Should I be ashamed of my millions, my dear Rabbi" (Amschel would conclude the imaginary conversation), "should I not rather look upon them as God's blessing? Recall what the wise Jesus ben Sirach said of great King Solomon (xlvii. 18) : 'By the name of the Lord God, which is called the Lord God of Israel, thou didst gather gold as tin, and didst multiply silver as lead.' I also will go, Rabbi, and in the name of the Lord God will gather gold as tin and silver as lead."

In the Talmud the passages that express the same point of view are frequent enough. Riches are a blessing if only their owner walk in God's ways, and poverty is a curse. Hardly ever are riches despised. Let us quote a few Talmudic sayings on the subject.

"Seven characteristics are there which are 'comely to the righteous and comely to the world.' One of them is riches" (*Aboth*, vi. 8).

" In prayer a man should turn to Him who owns wealth and possessions. . . . In reality both come not from business, but according to merit " (*Kidushin*, lxxxiia).

" R. Eleazer said, ' The righteous love their money more than their bodies ' " (*Sota*, xiia).

" Rabba honoured the wealthy, so did R. Akiba " (*Erubin*, lxxxvia).

" In time of scarcity a man learns to value wealth best " (*Aboth de Rabbi Nathan*).

Doctrines concerning wealth such as these could not but encourage a worldly view of life. This the Jewish view was, despite the belief in another world. There were indeed attempts at ascetic movements in Judaism (*e.g.*, in the 9th century the Karaites combined to live the life of monks ; * in the 11th century Bachja ibn Pakuda preached asceticism in Spain), but none of them ever took root. Judaism even in times of great affliction was always optimistic. In this the Jews differ from the Christians, whose religion has tried to rob them all it could of earthly joys. As often as riches are lauded in the Old Testament they are damned in the New, wherein poverty is praised. The whole outlook of the Essenes, turning its back upon the world and the flesh, was incorporated in the Gospels. One can easily recall passage after passage to this effect. (Cf. Matt. vi. 24 ; x. 9, 10; xix. 23, 24.) " It is easier for a camel to go through a needle's eye than for a rich man to enter into the Kingdom of God." This is the keynote of Christianity on the point, and the difference between it and Judaism is clear enough. There is no single parallel to the saying of Jesus in the whole of the Old Testament, and probably also none in the entire body of Rabbinic literature.

There is no need to expatiate on the different attitude of the good Jew and the good Christian towards economic

[* Sombart is mistaken in this. The characteristic of the Karaites was that they accepted and lived by the *letter* of the Torah.]

activities. The Christian is forced by all manner of mental gymnastics to interpret away the Essene conception of riches from his Scriptures. And what anxious moments must the rich Christian live through as he thinks of heaven locked against him ! Compare with him the position of the rich Jew, who, as we have seen, "in the name of the Lord God " gathers gold as tin and silver as lead.

It is well known that the religion of the Christians stood in the way of their economic activities. It is equally well known that the Jews were never faced with this hindrance. The more pious a Jew was and the more acquainted with his religious literature, the more he was spurred by the teachings of that literature to extend his economic activities. A beautiful illustration of the way religion and business were fused in the mind of pious Jews may be found in the delightful *Memoirs* of Glückel von Hameln, to which we have already referred. " Praise be to God, who gives and takes, the faithful God, who always made good our losses," she says. And again, " My husband sent me a long, comforting letter, urging me to calm my soul, for God, whose name be blessed, would restore to us what we had lost. And so it was."

V. The Rationalization of Life.

Since Judaism rests upon a contract between God and His people, *i.e.*, upon a two-sided legal agreement, each party must have definite responsibilities. What were those of the Jews ?

Again and again was the answer to this question given by God through His servant Moses. Again and again the Israelite was informed that two great duties were his. He was to be holy and to obey God's law. (Cf. Exod. xix. 6 ; Deut. iv. 56.) God did not require sacrifices of him ; He demanded obedience (Jer. vii. 22, 23).

Now it is generally known that in the course of events the Jews came to regard righteousness as a minute fulfilment of the Law. The inward holiness that may have existed in early days soon vanished before formalism and legalism. Holiness and observation of the Law became interchangeable terms. It is generally known, too, that this legalism was a device of the Rabbis to protect the Jews against the influences first, of Hellenism, then of Christianity, and finally, when the Second Temple was destroyed, to maintain by its means the national consciousness. The struggle with Hellenism resulted in Pharisaism ; the struggle with Pauline Christianity which aimed at replacing the Law by faith, transformed the religion of the Pharisees into that of the Talmud, and the old policy of the Scribes " to encompass the whole of life with regulation " made greater progress than ever. In their political isolation the Jewish communities submitted entirely to the new hierarchy. They desired to see the end attained and so accepted the means. The school and the Law outlasted the Temple and the State, and Pharisaic Rabbinism had unlimited sway. Righteousness henceforth meant living in strict accordance with the Law. Piety, under the influence of the legally minded Scribes, was given a legal connotation. Religion became the common law. In the Mishna all this finds admirable expression. The commands of the Pentateuch and the commands deduced from these are all divine ordinances which must be obeyed without questioning. More and more stress is laid on externals, and between important and insignificant commands there is less and less differentiation.[456]

So it remained for two thousand years ; so it is to-day. Strict orthodoxy still holds fast to this formalism and the principles of Judaism know no change. The Torah is as binding to-day in its every word as when it was given to Moses on Sinai.457 Its laws and ordinances must be observed by the faithful, whether they be light or grave, whether they appear to have rhyme or reason or no. And they must be strictly observed, and only because God gave them. This implicit obedience makes the righteous, makes the saint. "Saintly or holy in the Torah sense is he who is able to fulfil the revealed will of God without any struggle and with the same joy as carrying out his own will. This holiness, this complete fusion of the will of man with the divine will, is a lofty goal attainable in its entirety by a few only. Hence the law of holiness refers in the first instance to the striving towards this goal. The striving all can do ; it demands a constant self-watchfulness and self-education, an endless struggle against what is low and vulgar, what is sensual and bestial. And obedience to the behests of the Torah is the surest ladder on which to climb to higher and higher degrees of holiness." 458

These words show clearly enough how holiness and legalism are connected ; they show that the highest aim of Israel still is to be a kingdom of priests and a holy nation ; and that the path to that end is a strict obedience to God's commandments. Once this becomes apparent, we can imagine the importance the Jewish religion has for the whole of life. In the long run, external legalism does not remain external ; it exercises a constant influence on the inner life, which obtains its peculiar character from the observance of the law.

The psychological process which led to the shaping of Judaism appears to me to be this. At first God's behests were those that mattered, regardless of their contents. But slowly the contents must needs make themselves manifest to the observer, and a clearly defined ideal of Life evolved itself from the word of

God. To follow this ideal, to be righteous, to be holy was the heart's desire of each believer.

Before continuing, let us strive to obtain some notion of what the pious Jew meant, and means, by holiness in the material sense.

Let us recall what was said in the last section about the "worldliness" of the Jewish religion. In accordance with this it can scarcely be holy to deny the natural instincts or to crush them, as other religions teach— *e.g.*, Buddhism or Primitive Christianity. Other-worldly asceticism was always antagonistic to Judaism. "The soul which has been given thee—preserve it, never kill it"—that is the Talmudic maxim on which to build up the conduct of life and which found currency at all times. 459

The negation of life cannot therefore be holiness. Nor can the exercise of man's passions and appetites be holiness. For if it were, it could not be put as an ideal before the righteous ; it would then be accessible to everybody. There remains therefore only one other possibility—to live your life of set purpose in accordance with some ideal plan based on supernatural rules, and either utilizing the desires within you or crushing them. In fine, holiness is the rationalization of life. You decide to replace the natural existence with its desires and inclinations by the moral life. To be holy is to become refined, and to realize this is to overcome all your natural tendencies by means of moral obedience. 460

A rugged Dualism—the terrible Dualism which is part and parcel of our constitution—characterizes the Jewish conception of ethical worth. Nature is not unholy, neither is she holy. She is not yet holy. She may become holy through us. All the seeds of sin are in her ; the serpent still lurks in the grass as he did long ago in the Garden of Eden. "God certainly created the evil inclination, but he also created the Torah, the moral law, as an antidote to it." [461] The whole of human life is one great warfare against the inimical forces of Nature : that is the guiding principle of Jewish moral theology, and it is in accordance with it that the system of rules and regulations was instituted by which life might be rationalized, de-naturalized, refined and hallowed without the necessity of renouncing or stifling it. In this we see the marked difference between the Christian (Essene) and the Jewish (Pharisaic) ideas of morality. The former leads quite logically away from the world into the silent hermitage and the monastery (if not to death) ; the latter binds its faithful adherent with a thousand chains to the individual and social life. Christianity makes its devotee into a monk, Judaism into a rationalist ; the first ends in asceticism outside the world ; the second in asceticism within it (taking asceticism to mean the subjugation of what is natural in man).

We shall gain a clearer insight of what Jewish Ethics (and therefore also the Jewish religion) stands for if we examine its regulations one by one.

The effect of Law is twofold. Its very existence has an influence ; so have its contents.

That there is a law at all, that it is a duty to obey it, impels one to think about one's actions and to accomplish them in harmony with the dictates of reason. In front of every desire a warning finger-post is set ; every natural impulse is nullified by the thousand and one milestones and danger-signals in the shape of directions to the pious. Now, since obedience to a multifariousness of rules (the well-known commands compiled by Maimonides numbered 365—of which 243 are still current—and his prohibitions 248) is wellnigh impossible without a pretty good knowledge of what they are, the system includes the command to study the Holy Writ, and especially the Torah. This very study itself is made a means of rendering life holy. " If the evil inclination seizes hold of you, march him off to the House of Study," counsels the Talmud.

The view that all the enactments were for the purpose of ennobling the life of the faithful was accepted at all times, and is still held to-day by many orthodox Jews.

" God wished to refine Israel, therefore He increased the number of the commandments " (*Makkoth*, 23*b*).

" The commandments were given by God to ennoble mankind " (*Vajikra Rabba*, 13).[462]

" It would have been better for a man never to have been born, but once he is in the world let him continually examine his actions " (*Erubin*, 13*b*).

" Every night a man should critically examine his deeds of the day " (*Magen Abraham* on *Orach Chajim*, 239, § 7).[463]

" 'Observe' and 'remember' were ordained in a single utterance." [464]

Deum respice et cura [465-466] is still the motto of the Jew. If he meets a king or sees a dwarf or a negro, passes a ruined building or takes his medicine or his bath, notes the coming storm or hears its roaring thunder, rises in the morning and puts on his clothes or eats his food, enters his house or leaves it, greets a friend or meets a foe—for every emergency there is an ordinance which must be obeyed.

Now what of the contents of the ordinances? All of them aim at the subjugation of the merely animal instincts in man, at the bridling of his desires and inclinations and at the replacing of impulses by thoughtful action ; in short, at the " ethical tempering of man."

You must think nothing, speak nothing, do nothing without first considering what the law about it is, and then apply it to the great purpose of sanctification.

You must therefore do nothing merely for its own sake, spontaneously, or from natural instinct.

You must not enjoy Nature for the sheer pleasure of it. You may do so only if you think thereby of the wisdom and the goodness of God. In the spring when the trees put on their blossom the pious Jew says, " Blessed art Thou, O Lord our God, . . . who hast made Thy world lacking in nought, but hast provided therein goodly creatures and trees wherewith to give delight to the children of men." At the sight of the rainbow he brings to mind the Covenant with God. On high mountains, in vast deserts, beside mighty rivers—in a word, wherever his heart is deeply moved by Nature's wonders—he expresses his feelings in the benediction, " Blessed art Thou, O Lord our God, . . . who hast made the Creation."

You must not enjoy art for its own sake. Works of plastic art should be avoided, for they may easily lead to a breach of the second commandment. But even the poet's art is not looked upon with favour, except it refer to God. All reading is good, provided it has some practical end in view. " It is best to read the books of the Torah or such as refer to them. If we desire to read for recreation, let us choose books that are able to teach us something useful. Among the books written for amusement and to while away the time there are some that may awake sinful wishes within us. The reading of these books is forbidden." 467

You must not indulge in harmless pleasures. " The seat of the scornful [Psa. i. 1],—the theatres and circuses of the heathen are meant." Song, dance and wine, save when they are connected with religious ceremonial, are taboo. " Rabbi Dosa ben Hyrkanus used to say, Morning sleep and midday wine and childish talk and attending the houses where the ignorant foregather put

a man out of the world." [468] " He that loveth
pleasure shall be a poor man ; he that loveth wine and
oil shall not be rich " (Prov. xxi. 17).

If this be so, those qualities which may lead a man
to "unseemly" conduct are useless or even harmful.
Such are enthusiasm (for while a man is in this state he
may do something useless), [469] kindness of heart (you
must exercise kindness only because the idea of benevo-
lence actuates you ; you must never let pity carry you
away, so that the nobility and dignity of the ideal law
may always be before you) ; [470] a sensual temperament ("the source of passion—and of sin—is in sen-
suality "),[471] ingenuousness, in short anything that marks
the natural (and therefore unholy) man.

The cardinal virtues of the pious are, on the other hand,
self-control and circumspection, a love of order and of
work, moderation and abstemiousness, chastity and sobriety.

Self-control and circumspection especially in regard
to your words is a constant theme of the moralists. " In
the multitude of words there wanteth not transgression :
but he that refraineth his lips doth wisely " (Prov.
x. 19). [471A]

No less insistent was the later tradition. " Raba held
that whoso carries on an unnecessary conversation trans-
gresses a command " (*Joma*, 19*b*). "Our sanctification," says a modern book for popular edification,
" depends to a large extent on the control of our tongues,
on the power of holding our peace. The gift of speech
. . . was given to man for holy purposes. Hence all
unnecessary talk is forbidden by our wise men." [472]

But self-control and circumspection generally are urged
on the pious Jew.

" Who is the strongest of the strong ? He who controls his
passions " (*Aboth de R. Nathan*, xxiii. 1).

"The thoughts of the diligent tend only to plenteousness : but every one that is hasty hasteth only to want" (Prov. xxi. 5).

"He that hasteth with his feet sinneth" (Prov. xix. 2).

And as for industry and thrift, innumerable are the exhortations to that end.

The Jew must wake the day, not the day the Jew—so taught the Rabbis, as a homily on Psalm lvii. 9.[473]

It is just the strongest instincts of man that must be curbed, directed into right channels, deprived of their natural force and made to serve useful ends. In short, they must be rationalized.

Take the instinct which desires to satisfy hunger. It is forbidden to appease the appetite merely because it happens to be there ; it should be appeased only for the body's sake. And when the good man sits down to eat, let him do so according to the precepts of his Maker. Hence the large number of rules concerning food ; hence the command to be serious at meals—to begin and to close with prayer ; hence the advice to be moderate and the appeal to banish the pleasure of feeding. "It is only through God's goodness that you are enabled to use His creatures as food, and therefore if your entire eating and drinking is not to be beastly, it must be hallowed ; it must be looked upon as the getting of strength for His service." [474] "The Jew should make the satisfaction of his appetite for food a sacrament ; should regard his table as an altar and the food thereon as sacrifice, which he enjoys only in order to obtain more strength for the fulfilment of his duties. [475-476] (Jewish cooking, by the way, is excellent.)

Finally—and this of course matters most—just like hunger, Love also must be rationalized, that is to say, its natural expression must be held in check. Nowhere more than in the erotic sphere does the hard dualism show itself so well. The world, and certainly the civilized nations, owes this conception of the sexual to the Jews (through the agency of Christianity, which was infected with the idea). All earlier religions saw something divine in the expression of sex, and regarded sexual intercourse as of the nature of a heavenly revelation. All of them were acquainted with Phallus-worship in a grosser or finer form. None of them condemned what is sensuous, or looked upon women as a source of sin. But the Jews from Ezra's day to this held, and hold, the opposite view.

To sanctify himself, to make himself worthy of his converse with God, Moses "drew not nigh unto his wife." And Job mentions as being in his favour that he made a covenant with his eyes not to look upon a maid. The whole Wisdom Literature abounds in warnings against women,* and the same spirit dominates the Talmud. "Better to die than to be guilty of unchastity" (*Sanhedrin*, 75*a*). Indeed, the three capital crimes for which even death does not atone are murder, idol-worship and adultery. "Hast thou business with women? See to it that thou art not with them alone" (*Kiddushin*, 82*a*). This dread runs through all the codes. The *Eben Ha-ezer* condemns to death by stoning any one who has had guilty intercourse with a woman related to him within the prohibited degrees. The very clothes or the little finger of a woman of such close consanguinity must not be looked at "to get pleasure from it." It is forbidden a man to allow himself to be waited on by a woman, or to embrace his aunt or his grown-up sister.

Teachers of to-day are no less explicit. "Guard yourself against any contact with impurity," says one

[* Sombart instances Prov. v. 3–4. But does not the passage clearly refer to *bad* women ?]

of the most popular of them. "Look at nothing, hear nothing, read nothing, think of nothing which may in any wise occupy your thoughts unchastely or make you familiar with what is not clean. Do not walk in the street behind a woman ; if you cannot help yourself, look not at her with desire.* Do not let your eye rest longingly on a woman's hair, nor your ears on her voice ; do not take pleasure in her form ; yea, a woman's very clothes should not be looked at if you know who has worn them. In all things go out of the way of Opportunity. . . . The two sexes should not jest together. Even in make-believe little pressures of the hand, winking of the eyes, embracing and kissing are sinful." 477

Warnings such as these were not neglected, as may be seen from the autobiographies of pious Jews, some of which may now be read in modern languages.478

But the point of it all must not be overlooked. Other religions also show signs of being terrified at women. Ever since the notion became prevalent that woman brought sin into the world there have always been morbid souls who spent their lives exciting themselves with all manner of lascivious imaginings but avoiding woman as though she were the devil incarnate. In other religions the man fled to the hermit's cave in the wilderness or to a monastery. In either case, his religion forced "chastity" upon him, with all the horrid resultants well known to students of monastic life. Not so Judaism. Judaism does not forbid sexual intercourse ; it rationalizes it. Not that it does not regard sexual intercourse as sinful. Sinful it must always be, but its sinfulness may to some extent be removed by sanctification. Hence Judaism advocates early

[* Cf. Robert Louis Stevenson : "To remember the faces of women without desire, . . . is not this to know both wisdom and virtue ?"]

marriages and regulates the relationship between husband and wife as something "ever in the great Taskmaster's eye."

"A man should not be without a wife, nor a woman without a husband ; but both shall see to it that God's spirit is in their union." That is the motto, and in accordance with it the Talmud and the later codes have multiplied rules and regulations for the guidance of married couples. In the 11th century (to mention but a few) R. Eleazar ben Nathan compiled a special code on the subject, the *Eben Ha-ezer*, and in the 13th century R. Nachman wrote a famous work on the sanctification of marriage.479 The laws of the *Eben Ha-ezer* were incorporated in the *Shulchan Aruch* and together with the glosses upon them receive recognition to-day. The main ideas throughout are those we have already considered : hallow thy body's strength in accordance with God's will ; be careful of thy manhood ; be God's servant at all times. 480

Such was the Jewish view of marriage, which has continued for more than two thousand years. It is well illustrated by that touching story in the Book of Tobit, which may form a fitting conclusion to our considerations under this head.

"And after that they were both shut in together, Tobias rose out of the bed, and said, Sister, arise, and let us pray that God would have pity on us.

"Then began Tobias to say, Blessed art Thou, O God of our fathers, and blessed is Thy holy and glorious name for ever ; let the heavens bless Thee, and all Thy creatures.

"Thou madest Adam, and gavest him Eve his wife for an helper and stay : of them came mankind : Thou hast said, It is not good that man should be alone ; let us make unto him an aid like unto himself.

"And now, O Lord, I take not this my sister for lust, but uprightly · therefore mercifully ordain that we may become aged together.

"And she said with him, Amen.

"So they slept both that night."—Tobit vii. 4–9.

It may be asked, Why have I treated this aspect of Jewish life at such great length? My answer is simple. I really believe that the rationalization of life, and especially of the sexual life, which the Jewish religion effects cannot be too highly estimated for its influence on economic activities. If religion is at all to be accounted a factor in Jewish economic life, then certainly the rationalization of conduct is its best expression.

To begin with, a number of good qualities or virtues which are indispensable to any economic order owe their existence to rationalization—*e.g.*, industry, neatness, thrift. But the whole of life, if lived in accordance with the ordinances of the "Wise," ministers to the needs of wealth-getting. Sobriety, moderation and piety are surely qualities which stand the business man in good stead. In short, the whole ideal of conduct preached in Holy Writ and in Rabbinic literature has something of the morality of the small shopkeeper about it—to be content with one wife, to pay your debts punctually, to go to church or synagogue on Sunday or Saturday (as the case may be) and to look down with immeasurable scorn on the sinful world around.

But Jewish moral teaching did not spend itself in the mere production of this type of the small respectable shopkeeper. It may even be questioned whether the type is altogether its work. At any rate, it is not of much consequence for economic development. Middle-class respectability as a matter of fact owes its origin to the narrow outlook of the petty trading class. Hence it can have but little to do with capitalism, except in so far as the qualities which that class possessed were the foundation on which capitalism could be built up. But capitalism did not grow out of the qualities, and therefore we must search in other directions for the causes which made the Jews pioneers of capitalism.

The first that suggests itself is the cultivation of family life among Jews, calling forth as it did energies so necessary to economic growth. The cultivation and refinement of family life was undoubtedly the work of the Jewish Rabbis, assisted, it must be added, by the vicissitudes of the Jewish people. In Judaism woman was first held in that high esteem which is the prime postulate for the existence of a sound family life and all that it means for man's conduct. The Rabbis by their laws and regulations affecting marriages, the marital relationship and the education of children and the rest, did all that was humanly possible in the way of outward limitation and influence to establish family life in all its purity. That marriage is considered more sacred among pious Jews than among people of other denominations is demonstrated by the statistics of illegitimate births. These are considerably fewer among Jews than among Christians.[481]

Year.	Country.	Illegitimate Births per Thousand.	
		Of the General Population.	Of the Jews.
1904	Prussia	2·51	0·66
1905	Würtemberg	2·83	0·16
1907	Hesse	2·18	0·13
1908	Bavaria	4·25	0·56
1901	Russia	1·29	0·14

If the figures for Russia be looked into a little more carefully it will be seen that illegitimate births among Jews vary very much from those among non-Jews. At the same time it must not be forgotten that there is a slight lowering of the standard in sexual morality among Jews. Thus, in Russia, of every 100 births there were illegitimate—

Year.	Greek Orthodox.	Catholics.	Protestants.	Jews.
1868	2·96	3·45	3·49	0·19
1878	3·13	3·29	3·85	0·25
1898	2·66	3·53	3·86	0·37
1901	2·49	3·57	3·76	0·46

Such then was one result of the family life current among Jews and introduced by them. The man contributed to it the best that was in him, and in return he drew from it invigorating strength, courage, and an inducement to maintain and to expand his position in life. Family life of this kind generated centres for masculine energy large enough to set in motion such a mighty economic system as capitalism. For this system calls for great energy, and we can scarcely imagine it being produced except through the agency of psychological influences which appeal not only to the social instincts but also to the family ideal.

It may perhaps be necessary to look below the psychological influences to the physical ones. How curiously moulded must the constitution of the Jew have become through the rationalization of his married life! We see this phenomenon—that a people with strong sexual inclinations (Tacitus speaks of it as *projectissima ad libidinem gens*) is forced by its religion to hold them in complete restraint. Extra-marital connexions are absolutely forbidden ; every one must content himself with one wife, but even with her intercourse is restricted.

The result of all this is obvious. Enormous funds of energy were prevented from finding an outlet in one direction and they turned to others. Knowing as we do the condition of the Jews throughout the Common Era, we shall not be wrong in assuming that economic activities were their chief channel. But we may go further. It is possible to prove that, quite generally, restrained sexual desires and the chase of profits go hand in hand. For the present we have had but little scientific investigation of this fact, so important for all modern sociological problems.[482] That a lordly way of life is usually accompanied by lavishness of money and of love, whereas such qualities as niggardliness, avarice and a setting of much store by money are the ubiquitous partners of a stunted sexual life—these are everyday experiences, and though it would be presumptuous to attempt to solve this most interesting problem with the aid of observations which must perforce be limited, yet for the purpose of my argument they ought not to be omitted, at least as an hypothesis.

We see then that a good deal of capitalistic capacity which the Jews possessed was due in large measure to the sexual restraint put upon them by their religious teachers. The effect of the rationalization of the whole of life on the physical and intellectual powers of the Jew must still be gone into by scientists ; [483] at present we have only beginnings of such studies. I refer to the influence of the very wise regulations of sexual intercourse, of eating and drinking and so on. (Incidentally it is worthy of note that Jewish law has long restricted the marriage of the unfit.)

One other point in conclusion. The rationalization of life accustomed the Jew to a mode of living contrary to (or side by side with) Nature and therefore also to an economic system like the capitalistic, which is likewise contrary to (or side by side with) Nature. What in reality is the idea of making profit, what is economic rationalism, but the application to economic activities of the rules by which the Jewish religion shaped Jewish life? Before capitalism could develop the natural man had to be changed out of all recognition, and a rationalistically minded mechanism introduced in his stead. There had to be a transvaluation of all economic values. And what was the result? The *homo capitalisticus*, who is closely related to the *homo Judæus*, both belonging to the same species, *homines rationalistici artificiales*.

And so the rationalization of Jewish life by the Jewish religion, if it did not actually produce the Jewish capacity for capitalism, certainly increased and heightened it.

VI. ISRAEL AND THE NATIONS.

One of the causes to which the Jew owed his economic progress was, as the reader will remember, the fact that Israel was for generations a stranger and an alien. If we seek to account for this aloofness we shall find its roots in the ordinances of the Jewish religion, shall find that this religion always maintained and broadened the line of separation. As Leroy-Beaulieu, who has studied this aspect of Jewish history with great success, has so well said, " La loi leur donnait l'esprit de clan." The very fact that they had their Law forced the Jews to live apart from the Gentiles. For if they desired to observe the Law they needs must keep to themselves. The Jews created the Ghetto, which from the non-Jewish point of view was a concession and a privilege and not the result of enmity.

But the Jews wished to live separated from the rest because they felt themselves superior to the common people round them. They were the Chosen Race, a People of Priests. The Rabbis did all that was required to fan the flame of pride—from Ezra, who forbade intermarriage as a profanation of Jewish purity, down to this very day, when the pious Jew says every morning, " Blessed art Thou, O Lord, King of the Universe, who hast not made me a Gentile (stranger)."

And so they lived separate and apart all through the centuries of the Diaspora, despite the Diaspora and (thanks to the bands which the Law laid upon them) because of the Diaspora—separate and apart, and therefore a group by themselves, or, if you will, a group by themselves and therefore separate and apart.

A group by themselves—they were that already at the time of the Babylonian Exile, which in reality established the internationalism of the Jew. Many of them, especially the wealthier ones, remained behind in Babylon of their own free will, but they retained their Judaism and professed it zealously. They kept up a lively intercourse with their brethren who had returned home, took a sympathetic interest in their fortunes, rendered them assistance and sent them new settlers from time to time.[484]

The bonds of union were in no wise relaxed in the Hellenistic Diaspora. " They kept closely together in the cities and throughout the world. No matter where they pitched their tents, their connexion with Zion was upheld. In the heart of the wilderness they had a native land where they were at home . . . By means of the Diaspora they entered into the world. In the Hellenistic cities they adopted the Greek tongue and Greek manners even if only as the outer garb of their Jewishness " (Wellhausen).

So it continued throughout the centuries of their exile. If anything the bond became strengthened. " *Scis quanta concordia* "—" You know how they hang together ! " cries Cicero.[485] So it was ; so it still is.

" All the Jewries in the Empire and beyond," we read of the rebellion of the year 130 A.D., "were stirred and more or less openly supported the insurgents on the banks of the Jordan." [486] Is it any different to-day when a Jew is expelled from some Russian town or other ?

A group by themselves and therefore separate and apart—this is true from earliest antiquity. All nations were struck by their hatred of others, of which they were for the first time accused by Hekateus of Abdera (300 B.C.). Many other ancient writers repeat the indictment, [487] almost always in the same words. Perhaps the best known passage is in Tacitus : " *Apud eos fides obstinata, misericordia in promptu. Sed adversus omnes alios hostile odium. Separati epulis discreti cubilibus, proiectissima ad libidinem gens, alienarum concubitu abstinent* " (*Historia*, V, i. 5). [Amongst themselves they are doggedly faithful and quick to pity, but all strangers they hate as enemies. They neither eat nor intermarry with strangers ; they are a people of strong passions, yet they withhold themselves from other men's wives.]

Jewish apologetics never attempted to combat these views : [488] there must therefore have been some foundation for them.

It is true that the Jews kept together so closely and shut themselves off very often on account of the unfriendly treatment they received at the hands of their hosts. But it was not so originally. The Jews wanted to live secluded from their neighbours because of their religion. That this was so appears from their attitude in those lands where they were well treated. Witness one or two instances in the ancient world, of which I have just given illustrations [Tacitus, etc.]. Witness the same tendency in the Middle Ages. Take

Arabia in the first century. The Jews there at the period named lived according to the religion which the *Tanaim* and *Amoraim* had formulated—keeping the dietary laws and festivals, the great White Fast and the Sabbath. "Although they could not complain of anything in this hospitable country they yet longed for the return to the Holy Land and awaited the advent of the Messiah every day. . . . They were in direct communication with the Jews of Palestine." [489] Or take Moorish Spain. While the Christians who lived among the Mohammedans forgot their mother tongue (Gothic Latin), no longer understood their sacred books, and were rather ashamed of their Christianity, the Spanish Jews were more and more devoted to their national language, their Holy Writ and their ancient religion.[490] This attitude was clearly reflected in the Jewish poetry and philosophy of the period, the greatest perhaps that mediæval Jewry can boast. In the midst of an Arabic-Spanish world in which they lived and enjoyed the respect of their fellow-citizens, they were strictly "national," that is religious ; they drew poetic inspiration from the Messianic hopes and were filled with an unconquerable longing for Zion.[491] One need only mention the great Jehuda Halevy, whose Odes to Zion are the highest expression of the genius of neo-Hebrew poetry.

Like a cloud sailing in the blue of the sky above, Judaism winds its way through history, refreshed by the memories of its hoary and holy past as by a soft breeze. To this very day the pious Jew blesses his children with the words, "The Lord make thee as Ephraim and Manasseh."

What was the effect on economic life of this seclusion and separation of the Jewish social organism ? Directly the Jews stepped outside the Ghetto gates their intercourse was with strangers. We have already dealt with the point elsewhere ; my reason for calling attention to it again is to show that this attitude was a direct consequence of the teaching of Judaism, that in treating the people among whom they lived as "others," the Jews were but obeying a divine behest. Here, too, their conduct was hallowed, and it received a sanction from the peculiar system of laws relating to "strangers."

The most important and most frequently discussed legal ordinance in this system was that affecting the taking of interest. In the old Jewish theocracy, 492 as in every society in early civilization, loans without interest were the regular means of rendering assistance by a man to his neighbour. But it may be observed that even in the earliest collection of laws interest was allowed to be taken from "strangers."

The Jewish code was no exception. The best example of this may be found in Deuteronomy xxiii. 20. Other passages in the Torah that have reference to interest are Exodus xxii. 25 and Leviticus xxv. 37. They all form the theme of a lively discussion which has been carried on from the days of the *Tanaim* down to the present. The chief instance and at the same time the crux of the matter is in the Talmud, in *Baba Mezia*, 70*b*, and my own feeling is that for the most part it is an attempt to discount the very clear statement of the Torah by all manner of sophistries. For what does the verse in Deuteronomy say ? "Unto a foreigner thou mayest lend upon usury ; but unto thy brother thou shalt not lend upon usury." The only doubt is in the wording of the original, which may mean with equal grammatical exactitude, "thou *mayest* lend upon usury" or "thou *shalt* lend upon usury." (It need hardly be added that "usury" with the translators was nothing more or less than our "interest.")

In either case, the pious Jew was allowed to take interest from non-Jews—that is the significant thing as far as we are concerned. Right through the Middle Ages he was not oppressed by the burden of the anti-usury prohibition which weighed upon the Christian. The Jewish law on the subject was never to my knowledge questioned by the Rabbis.493 On the other hand, there were periods when the "mayest" in the Deuteronomic passage was read as "shalt," periods when the Jew was urged to become a money-lender.

The authors who have dealt with this subject in modern times appear to have overlooked the fact that the Deuteronomic command has been received as one of the laws that regulate the life of the Jew, and that Tradition sanctions money-lending to a stranger on payment of interest. Of the 613 commandments, this is the 198th and may be found likewise in the *Shulchan Aruch*. Modern Rabbis 494 to whom the perfectly clear ordinance in Deuteronomy is somewhat inconvenient (one cannot quite understand why), attempt to explain it away by asserting that "strangers" in the passage is intended not for all non-Jews but only for heathens or idol-worshippers. If this be so, let it not be forgotten that there never was any very distinct conception as to who was, and who was not, an idol-worshipper. Besides, the pious Jew who has committed the 198th command to memory is not likely to draw the fine distinction urged by the learned Rabbis. Sufficient for him that the man to whom he lent money was no Jew, no "brother," no neighbour, but a Gentile.

Now think of the position in which the pious Jew and the pious Christian respectively found themselves

in the period in which money-lending first became a
need in Europe, and which eventually gave birth to
capitalism. The good Christian who had been addicted
to usury was full of remorse as he lay a-dying, ready
at the eleventh hour to cast from him the ill-gotten
gains which scorched his soul. And the good Jew?
In the evening of his days he gazed upon his well-
filled caskets and coffers, overflowing with sequins of
which he had relieved the miserable Christians or
Mohammedans. It was a sight which warmed his
heart, for every penny was almost like a sacrifice which
he had brought to his Heavenly Father.

Apart from this particular question, the stranger was
accorded special consideration in the Jewish legal code.
Duties towards him were never as binding as towards
your "neighbour," your fellow-Jew. Only ignorance
or a desire to distort facts will assert the contrary.
True, the conception of law and morality as it affected
the "stranger" varied from age to age. But there was
no change in the fundamental idea that you owed less
consideration to the stranger than to one of your own
people. That has remained the same from the day
when the Torah first became current to our own.
That is the impression that is conveyed by an unprejudiced study of the law concerning strangers in the
Holy Writ, the Talmud, the Codes and the Responsa
literature. There certainly are passages in the Torah
which breathe equality between the home-born and
the stranger (Exod. xii. 49, xxiii. 9; Lev. xix.
33, 34, xxv. 44–6; Deut. x. 18, 19). But in a
question of *halacha* (legal enactment) such as this is,
the oral tradition cannot be neglected. Secondly, the
passages instanced above all refer to the *Ger*, the non-
Jew who had settled in Palestine, seeing that the Jews
knew the heart of a *Ger*, "for ye were *Gerim* in the

land of Egypt." [In the sentence about interest the word used is *Nachari,* some one from another nation.] As time went on it was but natural that there should be an increase of the cases in Jewish law in which the non-Jew was at a disadvantage as compared with the Jew. So much so that in the latest code they occupy a good deal of space.[494A]

What was the importance in economic life of the laws concerning strangers? It was twofold. First, intercourse with strangers was bereft of all considerations, and commercial morality (if I may put it so) became elastic. I admit that there was no absolute necessity for this to come about, but all the conditions were given for it to do so, and it must have been an everyday occurrence in certain circles. "If a non-Jew makes an error in a statement of account, the Jew may use it to his own advantage; it is not incumbent upon him to point it out." So we may read in the *Tur,* and though Joseph Caro did not include this in his law-book, it crept in later as a gloss from the pen of Isserlein. Is it not obvious that the good Jew must needs draw the conclusion that he was not bound to be so particular in his intercourse with non-Jews? With Jews he will scrupulously see to it that he has just weights and a just measure; [495] but as for his dealings with non-Jews, his conscience will be at ease even though he may obtain an unfair advantage. It is not to be denied that in some cases honesty towards non-Jews was inculcated.[495A] But to think that this should have been necessary! Besides, this is the actual wording of the law: "It is permissible to take advantage of a non-Jew, for it is written, Thou shalt not take advantage of thy brother." (The context refers not to overreaching, but only to the asking of higher prices from a non-Jew.)

This conception must have been firmly rooted in those districts (*e.g.*, in Eastern Europe) where the study of the Talmud and the casuistry it engendered were universal. The effect it had on the commerce of the Jew has been described by Graetz, surely no prejudiced witness. "To twist a phrase out of its meaning, to use all the tricks of the clever advocate, to play upon words, and to condemn what they did not know. . . such were the characteristics of the Polish Jew. . . Honesty and right-thinking he lost as completely as simplicity and truthfulness. He made himself master of all the gymnastics of the Schools and applied them to obtain advantage over any one less cunning than himself. He took a delight in cheating and overreaching, which gave him a sort of joy of victory. But his own people he could not treat in this way : they were as knowing as he. It was the non-Jew who, to his loss, felt the consequences of the Talmudically trained mind of the Polish Jew." [496]

In the second place, the differential treatment of non-Jews in Jewish commercial law resulted in the complete transformation of the idea of commerce and industry generally in the direction of more freedom. If we have called the Jews the Fathers of Free Trade, and therefore the pioneers of capitalism, let us note here that they were prepared for this rôle by the free-trading spirit of the commercial and industrial law, which received an enormous impetus towards a policy of *laissez-faire* by its attitude towards strangers. Clearly, intercourse with strangers could not but loosen the bonds of personal duties and replace them by economic freedom. Let us glance at this in greater detail.

The theory of price in the Talmud and the Codes, in so far as it affected trade between Jew and Jew, is exactly parallel to the scholastic doctrine of *justum pretium* which was prevalent in Europe throughout the Middle Ages. But as between Jew and non-Jew, there was no just price. Price was formed as it is to-day, by " the higgling of the market." 496ᴬ

Be that as it may, the important thing to observe is that already in the Talmud, and still more distinctly in the *Shulchan Aruch*, conceptions of the freedom of industry and enterprise, so entirely alien to the Christian law of Mediæval Europe, are met with. It is a subject deserving of close study and should be taken up by a specialist. For my part, I can do no more here than refer to a few instances. But few though they be, they seem to me to be conclusive evidence on the point in question. My first reference is to a passage in the Talmud which fully recognizes free competition among sellers.

Mishna.—" R. Judah was of opinion that a shopkeeper should not distribute nuts among children, because by so doing he gets them into the habit of coming to him. But the Rabbis allow it. Moreover, it is not lawful to spoil prices. But the Rabbis say, ' Blessed be his memory.' "

Gemara.—"The question at once arises, what was the reason for the attitude of the Rabbis in the first case ? The answer is that the shopkeeper may say to his competitor, ' I give the children nuts, you can give them plums.' And what is the reason of the Rabbis in the second case ? The Mishna forbids price alteration, and yet they say, ' Blessed be his memory.' The answer is, they bless his memory because he reduces prices " (*Baba Mezia*, 60a and b).

In the Codes the reasons have been omitted, and the dry statement of law only is found. " A shopkeeper is allowed to make presents of nuts and other things to the children who come to purchase in his shop, in order to win their custom. Moreover, he may sell at a price below the current one, and the competing tradesmen can do nothing" (*Choshen Mishpat*, 225, § 18).

Similarly, in the laws regulating the conduct of traders who bring their goods to the market town, the following may be read : "Should the strangers sell more cheaply than the native dealers, or should their goods be of a better quality, the natives may not prevent them, for the Jewish public derives benefit therefrom" (*Choshen Mishpat*, 156, § 7).

Once more. "If a Jew is prepared to lend money to a non-Jew at a lower rate of interest than some one else, the latter can do nothing against it" (*Choshen Mishpat*, 156, § 5).

Finally, Jewish law favours industrial *laissez-faire.* So we find in the *Shulchan Aruch :* "If any one commenced a handicraft in his street and none of his neighbours protested, and then one of the other residents in the street wishes to carry on the same calling, the first may not complain that the new-comer is taking the bread out of his mouth, and try to prevent him" (*Choshen Mishpat*, 156, §5).

Clearly, then, free trade and industrial freedom were in accordance with Jewish law, and therefore in accordance with God's will. What a mighty motive power in economic life !

VII. Judaism and Puritanism.

I have already mentioned that Max Weber's study of the importance of Puritanism for the capitalistic system was the impetus that sent me to consider the importance of the Jew, especially as I felt that the dominating ideas of Puritanism which were so powerful in capitalism were more perfectly developed in Judaism, and were also of course of much earlier date.

A complete comparison of the two "isms" is not within my province here. But I believe that if it were made, it would be seen that there is an almost unique identity of view between Judaism and Puritanism, at least, on those points which we have investigated. In both will be found the preponderance of religious interests, the idea of divine rewards and punishments, asceticism *within* the world, the close relationship between religion and business, the arithmetical conception of sin, and, above all, the rationalization of life.

Let me refer to an instance or two. Take the attitude of Judaism and Puritanism to the problem of sex. In one of the best hotels of Philadelphia I found a notice in my room to this effect: " Visitors who may have to transact business with ladies are respectfully requested to leave the door of their room open while the lady is with them." What is this but the old dictum of the Talmud (*Kiddushin*, 82*a*), " Hast thou business with women ? See to it that thou art not with them alone " ?

Again, is not the English Sunday the Jewish Sabbath ?

I would also recall the words of Heine,[496B] who had a clear insight into most things. " Are not," he asks in his *Confessions*, " Are not the Protestant Scots Hebrews, with their Biblical names, their Jerusalem, pharisaistic cant ? And is not their religion a Judaism which allows you to eat pork ? "

Puritanism *is* Judaism.

Whether the first was influenced by the second, and if so, how, are most difficult questions to answer. It is well known, of course, that in the Reformation period there was close intercourse between Jews and certain Christian sects, that the study of Hebrew and the Hebrew Scriptures became fashionable, and that the Jews in England in the 17th century were held in very high esteem by the Puritans. Leading men in England like Oliver Cromwell built up their religious views on the Old Testament, and Cromwell himself dreamed of a reconciliation between the Old and the New Testaments, and

of a confederation between the Chosen People of God
and the Puritan English. A Puritan preacher of the
day, Nathaniel Holmes by name, wished for nothing
better than, in accordance with the letter of the prophetic
message, to become a servant of God's people and to
serve them on bended knee. Public life became Hebraic
in tone no less than the sermons in churches. And if
only speeches in Parliament had been in Hebrew, you
might have believed yourself in Palestine. The "Level-
lers," who called themselves "Jews" (in opposition to
their opponents whom they termed "Amalekites"),
advocated the adoption of the Torah as the norm of
English legislation. Cromwell's officers suggested to
him to appoint seventy members of his Privy Council
according to the number of the members of the Synhe-
drin. To the Parliament of 1653 General Thomas
Harrison, the Anabaptist, was returned, and he and his
party clamoured for the introduction of the Mosaic
legislation into England. In 1649 it was moved in the
House of Commons that the Lord's Day should be
observed on Saturday instead of on Sunday. On the
banners of the victorious Puritans was inscribed "The
Lion of Judah." [497] It is significant that not only
the Bible, but the Rabbinical literature as well, was extensively read in large circles of the clergy and laity.

Altogether, then, there appears to be sufficient evidence
for the deduction of Puritan doctrines from Jewish
sources. The specialists must decide. Here I have
been able to do no more than give a hint or two. And
in conclusion I would draw attention to a little humorous
publication, which appeared in the year 1608 and the
contents of which would seem to demonstrate the close
connexion between Judaism and Calvinism (which is only
Puritanism). It is called, *Der Calvinische Judenspiegel*
(the Calvinistic Jewish Mirror), and on page 33 a com-

parison is drawn between the two religions in the following droll fashion. [The old German is delightful.] "If I am to say on my honour why I am become a Calvinist, I shall have to confess that the one and only reason which persuaded me was that among all the religions I could find none which agreed so much with Judaism, and its view of life and faith. (Here follow a number of parallel statements, partly serious and partly satirical). 8. The Jews hate the name of Mary and tolerate her only when she is made of gold and silver, or when her image is impressed on coins. So do we. We too like Mary farthings and crowns, to which we pay all due respect, for they are useful in business. 9. The Jews everywhere are at pains to cheat the people. So are we. For that very reason we left our country to wander in other lands where we are not known in our true colours, so that by our deceit and cunning . . . we might lead astray the ignorant yokels, cheat them and bring them to us. . . ."

CHAPTER XII

JEWISH CHARACTERISTICS

I. The Problem

THE decision to deal in a work of a scientific character with the problem suggested by the title of the present chapter has not been arrived at without a great effort. For it has of late become the fashion to seize upon anything even but faintly savouring of the psychology of nations as the plaything for the lighter moods of dilettanti, whilst descriptions of the Jewish genius have been hailed as the newest form of political sport by coarser spirits, whose rude instincts cannot but give offence to all those who, in our gross age, have managed to preserve a modicum of good taste and impartiality. Unjustifiable juggling with categories in race psychology has already led to the conclusion that it is impossible to arrive at any scientific results in this field of study. Read the books of F. Hertz, Jean Finot and others [498] and you will lay them down with the feeling that it is useless to attempt to find common psychological characteristics among any conglomeration of humans ; that French *esprit* is a myth—in fact that there are no Frenchmen, just as there are no Jews. But cross the street, and lo and behold, you are face to face with a specific type ; read a book or stand before a picture and almost unconsciously you say, How very German, how thoroughly French !

Is this only the imagining of our fancy ? [499-500]

Nay more. If we think for a moment of human history we must needs construct for ourselves the hypothesis of a sort of " collective soul." When, for example, we talk of the Jewish religion we are bound to connect it with the Jewish people whose genius gave it birth. Or, when we say the Jews had an influence on modern economic development, it follows surely that there must have been something essentially Jewish that brought it about. Otherwise we might as well assert that it would have made no difference to the economic history of Western Europe if Eskimos had taken the place of Jews, or perhaps even gorillas would have done equally well !

This *reductio ad absurdum* shows plainly enough that there must be some specifically Jewish characteristic. But let us consider the matter from a slightly different point of view. Let us glance at the objective circumstances in the Jewish aptitude for modern capitalism. There was first, as we have seen, the dispersion of the Jews over a wide area. Now without recourse to subjective forces the Diaspora can be as little explained as the effects of the Diaspora. And one thing is evident. The dispersion of a people in itself does not necessarily have either economic or cultural results ; nay, very often dispersion may lead to fusion and ultimate disappearance.

It has been claimed—and with truth—that it was the dispersion of the Jews which fitted them to become intermediaries. Granted, but did it also tend to make of them negotiators and private advisers of princes, callings which have from time immemorial been the stepping-stones of the interpreter to higher posts? Were the capacities essential to these new offices not inherent in the Jews themselves?

We have admitted that the dispersion of the Jews was responsible for no little of their success in international commeree and credit. But is not the postulate to this success the fact that the Jews everywhere kept together? What would have happened if, like so many other scattered races, they had not maintained their bonds of union?

Lastly, let us not forget that the Jews came among just those peoples who happened to be mature enough to receive capitalism. But even so, if Jewish influence was strong (and it is so still) in Holland, in England, in Germany, in Austria-Hungary—stronger far than their influence on the Spaniards, Italians, Greeks or Arabs—it was in a large measure due to the contrasts between them and their hosts. For it would seem that the more slow-witted, the more thick-skulled, the more ignorant of business a people is, the more effective is Jewish influence on their economic life. And can this be satisfactorily accounted for except through special Jewish peculiarities?

No matter what was the origin of their innate dissimilarity from their hosts, the salient point is that this strangeness should have obtained lasting influence in economic life. Once more it is impossible to fathom this without the assumption of inherent Jewish characteristics. That a people or a tribe is hated and persecuted does not furnish sufficient reason for spurring them on to redoubled efforts in their activities. On the contrary, in most cases this contempt and ill-treatment but serve to destroy morals and initiative. Only where man is possessed of exceptional qualities do these become, under the stress of circumstance, the source of regenerated energy.

Again, look at their semi-citizenship. Does not the identical argument hold good here also? It is so obvious as to become almost a truism. Nowhere did the Jews enjoy the same advantages as their fellow-citizens, and yet everywhere they achieved economically much more than the rest of the population. There can be but one explanation for this—the specifically Jewish characteristics.

On the other hand, the legal position of the Jews varied in different countries and at different times. In some States they were allowed to engage in certain occupations ; in others these same occupations were forbidden them ; in others again, such as England, they were on a perfectly equal footing with the rest of the people in this respect. And yet they devoted themselves almost everywhere to particular callings. In England and America they began their commercial mission by becoming bullion-merchants or storekeepers. And can this be accounted for in any other way than by once more pointing to their peculiar characteristics ?

As for the wealth of the Jews, that alone will hardly suffice to explain their great achievements in the sphere of economic activities. A man who possesses vast sums must have a number of intellectual qualities in addition, if his money is to be usefully employed in the capitalistic sense. That surely requires no proof.

Jewish characteristics must therefore exist. It remains only to discover what they are.

Our first thought of the Jews as a unit will naturally be associated with their religion. But before we proceed another step I should like to premise that on the one hand I shall limit the group lumped together under the Jewish religion, and on the other hand, I shall enlarge it. I shall limit it by only considering the Jews since their expulsion from Spain and Portugal, that is, from the end of the Middle Ages. I shall enlarge it by including within the circle of my observations the descendants of Jews, even if they themselves have left the faith.

Moreover, I should like to touch upon the arguments urged against the existence of Jewish peculiarities.

(1) It has been remarked that the Jews of Western Europe and America have to a large extent assimilated with the peoples among whom they dwell. This need not be denied, even if specifically Jewish characteristics were as clear as daylight. Is it not possible for social groups to intermingle? A man may be a German, have all the characteristics of a German, and yet be an individual in the group "international proletariat!" Or take another instance. Are not the German Swiss at one and the same time Swiss and German?

(2) The Jews in the Diaspora, it is maintained, are not a "nation" or a "people" in the commonly accepted meaning of the term,[501] since they are not a political, cultural or linguistic community. The reply to this objection is that there are many other qualifications besides those mentioned (*e.g.*, a common origin) which must be considered. But speaking generally, it is as well not to press a definition too closely.

(3) The differences between the Jews themselves have been made much of. It has been said that there is no homogeneity among Jews, that one section is bitterly opposed to the other. The Western Jews are different from the Eastern Jews, the Sephardim from the Ashkenazim, the Orthodox from the Liberals, the everyday Jew from the Sabbath Jew (to use a phrase of Marx). This also there is no need to deny. But it does not by any means preclude the possibility of common Jewish characteristics. Is it so difficult to conceive of wheels within wheels? Cannot a large group contain lesser groups side by side? Think of the many groups to which an Englishman may belong. He may be a Catholic or a Protestant, a farmer or a professor, a northerner or a southerner and Heaven only knows what else besides. But he remains an Englishman all the

same. So with the Jew. He may belong to one circle within the whole, may possess certain characteristics that mark all individuals in that circle, but he retains the specifically Jewish characteristics nevertheless.

Finally, I must make it plain that I have no intention of outlining all Jewish characteristics. I propose to deal with those only that have reference to economic life. I shall not content myself with the old-fashioned expressions, such as the Jewish " commercialism," the " bartering spirit " and the like. I say nothing of the practice of some to include the desire for profit as a characteristic of a social group. The desire for profit is human—all too human. In fact, I must reject all previous analyses of the Jewish soul (in so far as they touch economic life), and for the following reasons. First, what the Jew was well-fitted for was never clearly enough designated. " For trade " is much too vague a term to be of the slightest use. I have therefore tried to show, in a special chapter, the circle of economic activities for which Jews are specifically fitted. Secondly, mere description is not explanation. If I want to prove that a man has all the capabilities necessary to make him an admirable speculator on the Stock Exchange, it will not be enough if I say that he will make a fine jobber. It is like saying indigence is due to poverty. Yet that is how Jewish economic talents have been treated. Our method will be different. We shall try to discover certain properties of the soul which are congenial to the exercise of economic functions in a capitalistic organism.

And now, having cleared the way, I shall proceed to demonstrate what the real Jewish peculiarities are.

II. An Attempt at a Solution.

It is surprising to find that despite the enormity of the problem there is yet a great degree of unanimity in the different views about the Jews. In literature no less than in actual life, unprejudiced observers agree on one or other point of importance. Read Jellinek or Fromer, Chamberlain or Marx, Heine or Goethe, Leroy-Beaulieu or Picciotto—read the pious or the non-conforming Jew, the anti-Semitic or the philo-Semitic non-Jew—and you get the impression that all of them are conscious of the same peculiarities. This is comforting to one who is about to describe the Jewish genius once more. At any rate, he will say nothing that other people might not have said, even though his standpoint be slightly different. In my own case I shall attempt to show the connexion between the characteristics and the natural gifts of the Jews and the capitalistic economic system. I shall first try to sketch a detailed picture of Jewish qualities and then proceed to bring them into relation with capitalism.

Unlike most other writers on the subject I will begin by noting a Jewish quality which, though mentioned often enough, never received the recognition which its importance merited. I refer to the extreme intellectuality of the Jew. Intellectual interests and intellectual skill are more strongly developed in him than physical (manual) powers. Of the Jew it may certainly be said, "l'intelligence prime le corps." Everyday experience proves it again and again, and many a fact might be cited in its support. No other people has valued the learned man, the scholar, so highly as the Jews. "The wise man takes precedence of the king, and a bastard who is a scholar of a high-priest who is an ignoramus." So the Talmud has it. Any one who is acquainted with Jewish students knows well enough that this over-rating of mere knowledge is not yet a thing of the past. And if you could not become "wise," at least it was your duty to be educated. At all times instruction was compulsory in Israel. In truth, to learn was a religious duty ; and in Eastern Europe the synagogue is still called the Shool (Schule, School). Study and worship went hand in hand ; nay, study was worship and ignorance was a deadly sin. A man who could not read was a boor in this world and damned in the next. In the popular sayings of the Ghetto, nothing had so much scorn poured upon it as foolishness. " Better injustice than folly," and " Ein Narr ist ein Gezar " (A fool is a misfortune) are both well known.[502]

The most valuable individual is the intellectual individual ; humanity at its best is intellectuality at its highest. Listen to what a sensible Jew has to say when he pictures the ideal man, the superman if you like, of the future. He takes it all as a matter of course ; those who are differently constituted must surely tremble at the prospect. " In the place of the blind instincts . . . civilized man will possess intellect conscious of purpose. It should be every one's unswerving ideal to crush the instincts and replace them by will-power, and to substitute reflection for mere impulse. The individual only becomes a man in the fullest sense of the word when his natural predisposition is under the control of his reasoning powers. And when the process of emancipation from the instincts is complete we have the perfect genius with his absolute inner freedom from the domination of natural laws. Civilization should have but one aim—to liberate man from all that is mystic, from the vague impulsiveness of all instinctive action, and to cultivate the purely rational side of his being." [503] Only think. Genius, the very essence of instinctive expression, conceived as the highest form of the rational and the intellectual !

One consequence of this high evaluation of the intellect was the esteem in which callings were held according as they demanded more " headwork " or more " handwork."

The former were almost in all ages placed higher than the latter. It is true that there may have been, and still may be, Jewish communities in which hard bodily labour is done every day, but this hardly applies to the Jews of Western Europe. Even in Talmud times Jews preferred those callings which necessitated a lesser expenditure of physical energy. As Rabbi said, " The world needs both the seller of spices and the tanner, but happy he who is a seller of spices." Or again, " R. Meir used to say, A man should have his son taught a clean and easy handicraft" (*Kiddushin*, 82*b*).

The Jews were quite alive to their predominant quality and always recognized that there was a great gulf between their intellectuality and the brute force of their neighbours. One or two sayings popular among Polish Jews express the contrast with no little humour. " God help a man against Gentile hands and Jewish heads." " Heaven protect us against Jewish *moach* (brains) and Gentile *koach* (physical force)." *Moach v. Koach*—that is the Jewish problem in a nutshell. It ought to be the motto of this book.

The predominance of intellectual interests could not but lead in a people so gifted as the Jews to intellectual skill. " Say what you like about a Jew, you cannot say he is a fool." "A gallant Greek, a stupid Jew, an honest Gipsy—all are unthinkable " is a popular saying among Roumanians. And a Spanish proverb has it, "A hare that is slow and a Jew who is a fool : both are equally probable." [504] Who that has had dealings with Jews but will not confirm that on an average they possess a greater degree of understanding, that they are more intelligent than other people ? I might even call it astuteness or sagacity, as was remarked by one of the keenest observers of Jews [505] a century or more ago, who characterized them as " intellectual and endowed with great genius for things of the present age," though, he added, " to a less degree than in the past."

" The Jewish mind is an instrument of precision ; it has the exactness of a pair of scales " : most people will agree with this judgment of Leroy-Beaulieu. And when H. S. Chamberlain speaks of the under-development of Jewish " understanding" he must surely be using the term in a special sense. He cannot possibly mean by it quick thought, precise analysis, exact dissection, speedy combination, the power of seeing the point at once, of suggesting analogies, distinguishing between synonymous things, of drawing final conclusions. The Jew is able to do all this, and Jellinek, who rightly lays stress [506] on this side of the Jewish character, points out that Hebrew is particularly rich in expressions for activities demanding qualities of the mind. It has no fewer than eleven words for seeking or researching, thirty-four for distinguishing or separating, and fifteen for combining.

There is no doubt that these mental gifts make the Jews prominent as chess-players, as mathematicians [507] and in all calculating work. These activities postulate a strong capacity for abstract thought and also a special kind of imagination, which Wundt has so happily christened the combinatory. Their skill as physicians (ability at diagnosis) [508] may also be traced to their calculating, dissecting and combining minds, which " like lightning, illuminate dark places in a flash."

It is not unknown that often enough Jewish mental ability degenerates into hair-splitting. (When the mill has no corn to grind it grinds itself.) But this does not matter so much as another fact. The intellectuality of the Jew is so strong that it tends to develop at the expense of other mental qualities, and the mind is apt to become one-sided. Let us take a few instances. The Jew lacks the quality of instinctive understanding ; he responds less to feeling than to intellect. We can scarcely think of a Jewish mystic like Jacob Böhme, and the contrast becomes still more striking when we remember the sort of mysticism found in the Kabbala. In the same way all romance is alien to this particular view of life ; the Jew cannot well sympathize with losing oneself in the world, in mankind or in nature. It is the difference between frenzied enthusiasm and sober, matter-of-fact thought.

Akin to this characteristic is that of a certain lack of impressionability, a certain lack of receptive and creative genius. When I was in Breslau a Jewish student from the far East of Siberia came to me one day " to study Karl Marx." It took him nearly three weeks to reach Breslau, and on the very day after his arrival he called on me and borrowed one of Marx's works. A few days later he came again, discussed with me what he had read, brought back the book and borrowed another. This continued for a few months. Then he returned to his native village. The young man had received absolutely no impressions from his new surroundings ; he had made no acquaintances, never taken a walk, hardly knew in fact where it was that he was staying. The life of Breslau passed him by completely. No doubt it was the same before he came to Breslau, and will be the same throughout the future. He will walk through the world without seeing it. But he had made himself acquainted with Marx. Is this a typical case ? I think so. You may meet with it every day. Are we not continually struck by the Jew's love for the inconcrete, his tendency away from the sensuous, his constant abiding in a world of abstractions ? And is it only accidental that there are far fewer Jewish painters than literary men or professors ? Even in the case of Jewish artists is there not something intellectual about their work ? Never was word more truly spoken than when Friedrich Naumann compared Max Liebermann [the famous Jewish painter] with Spinoza, saying, "He paints with his brain."

The Jew certainly sees remarkably clearly, but he does not see much. He does not think of his environment as something alive, and that is why he has lost the true conception of life, of its oneness, of its being an organism, a natural growth. In short, he has lost the true conception of the personal side of life. General experience must surely support this view; but if other proofs are demanded they will be found in the peculiarities of Jewish law, which, as we have already seen, abolished personal relationships and replaced them by impersonal, abstract connexions or activities or aims.

As a matter of fact, one may find among Jews an extraordinary knowledge of men. They are able with their keen intellects to probe, as it were, into every pore, and to see the inside of a man as only Röntgen rays would show him. They muster all his qualities and abilities, they note his excellences and his weaknesses; they detect at once for what he is best fitted. But seldom do they see the whole man, and thus they often make the mistake of ascribing actions to him which are an abomination to his inmost soul. Moreover, they seldom appraise a man according to his personality, but rather according to some perceptible characteristic and achievement.

Hence their lack of sympathy for every status where the nexus is a personal one. The Jews' whole being is opposed to all that is usually understood by chivalry, to all sentimentality, knight-errantry, feudalism, patriarchalism. Nor does he comprehend a social order based on relationships such as these. "Estates of the realm" and craft organizations are a loathing to him. Politically he is an individualist. A constitutional

State in which all human intercourse is regulated by clearly defined legal principles suits him well.* He is the born representative of a " liberal " view of life in which there are no living men and women of flesh and blood with distinct personalities, but only citizens with rights and duties. And these do not differ in different nations, but form part of mankind, which is but the sum-total of an immense number of amorphous units. Just as so many Jews do not see themselves— do they not deny their obvious characteristics and assert that there is no difference between them and Englishmen or Germans or Frenchmen ?—so they do not see other people as living beings but only as subjects, citizens, or some other such abstract conception. It comes to this, that they behold the world not with their " soul " but with their intellect. The result is that they are easily led to believe that whatever can be neatly set down on paper and ordered aright by the aid of the intellect must of necessity be capable of proper settlement in actual life. How many Jews still hold that the Jewish Question is only a political one, and are convinced that a liberal régime is all that is required to remove the differences between the Jew and his neighbour. It is nothing short of astounding to read the opinion of so soundly learned a man as the author of one of the newest books on the Jewish Question that the whole of the anti-Semitic movement during the last thirty years was the result of the works of Marr and Dühring. " The thousand victims of the pogroms and the million sturdy workers who emigrated from their homes are but a striking illustration of the power of—Eugen Dühring " (!).509 Is not this opposing ink and blood, understanding and instinct, an abstraction and a reality ?

[* Is not this the general modern tendency ? Cf. Sir H. Maine's dictum : The progress of Society is from status to contract.]

The conception of the universe in the mind of such an intellectual people must perforce have been that of a structure well-ordered in accordance with reason. By the aid of reason, therefore, they sought to understand the world ; they were rationalists, both in theory and in practice.

Now as soon as a strong consciousness of the ego attaches itself to the predominating intellectuality in the thinking being, he will tend to group the world round that ego. In other words, he will look at the world from the point of view of end, or goal, or purpose. His outlook will be teleological, or that of practical rationalism. No peculiarity is so fully developed in the Jew as this, and there is complete unanimity of opinion on the subject. Most other observers start out with the teleology of the Jew ; I for my part regard it as the result of his extreme intellectuality, in which I believe all the other Jewish peculiarities are rooted. In saying this, however, I do not in the least wish to minimize the very great importance of this Jewish characteristic.

Take any expression of the Jewish genius and you will be certain to find in it this teleological tendency, which has sometimes been called extreme subjectivity. Whether or no the Indo-Germanic races are objective and the Semitic subjective,[510] certain it is that the Jews are the most subjective of peoples. The Jew never loses himself in the outer world, never sinks in the depth of the cosmos, never soars in the endless realms of thought, but, as Jellinek well puts it, dives below the surface to seek for pearls. He brings everything into relation with his ego. He is for ever asking why, what for, what will it bring ? *Cui bono ?* His greatest interest is always in the result of a thing, not in the thing itself. It is un-Jewish to regard any activity, be it what you will, as an end in itself ; un-Jewish to live your life without having any purpose, to leave all to chance ; un-Jewish to get harmless pleasure out of Nature. The Jew has taken all that is in Nature and made of it " the loose pages of a text-book of ethics which shall advance the higher moral life." The Jewish religion, as we have already seen, is teleological in its aim ; in each of its regulations it has the ethical norm in view. The entire universe, in the Jew's eyes, is something that was made in accordance with a plan. This is one of the differences between Judaism and heathenism, as Heine saw long ago. " They (the heathens) all have an endless, eternal ' past,' which is in the world and develops with it by the laws of necessity ; but the God of the Jews was outside the world, which He created as an act of free-will."

No term is more familiar to the ear of the Jew than *Tachlis*, which means purpose, aim, end or goal. If you are to do anything it must have a *tachlis* ; life itself, whether as a whole or in its single activities, must have some *tachlis*, and so must the universe. Those who assert that the meaning of Life, of the World, is not *tachlis* but tragedy, the Jew will reckon as foolish visionaries.

How deeply the teleological view of things is embedded in the nature of the Jew may be seen in the case of those of them who, like the Chassidim, pay no attention to the needs of practical life because " there is no purpose in them." There is no purpose in making a living, and so they let their wives and children starve, and devote themselves to the study of their sacred books. But we may see it also in all those Jews who, with a soul-weariness within them and a faint smile on their countenances, understanding and forgiving everything, stand and gaze at life from their own heights, far above this world.

I have in my mind such choice spirits among the literary men of our day as George Hirschfeld, Arthur Schnitzler and George Hermann. The great charm of their work lies in this world-aloofness with which they look down on our hustle and bustle, in the quiet melancholy pervading all their poetry, in their sentiment. Their very lack of will-power is only strength of will in a kind of negative form. Through all their ballads sounds the same soft plaint of grief : how purposeless and therefore how sad is the world ! Nature herself is tinged with this sorrow ; autumn always lurks in ambush though wood and meadow be bright with gay spring blossoms ; the wind plays among the fallen leaves and the sun's golden glory, be it never so beautiful, must go down at last. Subjectivity and the conception that all things must have an aim (and the two are the same) rob the poetry of Jewish writers of *naïveté*, freshness and directness, because Jewish poets are unable simply to enjoy the phenomena of this world, whether it be human fate or Nature's vagaries ; they must needs cogitate upon it and turn it about and about. Nowhere is the air scented with the primrose and the violet, nowhere gleams the spray of the rivulet in the wood. But to make up for lack of these they possess the wonderful aroma of old wine and the magic charm of a pair of beautiful eyes gazing sadly into the distance.

When this attitude of mind that seeks for a purpose in all things is united with a strong will, with a large fund of energy (as is generally the case with the Jew), it ceases to be merely a point of view ; it becomes a policy. The man sets himself a goal and makes for it, allowing nothing whatever to turn him aside from his course ; he is determined, if you like, stiff-necked. Heine in characterizing his people called it stubbornness, and Goethe said that the essence of the Jewish character was energy and the pursuit of direct ends.

My next point is mobility, but I am not quite sure whether this can be ascribed to all Jews or only to the Ashkenazi (German) Jews. Writers who have sung the praises of the Sephardim (Spanish Jews) always lay stress on a certain dignified air which they have, a certain superciliousness of bearing.[511] Their German brethren, on the other hand, have always been described as lively, active and somewhat excitable.[512] Even to-day you may meet with many Spanish Jews, especially in the Orient, who strike you as being dignified, thoughtful and self-restrained, who do not in the least appear to have that mobility, moral or physical, which is so often noticeable in European Jews. But mobility of mind—quick perception and mental versatility—all Jews possess.

These four elements, intellectuality, teleology, energy and mobility, are the corner-stones of Jewish character, so complicated in its nature. I believe that all the qualities of the Jew may be easily traced to one or more of these elements. Take two which are of special import in economic life—extreme activity and adaptability.

The Jew is active, or if you will, industrious. In the words of Goethe, "No Jew, not even the most insignificant, but is busy towards the achievement of some worldly, temporary or momentary aim." This activity often enough degenerates into restlessness. He must for ever be up and doing, for ever managing something and carrying it to fruition. He is always on the move, and does not care much if he makes himself a nuisance to those who would rest if they could. All musical and social "affairs" in our large towns are run by Jews. The Jew is the born trumpeter of progress and of its manifold blessings. And why? Because of his practical-mindedness and his mobility combined with his intellectuality. The last more especially, because it never strikes deep

root.   All intellectuality is in the long run shallowness ;
never does it allow of probing to the very roots of a
matter, never of reaching down to the depths of the soul,
or of the universe.   Hence intellectuality makes it easy to
go from one extreme to the other.   That is why you find
among Jews fanatical orthodoxy and unenlightened doubt
side by side ; they both spring from one source.

But to this shallow intellectuality the Jew owes perhaps
the most valuable of his characteristics—his adaptability—
which is unique in history.   The Jews were always a
stiffnecked people, and their adaptability no less than
their capacity to maintain their national traits are both due
to the one cause.   Their adaptability enabled them to
submit for the time being, if circumstances so demanded,
to the laws of necessity, only to hark back to their
wonted ways when better days came.   From of old the
Jewish character was at one and the same time resistant
and submissive, and though these traits may appear
contradictory they only seem so.   As Leroy-Beaulieu
well said, " The Jew is at once the most stubborn and the
most pliant of men, the most self-willed and the most
malleable."

The leaders and the " wise " men of the Jewish people
were in all ages fully alive to the importance, nay the
necessity, of this flexibility and elasticity, if Israel was to
continue, and they were therefore never tired of insisting
upon it.   Jewish literature abounds in instances.   " Be
as pliant as the reed which the wind blows in this direction and in that, for the Torah can be observed only by
him that is of a contrite spirit.   Why is the Torah
likened unto water?   To tell you that just as water
never flows up to the heights but rather runs down to the
depths, so too the Torah does not abide with the haughty
but only with the lowly." [513]   Or again, " When the
fox is in authority bow down before him." [514]   Once

more, " Bend before the wave and it passes over you ; oppose it, and it will sweep you away." [515]   Finally, a supplication from the Prayer Book runs as follows : " May my soul be as the dust to every one."

It was in this spirit that the Rabbis counselled their flocks to pretend to accept the dominant faiths in those countries where their existence depended on the renunciation of their own.   The advice was followed to a large extent, and in the words of Fromer, " The Jewish race, by simulating death from time to time, was able to live on and on."

There are very few, if any, make-believe Christians or Moslems to-day.   Nevertheless, the remarkable power of the Jew to adapt himself to his environment has more scope than ever.   The Jew of Western Europe and America to-day no longer wishes to maintain his religion and his national character intact ; on the contrary, he wishes, in so far as the nationalist spirit has not yet awakened in him, to lose his characteristics and to assimilate with the people in whose midst his lot happens to be cast.   And lo, this too he can successfully achieve.

Perhaps the clearest illustration of the way in which Jewish traits manifest themselves is the fact that the Jew in England becomes like an Englishman, in France like a Frenchman, and so forth.   And if he does not really become like an Englishman or a Frenchman, he appears to be like one.   That a Felix Mendelssohn should write German music, that a Jacques Offenbach French and a Souza Yankee-doodle ; that Lord Beaconsfield should set up as an Englishman, Gambetta as a Frenchman, Lassalle as a German ; in short, that Jewish talent should so often have nothing Jewish about it, but be in accord with its environment, has curiously enough again and again been urged as evidence that there are no specifically Jewish characteristics, whereas in truth it proves the very opposite in a striking fashion. It proves that the Jews have the gift of adaptability in an eminently high degree. The Jew might go from one planet to another, but his strangeness amid the new surroundings would not continue for long. He quickly feels his way and adapts himself with ease. He is German where he wants to be German, and Italian if that suits him better. He does everything and dabbles in everything, and with success. He can be a pure Magyar in Hungary, he can belong to the Irredenta in Italy, and be an anti-Semite in France (Drumont !). He is an adept in seizing upon anything which is still germinating, and bringing it with all speed to its full bloom.[516] All this his adaptability enables him to do.

I have already said that this peculiar capacity for adaptation is rooted in the four elements of the Jewish character. But perhaps the rationalism of the Jew is responsible for it to a greater degree than the other three. Because of his rationalism he is able to look at everything from without. If the Jew is anything, it is not because he must but because he determines to be so. Any convictions he may have do not spring from his inmost soul ; they are formulated by his intellect. His standpoint is not on solid earth but an imaginary castle in the air. He is not organically original but mechanically rational. He lacks depth of feeling and strength of instinct. That is why he is what he is, but he can also be different. That Lord Beaconsfield was a Conservative was due to some accident or other, or some political conjuncture ; but Stein and Bismarck and Carlyle were Conservatives because they could not help it ; it was in their blood. Had Marx or Lassalle been born in another age, or in another environment, they might quite easily have become Conservatives instead of Radicals. As a matter of fact, Lassalle was already coquetting with the idea of becoming a reactionary, and no doubt he would have played the part of a Prussian Junker as brilliantly as that of socialist agitator.

The driving power in Jewish adaptability is of course the idea of a purpose, or a goal, as the end of all things. Once the Jew has made up his mind what line he will follow, the rest is comparatively easy, and his mobility only makes his success more sure.

How mobile the Jew can be is positively astounding. He is able to give himself the personal appearance he most desires. As in days of old through simulating death he was able to defend himself, so now by colour adaptation or other forms of mimicry. The best illustrations may be drawn from the United States, where the Jew of the second or third generation is with difficulty distinguished from the non-Jew. You can tell the German after no matter how many generations; so with the Irish, the Swede, the Slav. But the Jew, in so far as his racial physical features allow of it, has been successful in imitating the Yankee type, especially in regard to outward marks such as clothing, bearing and the peculiar method of hairdressing.

Easier still, on account of his mental and moral mobility, is it for the Jew to make the intellectual atmosphere of his environment his own. His mental mobility enables him quickly to seize upon the " tone " of any circle, quickly to notice what it is that matters, quickly to feel his way into things. And his moral mobility? That helps him to remove troublesome hindrances, either ethical or æsthetical, from his path. And he can do this with all the more facility because he has only to a small degree what may be termed personal dignity. It means little to him to be untrue to himself, if it is a question of attaining the wished-for goal.

Is this picture faithful to life? The obvious adaptability of the Jew to the changing conditions of the struggle for existence is surely proof enough. But there is further proof in some of the special gifts which Jews possess. I refer to their undoubted talent for journalism, for the Bar, for the stage, and all of it is traceable to their adaptability.

Adolf Jellinek, in the book we have referred to more than once, has drawn a clever little sketch showing the connexion between the two. "The journalist," he says, "must be quick, mobile, lively, enthusiastic, able to analyze quickly and as quickly to put two and two together; must be able to enter *in medias res*, to have the gist of any question of the day or the central fact of a debate in his mind's eye; must be able to deal with his subject in clear and well-marked outlines, to describe it epigrammatically, antithetically, sententiously, in short arresting sentences, to breathe life into it by means of a certain amount of pathos, to give it colour by means of esprit, to make it spicy by means of seasoning." Are not all these Jewish traits?

The actor's calling, no less than the barrister's, depends for success on his ability to place himself quickly in a strange world of ideas, to take a right view of men and conditions without much difficulty, to form a correct estimate of them and to use them for his own end. The Jew's gift of subjectivity stands him here in good stead, for by its aid he can easily put himself in the position of another, take thought for him and defend him. To be sure, jurisprudence is the bulk of the contents of Jewish literature!

III. Jewish Characteristics as Applied to Capitalism.

Now comes the question, how and in what way did the Jewish characteristics enable Jews to become financiers and speculators, indeed, to engage as successfully in

economic activities within the framework of the capitalistic system as to be mathematicians, statisticians,
physicians, journalists, actors and advocates? To what
extent, that is, does a special talent for capitalistic enterprise spring from the elements in the Jewish character?

Speaking generally, we may say in this connexion
what we have already remarked about capitalism and
the Jewish religion, that the fundamental ideas of capitalism and those of the Jewish character show a singular
similarity. Hence we have the triple parallelism between
Jewish character, the Jewish religion and capitalism. What
was it we found as the all-controlling trait of the Jewish
people? Was it not extreme intellectuality? And is
not intellectuality the quality which differentiates the
capitalistic system from all others? Organizing ability
springs from intellectuality, and in the capitalistic system
we find the separation between head and hands, between
the work of directing and that of manufacturing. "For
the greatest work to be completely done, you need of
hands a thousand, of minds but only one." That sums
up the capitalistic state of things.

The purest form of capitalism is that wherein abstract
ideas are most clearly expressed. That they are part and
parcel of the Jewish character we have already seen ;
there is no occasion to labour the close kinship in this
respect between capitalism and the Jew. Again, the
quality of abstraction in capitalism manifests itself in
the substitution of all qualitative differences by merely
quantitative ones (value in exchange). Before capitalism
came, exchange was a many-sided, multi-coloured and
technical process ; now it is just one specialized act—
that of the dealer : before there were many relationships
between buyer and seller ; there is only one now—the
commercial. The tendency of capitalism has been to do
away with different manners, customs, pretty local and

national contrasts, and to set up in their stead the dead level of the cosmopolitan town. In short, there has been a tendency towards uniformity, and in this capitalism and Liberalism have much in common. Liberalism we have already shown to be a near relative of Judaism, and so we have the kindred trio of Capitalism, Liberalism, and Judaism.

How is the inner resemblance between the first and the last best manifested? Is it not through the agency of money, by means of which capitalism succeeds so well in its policy of bringing about a drab uniformity? Money is the common denominator, in terms of which all values are expressed; at the same time it is the be-all and end-all of economic activity in a capitalistic system. Hence one of the conspicuous things in such a system is success. Is it otherwise with the Jew? Does he not also make the increase of capital his chief aim? And not only because the abstractness of capital is congenial to the soul of the Jew, but also because the great regard in which (in the capitalistic system) money is held strikes another sympathetic note in the Jewish character—its teleology. Gold becomes the great means, and its value arises from the fact that you can utilize it for many ends. It needs but little skill to show that a nature intent on working towards some goal should feel itself drawn to something which has value only because it is a means to an end. Moreover, the teleology of the Jew brings it about that he prizes success. (Another point of similarity, therefore, with capitalism.) Because he rates success so highly he sacrifices to-day for to-morrow, and his mobility only helps him to do it all the better. Here again we may observe a likeness to capitalism. Capitalism is constantly on the look-out for something new, for some way of expanding, for abstaining to-day for the sake of to-morrow. Think of our whole system of credit. Does not this characteristic show itself there clearly enough?

Now remember also that the Jews were very much at home in the organization of credit—in which values or services which may, or can, become effective some time in the future are made available to-day. Human thought can plainly picture future experiences and future needs, and credit offers the opportunity through present economic activities of producing future values. That credit is extensively found in modern life scarcely requires pointing out. The reason too is obvious : it offers golden chances. True, we must give up the joys that spring from "completely throwing ourselves into the present." 517 But what of that ? The Jewish character and capitalism have one more point in common —practical rationalism, by which I mean the shaping of all activities in accordance with reason.

To make the whole parallelism even more plain, let me illustrate it by concrete instances. The Jew is well fitted for the part of undertaker because of his strength of will and his habit of making for some goal or other. His intellectual mobility is accountable for his readiness to discover new methods of production and new possibilities of marketing. He is an adept at forming new organizations, and in these his peculiar capacity for finding out what a man is best fitted for stands him in good stead. And since in the world of capitalism there is nothing organic or natural but only what is mechanical or artificial, the Jew's lack of understanding of the former is of no consequence. Even undertaking on a large scale is itself artificial and mechanical ; you may extend a concern or contract it ; you may change it according to circumstances. That is why Jews are so successful as organizers of large capitalistic undertakings. Again, the Jew can easily grasp impersonal relationships. We have already noted that he has the feeling of personal dependence only in a slight measure. Hence, he does not care for your hoary " patriarchalism," and pays little attention to the dash of sentimentality which is still sometimes found in labour contracts. In all relations between sellers and buyers, and between employers and employed, he reduces everything to the legal and purely business basis. In the struggle of the workers to obtain collective agreements between themselves and the masters, which shall regulate the conditions of their labour, the Jew is almost invariably on the side of the first.

But if the Jew is well fitted to be an undertaker, still more is he cut out for the part of the trader. His qualities in this respect are almost innumerable.

The trader lives in figures, and in figures the Jew has always been in his element. His love of the abstract has made calculation easy for him ; it is his strong point. Now a calculating talent combined with a capacity for working always with some aim in view has already won half the battle for the trader. He is enabled to weigh aright the chances, the possibilities and the advantages of any given situation, to eliminate everything that is useless, and to appraise the whole in terms of figures. Give this sober calculator a strong dose of imagination and you have the perfect speculator before you. To take stock of any given state of things with lightning speed, to see a thousand eventualities, to seize upon the most valuable and to act in accordance with that—such, as we have already pointed out, is the aim of the dealer. For all this the Jew has the necessary gifts of mind. I should like expressly to emphasize the close kinship between the activities of the clever speculator and those of the clever physician who can successfully diagnose a disease. The Jew, because of his qualities, is eminently fitted for both.

A good dealer must be a good negotiator. What cleverer negotiators are there than the Jews, whose ability in this direction has long been recognized and utilized ? To adapt yourself to the needs of a market, to meet any specified form of demand, is the one prime essential for the dealer. That the Jew with his adaptability can do this as well as any other is obvious. The second is the power of suggestion, and in this also the Jew is well qualified by his ability to think himself into the situation of another.

Wherever we look the conclusion forces itself upon us that the combination of no other set of qualities is so well fitted, as are those of the Jew, for realizing the best capitalistic results. There is no need for me to take the parallelism further ; the intelligent reader can easily do so for himself. I would only direct his attention to one point more before leaving the subject—the parallel between the feverish restlessness of Stock Exchange business, always intent on upsetting the tendency towards an equilibrium, and the restless nature of the Jew.

In another place I have sought to characterize the ideal undertaker in three words—he must be wide-awake, clever and resourceful. Wide-awake : that is to say, quick of comprehension, sure in judgment, must think twice before speaking once, and be able to seize upon the right moment.

Clever : that is to say, he must possess a knowledge of the world, must be certain of himself in his judgment and in his treatment of men, certain in his judgment on a given conjuncture ; and above all, acquainted with the weaknesses and mistakes of those around him.

Resourceful : that is to say, full of ideas.

The capitalistic undertaker must have three additional qualities : he must be active, sober and thorough. By sober, I mean free from passion, from sentiment, from unpractical idealism. By thorough, I mean reliable, conscientious, orderly, neat and frugal.

I believe this rough sketch will, in broad outline, stand for the capitalistic undertaker no less than for the Jew.

PART III

THE ORIGIN OF THE JEWISH GENIUS

CHAPTER XIII

THE RACE PROBLEM

PREFATORY NOTE

STRICTLY speaking the task I had set myself has now been completed. I have tried to show the importance of the Jews in modern economic life in all its aspects, and the connexion between Capitalism and " Jewishness." In other words, I have endeavoured to point out why it was that the Jews have been able to play, and still continue to play, so significant a part in economic life ; endeavoured to show that their great achievements were due partly to objective circumstances, and partly to their inherent characteristics.

But here new questions crop up in plenty, and I must not pass them by unanswered, if I desire my most valued readers may not lay aside my book with a feeling of dissatisfaction. It is obvious that any one who has accompanied me to the point where I maintain that specifically Jewish characteristics exist, and that they will account for the great influence of the Jews in the body economic, must be bound to ask, What is the true nature of these characteristics ? How have they come about ? What will their ultimate effect be ?

The answers to these questions may vary considerably. The Jewish characteristics we have noted may be nothing else but, as it were, a function without a corresponding organism ; may be only surface phenomena, skin-deep, without any root at all in the human beings that give expression to them ; may be but as a feather on a coat—easily blown away ; something which vanishes with the disappearance of the person.

Or they may become hardened into a habit and be deep-seated, but yet not sufficiently powerful to be hereditary. Contrariwise, they may be so marked as to pass from one generation to another. In this case, the question presents itself, when did they arise? Were these characteristics always in the Jew, were they in his blood, or have they only been acquired in the course of his history—either in what is termed ancient times, or later? Again, all hereditary qualities may last for ever, or be only of a temporary nature—may be, that is, permanent or only transient. Seeing that we are dealing with a social group, it will be necessary here, too, to answer the question, Is the group a racial entity? In a word, are the Jews a subdivision of mankind, differing by blood-kinship from other people ? Finally, in a problem of this sort we must deal with the possibility that the peculiar characteristics of the group may be due to admixtures with other groups, or to selection within the group itself.

The problem is many-sided : of that there can be little doubt. And the worst of it is that modern science can give no certain replies to the questions propounded. Attempts have of course been made, but they are not without prejudice, and any one even only superficially acquainted with the subject will be faced by more problems and puzzles than by solutions.

The most pressing need of the moment, so it seems to me—one which alone will be able to withdraw the Jewish Problem from the semi-darkness in which it is enshrouded—is to obtain a clear conception of the questions at issue, and to bring some order into the abundant material at hand. It is almost as though at the point where the general Jewish Question intersects the race problem, a thousand devils had been let loose to confuse the minds of men. As one authority [518] recently urged with regard to the doctrines of heredity : what is most needed is an exact precision concerning elementals. The same is the case to an enormous extent with .the question of whether the Jews are a race or not, and perhaps an outsider may contribute something to this end, just because he stands apart from the specialists. This thought emboldens me to attempt to give a résumé of all that is current to-day regarding Jews as a race—of all that is certain, and of the thousand and one theories, to say nothing of the numerous false hypotheses.

I. The Anthropology of the Jews.

Touching the origin of the Jews and their anthropology and ethnology, opinions at the present day are pretty well agreed as to the essential facts. It is generally assumed [519] that Israel, like Judah, arose from the admixture of different Oriental peoples. When, in the 15th century B.C., the Hebrews, then a Bedouin tribe, wished to settle in Palestine they found there an old population long since established—Canaanites, who were probably hegemonic, Hittites, Perizites, Hivites and Jebusites (Judg. iii. 5). Recent research has come to the conclusion, opposed to the older view, that the Israelitish clans largely intermarried with these peoples.

Later, when a portion of the population went into the Babylonian Exile, the admixture of races continued in Palestine. And as for the exiles (whose history in this connexion is of vital importance), we learn much from the latest cuneiform inscriptions concerning their attitude towards intermarriage. The inscriptions show, " without doubt," that there was a gradual fusion between the Jews and the Babylonians. The immigrants called their children by Babylonian names, and the Babylonians theirs by Persian, Hebrew and Aramaic names.[520]

Nothing like so clear are the views as to the relationship to each other of the peoples and clans of which the Jews were composed ; still less as to how they can be distinguished from other similar groups ; and least of all how they are to be called. A very heated controversy has recently raged about the term " Semites," with the result that in anthropological circles the word is no longer used. The Semite controversy, like that on the Aryans, only shows how vicious it is to allow linguistic concepts to interfere in the anthropological divisions of mankind. It is generally accepted that the Semites are all those peoples whose speech is Semitic, but that anthropologically they belong to different and differing groups.[521]

My own view is that the controversy as to the exact demarcation of the civilized Oriental peoples is a little futile. Nor does our ignorance on this point much matter. One thing however is certain—that all of them, the Egyptians, the Babylonians, the Assyrians, the Phœnicians and the Jews, by virtue of their origin and earliest history, belong to one class, which may perhaps be termed " Desert " or " Desert-edge " Peoples. The assumption that a fair, blue-eyed tribe from the North intermingled with these is now almost unanimously regarded as a fable. The theory of the ubiquity of the Germans [522] will have to be but coldly entertained as long as no more convincing proofs are forthcoming than the reddish hair of Saul, or the dolichocephalic skull of the mummy of Rameses II.

What, then, was the anthropological history of the group of peoples in which the Jews originated ? A common answer as regards the Jews was that they continued to mix with their non-Jewish neighbours in the Diaspora as they had done before. Renan, Loeb, Neubauer and others believe that the modern Jews are in large measure the descendants of heathen proselytes in the Hellenistic Age, or of marriages between Jews and non-Jews in the early centuries of the Common Era. The existence of fair Jews (to the extent of 13 per cent.), especially in Eastern Europe, lent probability to this opinion. But to-day, so far as I can make out, the entirely opposite view generally prevails— that from the days of Ezra to these the Jews have kept strictly apart. For more than two thousand years they have been untouched by other peoples; they have remained ethnically pure. That drops of alien blood came into the Jewish body corporate through the long centuries of their dispersion no one will deny. But so small have these outside elements been that they have not influenced to any appreciable degree the ethnical purity of the Jewish people.

It seems pretty clear now that in the past the number of proselytes admitted into Judaism was considerably over-estimated. There is no doubt that in the Hellenistic and early Christian periods Judaism won adherents among the heathen peoples. (The subsequent centuries were of no consequence at all, with the exception of one case only.) Both the Roman and the Jewish Law made provision for such converts. But we may assume with certainty that all of them were the so-called " Proselytes of the Gate "—that is, they worshipped God in accordance with Jewish teaching, but they were not circumcised, nor were they allowed to marry Jewesses. Nearly all of them eventually drifted into Christianity. As a matter of fact, in the time of Pius circumcision was again allowed to the Jews, but the rite was expressly forbidden to be performed on proselytes. In this way conversion to Judaism was made a punishable offence. This in all probability was not the intention of the framers of the prohibition, but its effect was soon recognized, and it was extended.[523] For Severus " forbade conversion to Judaism on pain of grave penalties."

But even if we allow foreign admixtures among the Jews in the early Christian Age, it could never have amounted to very much when we think of the millions of Jews who presumably existed at the time, and anyhow the stranger elements came from peoples closely akin to the Jews.

As for the centuries that followed the entry of the Jews into European history, we may take it that proselytizing ceased almost entirely. Throughout the Middle Ages therefore the Jews received but little of non-Jewish blood. The remarkable conversion of the Chozars in the 8th century cannot be regarded as an exception to this statement, for their realm was never very extensive. In the 10th century it was limited to a very small area in the western part of the Crimea, and in the 11th the tiny Jewish State disappeared altogether. Only a small remnant of the Chozars live in Kieff as Karaites. Hence, even if the whole of the Chozars professed Judaism, the ethnical purity of the Jews could have been affected but little. As a matter of fact, however, it is very doubtful whether any others than the ruling family, or the upper classes, became Jews.[524]

Mixed marriages thus remain as the only possible source whence Jewish blood might be made impure. Certainly marriages between Jews and non-Jews must have occurred in some periods of Jewish history. Mixed marriages were probably numerous—a not extravagant assumption—in those epochs in which the band of Jewish solidarity was somewhat loosened—say, the last pre-Christian century, or the 12th and 13th in Spain. Even so, such relaxations never lasted for any considerable time ; Jewish orthodoxy soon regained the upper hand, to the exclusion of non-Jews. What the Pharisees achieved in the first-named period resulted in the second from the Maimonides schism, and this had such reactionary consequences that marriages with Christian and Mohammedan women were annulled.[525]

But there are indications that such marriages were to be found. They were expressly forbidden at the early Spanish Councils. For instance, the 16th Canon of the Council of Elovia (304) provides that "the daughters of Catholics shall not be given in marriage to heretics, except they return to the Church. The same applies to Jews and schismatics." The 64th Canon of the Third Council of Toledo (589) forbids Jews to have Christian women either as wives or mistresses ; and if any children spring from such unions they must be baptized. Once more, the 63rd Canon of the Fourth Council of Toledo (633) makes it incumbent upon Jews who have Christian wives to accept Christianity if they wish to continue to live with them.[526] It seems hardly likely, however, that marriages against which these canons were issued were very numerous. And anyhow, as the children of such marriages were lost to Judaism, Jewish racial purity could not have suffered much by them.

Similarly, it is improbable that there was any admixture of Jews with the Northern peoples. There was an opinion current that the Jews in Germany up to the time of the Crusades lived among their Christian neighbours, and had free intercourse with them in every direction. But this view is hardly credible, and Brann, one of the best authorities on German Jewish history, has declared the assumption of even the least degree of assimilation at this period to be "an airy fancy, which must vanish into nothingness when the inner life of the Jews of those days is understood."[527]

There remain the fair Jews. They have been regarded as a proof of Jewish admixture with the fair races of the North. But no scholar of repute looks upon these as the outcome of legitimate unions between Jews and their Slav neighbours. On the other hand, one hypothesis [528] has found credence—that the fair Jews are the children of illegitimate unions between Jews and Russians, either in the ordinary way or forcibly on the occasion of pogroms. But the weakness of this assumption is obvious. Even if it did explain the existence of fair Jews in Russia, it would be of no use at all for accounting for fair Jews in Germany, in Southern lands, in North Africa and in Palestine.

There is really no necessity to look for an explanation of the fair Jews in the admixture of races. All dark peoples produce a number of variants, and this is a case in point.[529]

We come back then to the fact that for some twenty centuries the Jews have kept themselves ethnically pure. One proof of this is found in the similarity of the anthropological characteristics of the Jews all over the globe, and, moreover, in that the similarity has been remarkably constant through the centuries. " Differences in treatment or environment have not been able to blur a common type, and the Jews more than any other race stand as a proof that the influence of heredity is much more powerful than that of environment " (E. Auerbach).

The anthropological homogeneity of the Jewish stock at the present time has been established by numerous anatomical experiments and measurements.[530] The only doubtful question is whether the ancient contrast between Ashkenazim [German Jews] and Sephardim [Spanish Jews] extends to their anthropology. There are two conflicting opinions on the subject,[531] but I believe the basis of either is not sufficiently conclusive to justify an independent judgment. It must be added, though, that personal observation would seem to warrant the belief that there was some anthropological difference between the two. Look at your spare, elegant Spanish Jew, with his small hands and feet and his thin, hooked nose, and then at his German brother, stout and bow-legged, with his broad, fleshy Hittite nose. Do they not appear as two distinct types to the ordinary observer? There is as yet no scientific ground to explain the difference.

Another controversial argument is whether the Jews of to-day are a separate entity, distinct from their neigh-bours physiologically and pathologically. There can be no doubt that from this point of view Jews do exhibit certain peculiarities in many respects—early puberty, little liability to cancer, especially cancer of the womb, strong disposition for diabetes, insanity, and so forth. There are people, however, who cannot look upon these things as physiological and pathological Jewish traits, but explain them as resultants of the social position of the Jews, of their religious practices, and so on.[532] Here also the ground has not been sufficiently prepared to war-rant a definite statement.

It is different with the physiognomy of the Jew. Physiognomy, as is well known, is the outcome of two causes—of certain facial forms and of their particular expression. You cannot weigh or measure either, and therefore this is a matter that must be left entirely to common observation. Now, just as the colour-blind distinguish no colours, so those who cannot see differences in men's faces know nothing of physiognomy. When, therefore, some writers [533] say that in the case of three-quarters of cultivated and wealthy Jews they cannot with certainty tell that they are Jews merely from their faces, then there is nothing to urge in reply. But a keen observer will most decidedly be able to tell. Jewish physiognomy is still a reality, and few will deny it. Undoubtedly there are individuals among Jews who do not look one whit Jewish. But there are also very many individuals among Gentiles who look very Jewish. I should not like to go so far as some do, 534 and say that the Hapsburgs because of their heavy lips, or the Louis of France because of their hooked noses, were Jewish-looking. But among Oriental peoples (including possibly the Japanese) we do come across Jewish types. This in no wise detracts from the anthropological unity of the Jews. If it proves anything, it only points to a common origin of the Jews and the Oriental peoples. (It might be mentioned, by the way, that the lost Ten Tribes have been located in Japan—a somewhat fantastic conjecture, but having something in its favour in the striking similarity of the Japanese and Jewish types.) To consider the Jewish physiognomy as an expression of decadence, or to account for it, as Ripley does, as a result of Ghetto life, is not very conclusive in face of the undeniable Jewish types depicted on the monuments of ancient Egypt and Babylonia. Look at the picture of Jewish captives in the epoch of Shishak (973 B.C.), or of the Jewish ambassadors at the court of Salmanasar 535 (884 B.C.), and you will be convinced that from those days to our own, a period of nearly three thousand years, few changes have marked the Jewish type of countenance. This is but another proof of the proposition that the Jewish stock is an anthropological entity, and that its characteristics have been constant through the ages in a most extraordinary fashion.

II. The Jewish "Race."

In view of all this, may we speak of a Jewish race ? The answer would depend on the connotation of the word "race." But to define it is not easy, for there are probably as many definitions as there are writers on it.[536-537] It is, of course, open to any one to say, Such and such things I look upon as the mark of race, and if I apply my standard the Jews are or are not a race, as the case may be. But a procedure of this kind is more of the nature of a game. What is needed is a scientific definition. But how? Many methods have been tried— anthropological differences, skull measurements, biological experiments and their application—but all with no absolute result. It would, however, be a fallacy to conclude that because hitherto no satisfactory classification of the human species has been achieved, therefore no anthropological differences really exist. An Eskimo *is* different from a negro, and the South Italian from the Norwegian. We do not require anthropology to tell us that.

So with the Jews. It may be difficult to class them, but anthropological peculiarities of their own they surely have. When therefore one distinguished scholar [538] writes : " I recognize only a Jewish religious community ; of a Jewish race I know nothing," we must regard it as a hasty expression uttered in the heat of the moment. The objection to it is that we can easily place a " Jewish national community " with a common history beside the " Jewish religious community."

So with anthropological characteristics which mark off the Jew from the non-Jew. I am firmly of opinion that the Jews, no matter .where they may be found, are an anthropological group differing from, let us say, the Swede or the negro. " A religious community " will not suffice.

After all, is it not a controversy about words ? Some will have it that there is no Jewish race. Well and good. But they admit Jewish anthropological peculiarities. It is a thousand pities that there is no satisfactory term by which to describe them. "A people" will not serve, for the definitions of "people" are no less numerous than those of "race." But what does the name matter? The thing certainly is there, and I should have no hesitation in speaking of the Jewish race, or, if you will, of the Jewish "race."

Let me conclude this section with one or two wise words written by Arthur Ruppin,[539] that excellent authority on the Jew, words that appear to me to be among the best that have been uttered on the subject : "The term 'race' should not be stretched too far. If we include in it such groups as developed their special anthropological characteristics in prehistoric times, and have since kept themselves without admixture with other groups, then in reality there are no 'races' among white-skinned peoples, seeing that all of them have intermingled over and over again. As for the Jews, whether they had common racial features in prehistoric times and have preserved them through the centuries, is a detail of no great significance. What does matter is this—that it is certain that those who professed the Jewish religion formed a well-defined group distinct from their surroundings, even as late as the end of the 18th century, after many generations of strict avoidance of marriage with non-Jews. The community which has descended from this group may be called, for lack of a better name, a race, more particularly, 'the Jewish race.'"

III. How the Jewish Genius remained Constant.

The question of greatest interest in these anthropological considerations is to discover whether any connexion exists between the somatic characteristics of the Jew and his intellectual qualities. We want to make sure whether the latter are in his blood, so to say, *i.e.*, whether they are racial or no. To discover this it will be necessary to see whether the characteristics we have observed in modern Jews were to be found among Jews in ancient times also ; whether they reach back to their earliest history, or whether they appeared at a later date, and if so, when.

The result will be that we shall observe that Jewish intellectual qualities have remained constant, that certain characteristics, certain peculiar features of the Jewish soul may be traced as far back as the formation of the Jewish ethnical group. We cannot prove all this directly, because we have no reliable accounts of the Jewish popular character dating from early times. What we do possess are brief and scanty expressions of opinions, valuable, however, as far as they go. It is of great interest, for example, to note that the Pentateuch (in four places— Exod. xxxii. 9, xxxiv. 9 ; Deut. ix. 13 and 27) asserts of the Jews what Tacitus said of them later—that they are a stiffnecked people. No less interesting is Cicero's statement that they hang together most fraternally, or Marcus Aurelius's that they are a restless people, to whom he cries, "O ye Marcomanni, O ye Quadi, O ye Sarmatæ, at length have I found a race more restless than you ! " ; or finally Juan de la Huarte's that their intellect is keen and well fitted for worldly things.

The first point to note is :—

(1) The attitude of the Jews to the peoples among whom they dwelt all through the Diaspora. In the last century or so we have seen this to be one of aloofness. Before capitalism came and set them free, Jews were looked upon as " strangers," as " semi-citizens." They were hated and persecuted in all lands, but everywhere they knew how to preserve and maintain themselves.

How was it in antiquity ? How later ? The same spectacle confronts us, ever since the Jews came into contact with other peoples. Everywhere there was opposition, persecution and ill-treatment. To begin with

the Egyptians : " They abhorred the children of Israel "
(Exod. i. 12). Paul of Tarsus went so far as to say that
the Jews "were contrary to all men " (1 Thess. ii. 15).
In the Hellenistic period, in Imperial Rome—the same
story of hate and plunder and death. Philo and Josephus
both record dreadful Jewish pogroms in Alexandria in
the first century of our era. " Hatred of the Jew and
ill-treatment of him are as old as the Diaspora itself "
(Mommsen).

Under the Cæsars their lot was no different : " I am
just sick of these filthy, noisy Jews," said Marcus
Aurelius. Then, in the time of Theodoric, massacres
and wholesale plundering were the order of the day, as
later in the 7th century under the Longobards. And the
East was like the West ; the 6th century in Babylon was
as dark as the 7th in Northern Italy. Even in the
Pyrenean Peninsula, where they enjoyed much that was
good, the end was bitter : Christian and Moslem both
laid hands upon them.

These instances might be multiplied. They are all
expressions of hatred of the Jew in Christian and non-
Christian environments alike. Can the phenomenon be
explained without the assumption of the existence of
Jewish characteristics, which remained constant no matter
where the Jew was placed ? The answer must surely be
in the affirmative. The hatred of the Jew could not
have been the result of a passing mood on the part of all
these peoples.

Then again, everywhere and at all times the Jews were
semi-citizens. Sometimes indeed they were not in this
category because the law placed them there. On the
contrary. There were many cases in antiquity where
Jews were assigned privileged positions, by virtue of
which they were excused certain duties of the citizen (*e.g.*,
military service), or had exceptional advantages in regard

to legal enactments. Nevertheless they took no full share in the life of the State in which they were domiciled. The Greek inhabitants of Cæsarea, a city on Jewish soil and built under Jewish rule, denied citizen rights to the Jews, and Burnus, Nero's minister, upheld their decision.540 There was little change in this respect during the Middle Ages.

How are we to account for this generally prevailing treatment ? Differing States adopted a similar policy towards the Jew : does it not seem clear that it was due to some special characteristic of his ? If you like, say it was the strict adherence to the letter of the Jewish religion. But something it must have been.

And yet, despite all oppression, the Jew was not crushed. He knew how to maintain himself from the oldest times onward. Perhaps it was because of the curious mixture of stubbornness and elasticity which we have noted in Jews of modern days. They might be crushed never so relentlessly, but like a Jack-in-the-box they were soon up again. How they withstood the onslaught of the Roman Emperors, who used all the weapons at their command to stamp them out ! Despite their efforts, there was again in the 3rd century a Patriarch at Jerusalem recognized by the government, with a jurisdiction of his own. In antiquity, in the Middle Ages, in this our own time, the peoples have summed up their judgment of the Jew in the one word—stubborn : " *ostinato come un ebreo.*"

The peculiar mixture of determination and elasticity is most wonderfully exhibited by the Jews in their bearing towards governments, where their religion was concerned. To it they owed most of their enemies ; because of it they suffered hardships untold. Yet they would not give up their beloved faith. And when pressure was severe, many Jews pretended to have forsworn their religion only to be able to carry out its precepts in secret. We know of this conduct in connexion with the Marannos, but it is as old as the Diaspora itself. When you read of the thousands of crypto-Jewish heathens, crypto-Jewish Mohammedans, crypto-Jewish Christians, you are astounded at this unique event in human history. The more so as it was the most religious Jews, teachers and leaders, who had recourse to the sham conversions in order to save their lives. Recall the case of R. Eleazar ben Parta, who was active under Hadrian as a pretended heathen ; [541] that of Ismael ibn Negrela, who, as R. Samuel, held discourses on the Talmud and answered questions of religious practice, and as Vizier of the Mohammedan King Habus, began his master's ordinances with the formula *Chamdu-l-Illahi* and ended them with urging those to whom they were addressed to live according to the laws of Islam ; [542] that of the great Maimonides, who sought to give excellent reasons for his pretended conversion to Mohammedanism ; [543] that of Sabbatti Zevi, the false Messiah, who though he acknowledged Mahomet yet did not lose the respect of his followers ; that of the Neapolitan Jew Basilus, who made a pretence of having his sons baptized in order to be able to carry on the trade in slaves under their name,[544] since this branch of commerce was forbidden the Jews ; that of the thousands and thousands of Marannos who, after the expulsion of the Jews from the Pyrenean Peninsula, appeared to all the world as Christians and returned to the faith of their fathers at the very first opportunity that presented itself. What remarkable people must these have been who combined such determination with such elasticity !

We have thus noted that many Jewish characteristics developed to their fullest in the Diaspora. But

(2) Is the Diaspora itself explicable as a result of only

outward circumstances? Does it not itself rather bear witness to special characteristics? Or to put the question somewhat differently, would it have been possible to scatter any other people over the face of the earth as the Jews were scattered?

The experience of exile the Jews tasted in quite early days. Most people have heard of Tiglath-Pileser, who dragged a part of the Jewish population to Media and Assyria; of the later Babylonian Exile; of Ptolemy Lagi, who forced very many Jews to settle in Egypt and planted a Jewish colony in Cyrene; of Antiochus the Great, who brought two thousand Jewish families from Babylon and peopled with them the centre of Asia Minor, Phrygia and Lydia. Mommsen calls the settlement of Jews outside Palestine "an invention of Alexander or of his generals."

In all these cases the temptation is strong to ascribe the dispersion of the Jews to outward circumstances, seeing that in most of the cases the Jews were carried away from their homes against their will. There appears to be nothing therefore in these dispersions that would point to inherent Jewish characteristics. Such a conclusion would be hasty. Is there not this possibility—that if the Jews had not possessed certain qualities they might never have been transplanted? The enforced settlements must have had some purpose. Either they were beneficial to the land from which the Jews were taken, or (what was more probable) to the land or the town where they were settled. Either they were feared in their own country as firebrands of sedition, or they were accounted such valuable citizens for their wealth or their industry that they were made the nucleus of new settlements, or they were held to be so trusty that they were utilized by rulers to strengthen their hold on turbulent centres (as was done by Ptolemy Lagi in Cyrene).

But many Jews may have forsaken Palestine for what might be termed economic reasons : there was not sufficient room for the maintenance of an increasing population. Considering the size and the productiveness of Palestine, emigration on these grounds must have been of frequent occurrence.　But this points to a national characteristic— viz., an increasing population due, as is known, to physiological and psychological causes alike.　Furthermore, that economic pressure led to emigration was traceable to another national peculiarity.　In this respect the Jews have been compared to the Swiss.　They, too, leave their homes because the country is unable efficiently to maintain them all.　But they only emigrate because they have the energy and the determination to do better for themselves.　The Hindoo does not emigrate.　If the population increases, he is content with his smaller portion of rice.

But to regard all Jewish dispersion as enforced is probably one-sided.　We cannot possibly explain so general a phenomenon, which moreover remains the same through the ages, without assuming a voluntary migration.　What precisely this was due to—whether to a migrative instinct, or to inability to remain on one piece of soil for long—does not much matter.　But some special characteristic will have to be associated with this people to account for their travelling so easily from land to land, no less than for their settlement in large cities, a proclivity shown by the Jews already in very early times.　Herzfeld, who has compiled probably the most complete list of Jewish settlements in the Hellenistic Age, draws attention to the striking fact that of the settlements 52 are in towns, and of these 39 were wealthy commercial centres.[545]

It would appear from all this that Jewish characteristics were by no means developed in the Diaspora, or, as the Jewish historians assume, in the Middle Ages, but

that the Diaspora itself was the result of these characteristics. The characteristics were there first, at least in
embryo.

(3) So, too, with their religion. When it is asserted
that the Jew of to-day is a product of his religion, that
he has been made what he is, almost artificially, by means
of a well thought-out policy of some man or group of
men, and not organically, I am ready to admit the
statement. My own presentation of this very subject
in a previous chapter attempted to show what enormous
influence the Jewish religion had, more especially on the
economic activity of the Jew. But I want to oppose
the view promulgated by H. S. Chamberlain with all
my power. I want to make it clear that the religion
of the Jew would have been impossible but for the
special characteristics of the Jew. The fact that some
man, or group of men, was able to give expression to
such wonderful thoughts necessarily postulates that the
individual or the group was specially gifted. Again, that
the whole people should accept their teachings not merely
by way of lip-service, but with deep and sincere inwardness—can we explain this except by the supposition of
special national characteristics ? To-day we can no longer
free ourselves from the opinion that every people has, in
the long run, the religion best suited for it, and that if it
adopts another religion it keeps on changing it to suit it
to its needs.

I believe, therefore, that we may deduce the special
characteristics of the Jewish people from the special characteristics of the Jewish religion. From this standpoint
many traits of the Jewish character adduced from Jewish
legends may be placed very far back, certainly as early as
the Babylonian Exile. That I shall proceed in this as the
authors of anti-Semitic catechisms do, and infer from the
somewhat questionable story of Isaac, Jacob and Esau,

and their cheating of each other, a tendency on the part
of the Jews for swindling, need not be feared. No one,
I hope, will think so badly of me. Cheating is an element found in all mythologies. We need only cast our
eyes on Olympus or Valhalla to see the gods cheating
and swindling each other in the most shameless fashion.
No. What I mean is that the fundamental characteristics
of the Jewish religious system which we have already
examined—Intellectuality, Rationalism, Teleology—are
also the characteristics of the Jewish people, and they
must have been in existence (I would repeat, at least in
embryo) even before the religion was developed.

(4) My next point is the remarkable similarity in the
economic activities of the Jews throughout almost all
the centuries of history. In asserting that this is a
proof that Jewish characteristics were constant, I am
setting myself in opposition to the prevailing views. I
differ not only from those who believe that the economic
activities of the Jews have changed in the course of time,
but also from those who agree with me that it was a
constant factor in their development. From the latter
I differ because we do not agree as to what those
activities were.

What is the generally accepted view of Jewish economic
history? I believe it may be traced to Heine, and is
something to this effect. Originally the Jews were an
agricultural people. Even in the Diaspora, it is said, the
Jews tilled the soil, avoiding all other pursuits. But in
the 6th and 7th centuries of our era they were forced
to sell their holdings and had, willy-nilly, to look out
for other means of livelihood. What did they do?
They devoted themselves to trade, and for something
like five centuries continued in this calling. Again Fate
pressed heavily upon them, for the Crusades engendered
much anti-Jewish feeling in commercial circles, and the

growing trading class in each country organized themselves into gilds, and excluded the Jews from the markets,
which they retained as the exclusive preserves of members
of their corporations. Once more the Jews had to cast
about for new occupations. All channels were closed to
them; the only possibility left was to become money-
lenders. So they became money-lenders, and before long
enjoyed privileges as such because the usury laws meted
out special treatment to them.

Such is the almost semi-official view prevalent in Jewish
circles, certainly among assimilationists, but also among a
goodly number of Jewish nationalists.

There is another view to which some historians, Jewish
and Gentile (among the former Herzfeld), have given
currency. It is that the Jews have always been a commercial people, from the age of King Solomon onwards,
throughout the Diaspora, down to our own times.

I regard both views as wrong, certainly as one-sided,
and I hope to give my reasons in a sketch of the economic
history of the Jews which I shall furnish.

From the period of the Kings to the end of the
national independence—we may even say up to the
codification of the Talmud—the Jewish people were a
self-contained, self-sufficing economic unit. Its surplus
commodities it sent to foreign lands, and its constituent
units produced all they needed, or at best, supplemented
their own work by simple bartering with their neighbours.
We should describe the whole by saying that we had here
single economic units satisfying their own wants, with
which was connected a certain amount of hired labour;
there was something of the nature of the manorial system,
and there were some handicrafts. Where these are found
little trade is possible. But how about the numerous
merchants in Palestine, of whom we read in the time
of the Kings? How account for them? To speak of

merchants in the ordinary interpretation of the term is
to misunderstand the nature of the economic organization
of the country in Solomon's day.   It was nothing but
an extensive manorial system, something like that of
Charlemagne, and obviously required the distribution of
commodities.   But this was not commerce.   " The chief
officers (they corresponded to the *villici*) that were over
Solomon's work were 550. . . . And King Solomon
made a navy of ships in Ezion-geber. . . . And Hiram
sent in the navy his servants, shipmen that had knowledge
of the sea, with the servants of Solomon.   And they
came to Ophir and they fetched from thence gold, four
hundred and twenty talents, and brought it to King
Solomon " (1 Kings ix. 23, 26–28).

This and similar passages have been taken to denote
a flourishing international commercial intercourse, even
a monopoly of trade.   But there is no need of this
explanation at all.   It is perfectly simple when we think
of the royal household as a manor on a large scale,
from which the servants, in company with those from
another large manor, were sent forth to distant lands
in order to bring back commodities that were needed
at the King's court.   The economic independence of
the royal household further appears in the story of the
building of the Temple.   Solomon asks Hiram to send
him " a man cunning to work in gold, and in silver
and in brass, and in iron and in purple, and in crimson
and in blue, and that can skill to grave all manner of
gravings, to be with the cunning men that are with
me. . . . Send me also cedar-trees, fir-trees and algum-
trees, out of Lebanon : for I know that thy servants
can skill to cut timber in Lebanon ; and behold my
servants will be with thy servants. . . . And behold
I will give to thy servants, the hewers that cut timber,
twenty thousand measures of beaten wheat, and twenty

thousand measures of barley, and twenty thousand baths of wine, and twenty thousand baths of oil" (2 Chron. ii. 7 ff.). The same applies to a later passage in the same book (2 Chron. viii. 4), " And Solomon built Tadmor in the wilderness and all the store cities which he built in Hamath." Store cities tell of the manor and its wealth in kind rather than of commerce.

The other passages on which the theory is based that an extensive trade was carried on in later times hardly warrant this deduction.[545A] True, we learn that the Babylonian exiles were wealthy (Ezra i. 46 ; Zech. vi. 10, 11), but no indication is given of their callings. There is not one iota of evidence in the Bible for the contention of Graetz that they had obtained their riches in commerce. Perhaps the cuneiform inscriptions brought from Nippur may support such an assumption. But to refer the prophecy of Ezekiel about the destruction of Tyre (Ezek. xxvi. 2) to jealousy of the Phœnicians, and then on that basis to establish the suggestion that even in the pre-Exilic period Palestine was largely a trading country, appears to me to be somewhat bold.

That we cannot be too careful in reasoning of this kind is made abundantly manifest by the interpretation put upon the famous passage in Proverbs (vii. 19, 20), where the wiles of the adulteress are described. "For the goodman is not at home, he is gone a long journey ; he hath taken a bag of money with him : he will come back at the full moon." Was the husband a merchant ? Perhaps, but he may have been a farmer who had left home to pay his rent to the bailiff in a distant town, and at the same time to buy a couple of oxen there.

There is no clear proof, therefore, for the existence of commerce as a specialized calling. On the other hand, there are passages which support my view that the manorial system was prevalent even at a later period. Take, for example, Nehemiah ii. 8, where the letter is mentioned in which Asaph, the keeper of the King's forest, is asked to give timber to make beams for the gate of the castle. The injunction in Leviticus (xix. 35, 36) about just weights and measures does not in itself militate against this theory.

But this does not mean that there were no traders. There must have been, even in the period of the Kings, but they were only retail dealers. Do we not read of them in the Book of Kings (1 Kings xx. 34), where the defeated Ben-hadad, King of Syria, offers Ahab to build streets for bazaars in Damascus as his father had done in Samaria? Or in Nehemiah (iii. 32), where we are told that the goldsmiths and the merchants built their shops in a particular quarter? How this last statement can be construed to mean that there must have been highly respected merchant gilds (Bertholet) I cannot understand. You can almost see the small shopkeepers at the Sheep Gate.

That there was an international exchange of commodities, even in the earliest times, cannot of course be denied. There must have been extensive trade and great merchants, who exchanged the surplus produce of Palestine for the articles of luxury which they brought with them.546 " Judah, and the land of Israel, they were thy (Tyre's) traffickers : they traded for thy merchandise wheat of Minnith and pannag [a kind of confection] and honey and oil and balm " [Ezek. xxvii. 17]. But the extraordinary thing is that these great merchants were never Jews, but always foreigners. The caravans that crossed the country were led by Midianites, Sabæans, Dedanites, men of Keder, but not by Jews.547 Even retail trade, when the Proverbs were written, was in the hands of Canaanites. Ousted from trade in their own land, the Jews were hardly likely to have had any influence in the international trade of those times. The great international merchants were Phœnicians, Syrians or Greeks.[548] "Absolute proofs that Jewish emigration was chiefly for commercial ends are wanting entirely."[549] In view of all this I see no reason for regarding the passage in Josephus, which describes the position of the Jews in his days, as prejudiced and one-sided. It was in all probability true to fact. What does he say? "As for ourselves, therefore, we neither inhabit a maritime country, nor do we delight in merchandise" (*Contra Apion*, i. 12).

The centuries that followed brought little change in these conditions. In the Talmud those sayings predominate that would point to the prevalence among Jews, at least in the East, of small independent economic units, each sufficient for its own needs. It would be a mistake to speak of commercial activity. Granted we hear[550] that man accounted blessed who is able to become a spice-seller, and need not do laborious work. But surely the retail trader is meant, and not the great merchant. In fact trade, and more particularly over-sea trade, found little favour with the Rabbis. Some even go so far as to damn all manner of markets, pinning their faith to that economic organization where there is no need for the exchange of commodities. "R. Achai ben Joshia used to say, Unto whom may he be likened who buys fruit in the market? Unto a little child whose mother has died, which, when taken to the houses of other mothers who feed their own babes, yet remains unsatisfied. Whoso buys bread in the market is like to a man who digs the grave in which he will be buried."[551] Rab (175–247) constantly impressed upon his second son that "better was a small measure from the field than a large one from the vat" (*i.e.*, warehouse).552 Or again, " The Rabbis taught : four kinds of grain bring no blessing—the payment of a scribe, the fee of an interpreter, the earnings that flow from orphans' property and the profits derived from over-sea trade." Why the latter ? " Because miracles do not happen every day." 553

So much for the East. What of the West ? Here, too, the Jews were not great merchants. Throughout the Imperial period and the succeeding early Middle Ages the Jew, like the Syrian, if he were a " trader " was only a poor chapman, a mere grasshopper who got entangled between the feet of the royal merchants of Rome, just like the small Polish dealer of the 17th and 18th centuries, who made himself a nuisance to the merchants of that day. All that we can discover regarding Jewish trade in the early mediæval period fits beautifully into the picture. The Jews, in short, were never merchants so long as commerce, and especially intermunicipal and international commerce, remained partly a robbing expedition and partly an adventure— that is to say, until modern times.

If this is so—if the Jews never were a trading people from of old—are those correct who hold that they were agriculturists ? Certainly, in so far as their economic organization was the manorial one. But that is not all. The occupation to which Jews devoted themselves in later times and which, in the view of Jewish historians, was forced upon them against their will, was well-known and practised even in the earliest periods. I refer to money-lending, and I attach the greatest importance to the establishment of this fact. The economic history of the Jews throughout the centuries makes it appear that money-lending always played a very great, nay, an extraordinarily great, part in the economic life of the people. We meet with it in all phases of Jewish history, in the age of national independence as in the Diaspora. Indeed, a community of peasant proprietors is fine game for money-lenders. Always the creditors are Jews, anyhow after the Exodus. In Egypt it appears the Jews were the debtors, and when they left, as the official report narrates, they carried away what had been lent to them. "And I will give this people favour in the sight of the Egyptians, and it shall come to pass when ye go, ye shall not go empty" (Exod. iii. 21). "And the Lord gave the people favour in the sight of the Egyptians, so that they let them have what they asked . . ." (Exod. xii. 36). Thereafter the position changed. Israel became the creditor and other peoples became his debtors. Thus the promise made by God was fulfilled, the promise that may rightly be called the motto of Jewish economic history, the promise which indeed expresses the fortunes of the Jewish people in one sentence : "The Lord thy God will bless thee as He promised thee : and thou shalt lend unto many nations, but thou shalt not borrow" (Deut. xv. 6).554

The oldest passage which points to a highly developed system of borrowing in ancient Israel is that in Nehemiah (vi. 15) :—

"Then there arose a great cry or the people and of their wives against their brethren the Jews. For there were that said, We, our sons and our daughters, are many : let us get corn, that we may eat and live. Some also there were that said, We are mortgaging our fields, and our vineyards and our houses : let us get corn because of the dearth. There were also that said, We have borrowed money for the king's tribute upon our fields and our vineyards. Yet now our flesh is as the flesh of our brethren, our children as their children : and lo, we bring into bondage our sons and our daughters to be servants, and some of our daughters are brought into bondage already : neither is it in our power to help it, for other men have our fields and our vineyards. And I was very angry when I heard their cry and these words. Then I consulted with myself and contended with the nobles and the rulers, and said unto them, Ye exact usury, every one of his brother. . . . Restore, I pray you, to them even this day their fields, their vineyards, their olive-yards and their houses, also the hundredth part of the money, and of the corn, the wine and the oil, that ye exact of them."

The picture here drawn is clear enough. The people were divided into two sections, an upper wealthy class, which became rich by money-lending, and the great mass of agricultural labourers whom they exploited. This state of affairs must have continued, in despite of Nehemiah and other reformers, throughout the whole history of the Jews in Palestine and Babylon. We need only refer to the Talmud for proof. In some of the Tractates, after the study of the Torah nothing occupies so much space as money-lending. The world of ideas which the Rabbis had was crammed full with money business. A decision of Rabina (488–556), one of the last of the Amoraim (*Baba Mezia*, 70*b*), sounds almost like the creation of a money-lending monopoly for the Rabbis. Throughout the three Tractates called *Baba*, there are numerous examples from the business of money-lending and from the rise and fall of interest, and numerous discussions about money and problems of money-lending. The unprejudiced reader of the Talmud cannot but come to this conclusion : in the Talmudic world there must have been a good deal of money-lending.

With the Diaspora the business only extended. How far money-lending was regulated among the Jews in the Egyptian Diaspora, four or five centuries before the Common Era, may be seen from the Oxford Papyrus (MS. Aram. cl. P) 555 :—

". . . Son of Jatma . . . you gave me money . . . 1000 segel of silver. And I am ready to pay by way of interest 2 hallur of silver /

per month for each segel until the day whereon I repay the money to you. The interest / for your money is thus to amount to 2000 hallur every month. And if in any month I pay you no / interest, then the amount of interest shall be added to the principal and shall bear interest itself. I undertake to pay you month by month / out of my salary which I receive from the Treasury, and you will give me a receipt (?) for the whole / sum and for the interest that I will pay you. And if I have not repaid the whole of your / money by the month of Roth in the year . . . then your money shall be doubled (?) / and also the interest I have yet to pay, and month by month I must be made to pay the same / until the day I repay you the whole / Witness, etc."

In the Hellenistic and Imperial periods rich Jews were found supplying crowned heads with money, and the poorer Jews lent to the lower classes. The Romans were not unacquainted with Jewish business.556 It was the same in the pre-Islamic period among the Arabs, to whom the Jews lent money at interest, and who regarded this business as being natural to the Jew, as being in his blood.557

When the Jews first appeared on the scene in Western Europe it was as money-lenders. We have already noted that they acted as financiers to the Merovingians, which means, of course, mainly as creditors.558 They went further in Spain ; there, where they had complete freedom of movement, the common people were soon in their debt. Long before there was a Jewish (*i.e.*, money-lending) question in other States, the legislative authorities in Castile were dealing with the problem of debts owing to Jews, and dealing with it in such a way as to show that it was of no small practical importance.559 That money-lending became the principal calling of the Jews after the Crusades will be admitted on all hands.

We come, then, to this conclusion, that from the earliest times money-lending was a prime factor in the economic history of the Jews.

The time has really arrived when the myth that the Jews were forced to have recourse to money-lending in mediæval Europe, chiefly after the Crusades, because they were debarred from any other means of livelihood, should be finally disposed of. The history of Jewish money-lending in the two thousand years before the Crusades ought surely to set this fable at rest once and for all. The official version that Jews could not devote themselves to anything but money-lending, even if they would, is incorrect. The door was by no means always shut in their faces; the fact is they preferred to engage in money-lending. This has been proved by Professor Bücher for Frankfort-on-the-Main, and the same may be done for other towns as well. The Jews had a natural tendency towards this particular business, and both in the Middle Ages and after rulers were at pains to induce Jews to enter into other callings, but in vain. Edward I made the attempt in England ; [560] it was also tried in the 18th century in the Province of Posen,[561] where the authorities sought to direct the Jews to change their means of livelihood by offering them bounties if they would. Despite this, and despite the possibility of being able to become handicraftsmen and peasants like all others, there were, in 1797, in the southern towns of Prussia, 4164 Jewish craftsmen side by side with 11,000 to 12,000 Jewish traders. The significance of these figures is borne in upon us when we note that though the Jewish population formed some 5 or 6 per cent. of the whole, the Christian traders totalled 17,000 or 18,000.

It may be urged, however, that the practice of usury, even when it is carried on quite voluntarily, need not be accounted for by special racial attributes. Human inclinations of a general kind will amply explain it. Wherever in the midst of a people a group of moneyed men dwell side by side with others who need cash, be it for consumption, be it for production, it soon comes about, especially where the legal conditions governing money-lending are of a primitive kind, that the one class becomes the debtors and the other the creditors.

True. Wherever rich and poor lived together, the latter borrowed from the former, even when there was as yet no money in existence—in which case the debts were in kind. In the earliest stages of civilization, when the two classes felt themselves members of the same brotherhood, the lending was without interest. Later, especially when some intercourse with strangers sprang up, the borrower paid the lender a certain quantity of corn or oil or (where a money economy had already established itself) gold over and above the principal, and the custom of giving interest gradually became universal.

In this there is no difference between the ancient, the mediæval or the modern world. All three were acquainted with money-lending and "usury," which was never confined to the members of any one race or religion. Think of the agrarian reforms in Greece and Rome, which prove conclusively that the economic conditions in these countries at certain times were exactly like those in Palestine in the days of Nehemiah.* In the ancient world the temples were the centres of the money-lending business, for in them were stored vast quantities of treasure. If at the Jerusalem Temple money-lending was carried on—what is by no means established : the Talmudic tractate (*Shekalim*) which deals with Temple taxes clearly forbids the utilization of what remained over from certain sacrifices for purposes of business—I say *if* such were the case, then there was nothing extraordinary in this : all temples in antiquity lent money. The temples of Babylonia, we are informed,[562] were like

[* Cf. A. E. Zimmern, *The Greek Commonwealth*, p. 111 ff.]

so many great business houses. The temples at Delphi, at Delos, at Ephesus, at Samos were no different.563 And in the Middle Ages the churches, the monasteries, the houses of the various Knights and other religious orders took the place of the ancient temples in this respect. Despite the prohibitions of the Church against usury, they were the centres of a brisk trade in money. Is it any different to-day? The German peasant on the marshes of the North Sea coast who has managed to make a little money knows of nothing better to do with it than to lend it at interest to a needy neighbour.

To increase one's fortune by means of interest on loans is so easy and pleasant, that everybody who is able makes the attempt. Every period wherein the demand for money is great gives opportunity enough (the periods, that is, of the so-called credit crises—regularly followed, by the way, in recent European history by Jewish persecutions).

Everybody, then, does it—gladly does it. The desire to take interest on money is pretty generally prevalent. But is the ability to do so? This leads me to my next proof in support of the view that Jewish characteristics have remained constant—

(5) The capacity of the Jew for money-dealing.

It is well-known that in the Middle Ages many authorities, whether individual rulers or corporations, almost begged the Jews to come to their city in order to carry on money-lending. All sorts of privileges were held out to them. The Bishop of Speyer is a case in point. He thought it would give his city a certain *cachet* to count a number of rich Jews among its inhabitants. Some of the cities of Italy in the 15th and 16th centuries actually made agreements with the wealthiest Jewish money-lenders that they should come and establish loan-banks and pawnshops.563A

Why should these requests have been made, and these privileges offered? Why should just Jews and no others have been invited to found money-lending concerns? No doubt to some extent it was because good Christian men were not willing to soil their souls by the nefarious trade, and Jews were called in to stand between them and damnation. But was this all? Does it not appear rather that the Jews had a special capacity for the business? They were the cleverest, the most gifted money-lenders, and that is why they were in demand. How else should we be able to account for their success, which for centuries brought them so much riches? Anybody can be a lender, but not everybody can be a successful lender. For that special capacities and attributes are necessary.

Turn to the pages of the Talmud and you will find that money-lending was no mere dilettante business with the Jews. They made an art of it; they probably invented (certainly they utilized) the highly organized machinery of lending.

The time has come, it seems to me, for a trained economist to deal thoroughly with the economic side of the Talmud and of Rabbinic literature generally. I hope this book may act as some spur to this end. All I can do here is to point the way, so that some successor of mine may find it the more easily. I shall briefly note some of the passages which appear to me to bear witness to an extensive acquaintance with economic problems, and more particularly those bearing on credit. When we recall the period in which the Talmud came into being (200 B.C. to 500 A.D.) and compare what it contains in the field of economics with all the economic ideas and conceptions that the ancient and the mediæval worlds have handed down to us, it seems nothing short of marvellous. Some of the Rabbis speak as though they had mastered Ricardo and Marx, or, to say the least, had been brokers on the Stock Exchange for several years, or counsel in many an important money-lending case.   Let me cite an instance or two.

(*a*) A profound acquaintance with the nature of the precious metals.   " R. Chisda said, There are seven kinds of gold : ordinary gold, best gold, gold of Ophir (1 Kings x. 11), fine gold (1 Kings v. 18), drawn gold, heavy gold and Parvayin gold " (*Joma*, 45*a*).

(*b*) The idea that money is a common denominator in terms of which commodities are exchanged is fully developed.   The best proof of this is the legal decision that the act of purchasing becomes complete not as soon as the price has been paid, but when the commodity is delivered.   The whole of the 4th section of *Baba Mezia* is illustrative of this point.

(*c*) There is a clear conception of the difference between credit for production and for consumption. In the case of the first, interest is permitted ; not so, from a Jew, in the case of the second.   " If A rents a field from B at a rental of 10 measures of wheat and then requests B to lend him 200 zuz for the improvement of the field, promising a total payment of 12 measures of wheat—that is permissible.   But may you offer to give more in renting a shop or hiring a ship ? Rab Nachman (235–320), on the authority of Rabba bar Abuha, was of opinion that sometimes it was permissible to give more for a shop in order to be able to hang pictures up in it, and for a ship too, in order to place a mast on it.   The pictures in the shop will attract many people and so increase profits, and the mast on the ship will enhance the ship's value " (*Baba Mezia*, 69*b*).

(*d*) Law and rules of practice point to an extra-ordinarily developed system of credit agreements.   After reading the 4th and 5th sections of *Baba Mezia* you feel as though you had just laid down the report of an Enquiry into Money-lending in Hesse twenty or thirty years ago, where a thousand and one gins and traps were introduced into money-lending compacts. The *Prosbol*, too (by means of which it was possible to ensure the existence of a debt even over the year of release), is a sign of a highly organized system of lending (Section 10 of *Sheviith*).

(*e*) The treatment of deposits is handled in a way which shows practical knowledge of the subject. " If any one deposits moneys with a banker, the latter may not make any use of them if they are in one bundle. If, however, they are loose, he may, and if they are lost he is held responsible. But if the moneys are deposited with a private individual, whether they are in one bundle or loose, he may make no use of them whatever ; and if they should be lost he is not bound to replace them. R. Meir (100–160) held that a shopkeeper was regarded as a private individual in this respect ; but R. Judah (136–200) was of the contrary opinion, and said that the shopkeeper was like the banker. . . . " (*Baba Mezia*, 43*a*).

(*f*) Finally I would mention the Jewish gift for figures. The Talmudists all had it, but it was to be found in earlier ages also. The exact statistical lists in the Bible and the later literature must have struck every one. One French writer remarks on the topic : " The race possessed a singular capacity for calculation —a genius, so to say, for numbers." 563[B]

Apart from all these considerations, the very success of the Jews in their money-lending activities effectively demonstrates a special capacity for the business. And the success was manifested in

(6) Jewish wealth.

That ever since the race began some Jews amassed huge fortunes can be easily shown, nor can it be doubted that the average wealth of all Jews was fairly high. In all ages and in all lands Jewish riches were proverbial.

We may begin with King Solomon, whose wealth was renowned even among wealthy Oriental potentates— although he did not acquire it by successful trading (though you never can tell!). Later we read that some of the Jewish exiles in Babylon were in a short time able to send gold and silver to Jerusalem (Zech. vi. 10, 11). That Jews played a great part in the economic life of the Euphrates country during the Exile appears from the commercial contracts dug up at Nippur.[564] Those who returned with Ezra brought great opulence with them (Ezra i. 6–11), and in the subsequent period the wealth of the priests was notorious.[565] Noticeable are the large number of rich men, some of them very rich, among the Talmudic Rabbis. It would not be difficult to compile quite a respectable list of such of them as were renowned for their wealth. Certainly, in my view, the rich Rabbis were in the majority.[566]

In the Hellenistic Diaspora likewise the impression cannot be avoided that the standard of wealth among Jews was pretty high. Wherever Jews and Greeks lived side by side, as in Cæsarea,[567] the former were the more opulent. There must have been a specially great number of wealthy Jews among those of Alexandria. Of very rich Alabarchs we are actually told, and we have already mentioned the position of the Alexandrian Jews as financiers of crowned heads.

It was not·one whit otherwise in the early Middle Ages. We have it on record that many Jews in those days were blessed with the good things of the world in abundance. In Spain they offered money to Reccared if he would annul anti-Jewish legislation,[568] and in the early period of Mohammedan rule we learn that the Arabs envied them their wealth.[569] Cordova, in the 9th century, had "several thousand (?) Jewish families who were well off." [570] And more to the same effect.[571]

There is no need to labour the statement that in the later Middle Ages the Jews were wealthy. It is a generally accepted fact.[572] And for what is called the modern period I have myself adduced proofs enough in this book.

We shall be justified in the conclusion, therefore, that from King Solomon to Barney Barnato Jewish opulence runs through history like a golden thread, without ever once snapping. Is this merely accidental? If not, what was it due to—subjective or objective causes?

Objective factors, *i.e.*, outward forces, have certainly been hinted at to explain Jewish wealth. In the first place, the Jews were early taught to look for their chief happiness in the possession of money; in the second, the insecurity of their position forced them to accumulate their wealth in easily movable forms—in gold or ornaments, which they could take about with them, which they could hide or carry off without much difficulty. These causes undoubtedly go a good way to account for the growth of Jewish wealth, but they by no means suffice to explain it completely. We must not forget that the outward forces referred to above, in order to produce the result they did, could not but have influenced a people possessing certain special gifts. But let that pass. Again, the facts instanced could only have been of any effect in the Diaspora. Let that also pass. The great weakness of this explanation is that it tells us merely why the Jews had any desire to become wealthy, and, incidentally, that their wealth took a particular form. The desire in this case is of little moment; it does not make clear why it was realized. Hence we must look for other causes. Besides, the desire to become rich has been universal ever since Alberich robbed the Maidens of the Rhine-gold.

Another explanation has therefore been suggested for Jewish wealth. The Jews, it has been rightly pointed out, for centuries occupied a position of inequality with their Christian neighbours, and therefore had less occasion to spend as much as the latter. The conception of social status, with varying standards of comfort for each, was unknown among them, and therefore also the thousand and one artificial wants that were associated with the idea. " It is certain," remarks a writer who has dealt with this aspect of the problem in a most delicate fashion,573 " that a Jew, compared with a Christian of the same income, was bound to become the richer of the two, seeing that the Christian had very many opportunities of spending money which were denied to the Jew, for the simple reason that the former belonged to the ruling class, and the latter was only tolerated. As for the rich Jew, his circumstances were different from those of the Christian, for he had no need to consider what was demanded in his social class. Thus, any luxuries he cared to enjoy were not necessarily in accordance with his status."

Doubtless this is one explanation of the wealth of the Jews, and will account also for the specifically Jewish economic standpoint, which we have noted above. To it were due such ideas as that of free competition, that your expenses should be limited by your income—a conception utterly foreign to a feudal society—and that saving, associated with Jews from earliest times, was good. Let me recall an old German proverb:—

" Selten sind sieben Dinge :
Eine Nonne, die nicht singe,
Ein Mädchen ohne Liebe,
Ein Jahrmarkt ohne Diebe,

Ein Geissbock ohne Bart,
Ein Jude der nicht spart,
Ein Kornhaus ohne Mäuse,
Und ein Kosak ohne Läuse."

[" Rare are seven things :
A nun who never sings,
A maid without a lover,
A fair without a robber,
A goat of beard bereft,
A Jew that knows no thrift,
A granary without mice,
And a Cossack without lice."]

To the saving habit of the Jews may be traced the tendency to accumulate capital. One sometimes hears it said that Jewish money remains in a business longer than Christian money, and increases more quickly to boot. In olden times the Jew could not enter the charmed circle of the feudal landed gentry, and so his money was not spent in keeping up the appearances demanded by his status. If he saved, his money had perforce to be invested in commercial enterprise, unless, of course, he lent it out directly at interest, as the Jews of Hamburg of the 17th century were in the habit of doing. Glückel von Hameln and her friends, whenever they had any surplus, always lent it out on security. The money fructified and increased.

All these considerations are valuable as far as they go. But they do not go far enough satisfactorily to explain the phenomenon of Jewish wealth. It is all very well pointing to objective forces in any problem. We must not forget, however, that those forces might not effect the particular result they did if the men and women whom they influenced were not constituted in a particular way. A people does not become thrifty because of the stress of outward circumstances alone.

The merest tyro knows that. Besides, nowadays, when the Ghetto walls have long since fallen, and the Jew enjoys perfect equality ; when he may become a landed proprietor and regulate his life in accordance with the most rigid requirements—nowadays, too, I say, Jews are thriftier than Christians. Look at a few statistics. In Baden, in the years 1895 to 1903, capital increased in the case of Protestants from 100 to 128·3 per cent., in the case of Jews from 100 to 138·2 per cent. This is striking enough, but it becomes even more so when we remember that during the same period the incomes of Protestants grew from 100 to 146·6 per cent., those of Jews from 100 to 144·5 per cent.

When all is said the possible causes hitherto mentioned would only explain why already existing wealth was increased. Not one can satisfactorily answer the question, How was it in the first place obtained ? There is only one answer. Wealth is got by those who have a talent for it. From the wealth of the Jews, therefore, may be deduced special Jewish characteristics or attributes.

IV. Is the Jewish Genius Natural or Artificial ?

What is the result of all our considerations in the previous section ? That in all probability the anthropological character of the Jews, no less than their intellectual attributes, has remained constant for thousands of years.

What does this prove ? Are we to conclude that the Jewish genius is rooted in race ? Those who have a dogmatic faith in race unhesitatingly say yes. We, however, who are trying to proceed scientifically, must say no. Nothing as yet has been proved.

A brief reference to the methods of some of the believers in the race-theory 574-585 will show how unreliable their conclusions are. They start out with the assumption that the Jews are a race. Since every race must have specific characteristics, Jews have theirs. In other words, their specific characteristics are rooted in their race. But for this there is no actual proof. If the truth must be told, we know nothing whatever of the connexion between somatic or anthropological features and intellectual capacities.

What the race-theorists have produced is a new sort of religion to replace the old Jewish or Christian religion. What else is the theory of an Aryan, or German, " mission " in the world but a modern form of the "chosen people" belief? All well and good, but let no one be deceived into imagining that this is science. It is faith, and faith and science had best be kept apart.

As we have said, there is no certain connexion between somatic attributes and intellectual capacities. The constancy of each may be purely accidental; it may arise anew in every generation or may be carried on by the aid of tradition. And among a people who were attached to tradition as the Jews were, this assumption seems likely enough. The Jews were shut off from others, they possessed a strong love of family, their religious practices were scrupulously observed, the Talmud was energetically studied in every generation—all these supplied, as it were, the machinery for carrying on certain peculiarities from one generation to another merely by education alone.

This is one view. Yet Jewish characteristics *may* spring from the blood. Again, there are those who would trace them to environment. The Jewish religion, Ghetto life, the dealing in money for so many centuries have all three been instanced to account for the specifically Jewish type of character. There may be something in this. Only possibly, as I have tried to show, these influences instead of being causes may be results.

I propose in the next chapter to analyse the Jewish genius, laying special stress on the following points in the order given : (1) The original aptitudes of those races from which the Jews sprang as exhibited in their mode of life. (2) How the various elements mingled. (3) Which of these aptitudes survived under the influences of Jewish history. Finally, if these considerations should prove insufficient, we shall venture the hypothesis : (4) that certain characteristics grew up in the course of history. We shall see, however, that there will be no need to have recourse to this hypothesis, since the Jewish genius can be adequately explained along the first three lines. If this be so, then one result will have been established : that the Jewish characteristics are rooted in the blood of the race, and are not in any wise due to educative processes.

CHAPTER XIV

THE VICISSITUDES OF THE JEWISH PEOPLE

IF any one wished in a sentence to account for the importance of the Jews in the world's civilization, and more particularly in economic life, he could do so by saying that it was due to the transplanting of an Oriental people among Northern races, and the culture union of the two. A similar assertion has been made regarding the civilizations of the classical world, of the Greek more especially, and also of that of the Italian Renaissance. It has been suggested that they resulted from the mixture of Northern peoples, who had wandered into a Southern environment, with the autochthonous inhabitants—a brilliant hypothesis, not without an element of truth in it.

But the statement concerning the Jews is no hypothesis: it is an established fact, capable of abundant proof. The capitalistic civilization of our age is the fruit of the union between the Jews, a Southern people pushing into the North, and the Northern tribes, indigenous there. The Jews contributed an extraordinary capacity for commerce, and the Northern peoples, above all the Germans, an equally remarkable ability for technical inventions.

It is clear, therefore, what we must have in view in our considerations of the Jewish genius and its enormous influence. Not whether the Jews were Semites, or Hittites, or of some other stock, not whether they are " pure," or " mixed," is the important thing, but that

they are an Oriental folk transplanted into an environment both climatically and ethnically strange, wherein
their best powers come to fruition.

They are an Oriental people—that is to say, one of
those peoples whose habitat was in that part of the globe
lying between the Atlas Mountains in the West, and the
Persian Gulf in the East ; one of those races baked by
the sun in the dry, burning climate of the great
deserts of North Africa, Arabia and Asia Minor, or of
their border-lands ; the races which brought their special
characteristics to maturity amid their peculiar environment which had never altered since the Ice Age, a period
of some twelve or sixteen thousand years.

The whole of this region, from which the Jews also
hailed, is an extensive sandy desert, with here and there
an oasis where man and beast can dwell. In the larger
of these watered valleys arose, as is well known, the
earliest civilizations of the world—in Egypt, in Mesopotamia and in Palestine. All three are comparatively
small fertile patches ; all are true oases in the desert,
and theirs was an essentially oasis civilization. The cultiv-
able area of Egypt was about as large as the Prussian
Province of Saxony is to-day [about 5,500,000 acres,
according to the *Statesman's Year Book*] ; Mesopotamia
at its widest extent was only about half the size of
the Plain of Lombardy [about 4500 square miles,
according to the same authority] ; Palestine, the land
of the whole people of Israel, was smaller still, being
no larger than perhaps Baden [about 5000 square miles];
while Judæa, the Southern Kingdom, and therefore the
home of the Jews, was as extensive as the Duchies of
Anhalt and Saxe-Coburg and Gotha together [about
1600 square miles]. But these oases, and Palestine more
especially, were themselves broken by deserts, Judæa being
particularly badly treated by Nature. Its southern end

extended past Hebron and Beersheba, right into the modern sandy waste.

All agriculture in these countries was the tillage of oases. What does this mean? It means that the soil collected by almost artificial means, and that the great aim of the farmer was to gather the water necessary for the growth of vegetation. This was the case in Palestine, where the cultivation of the soil depended on the water-supply. Drought is the scourge that the farmer fears most. Every year he trembles lest the arid waste should stretch its arms and embrace his strip of land, tended with so much care and tribulation. Every moment he is in dread lest the desert send him its scorching winds, or its locust-swarms. And above all, he fears the desert wastes because of the marauding bands who may fall upon him, robbing, killing, pillaging as they cross the country, sometimes even taking possession of his holding if the fancy seize them. These children of the desert, whom we now call Bedouins, and of whom the oasis-dwellers were once themselves a part, were nomadic shepherds. Their raids hastened the rise of strong cities with stout walls, behind which the inhabitants of the plain could take refuge. Sometimes the desert crept right into them, and so at all times they were filled with the spirit of the sandy wastes.

Such a tribe of restless wandering Bedouins were the Hebrews, when about the year 1200 B.C. they fell upon Canaan, plundering and killing as they went, and finally deciding to settle there, and rest from all their wanderings. Which meant, that if possible they would do nothing, but that the natives would work for them —the aim of every conquering people. Such was Jehovah's promise : " I will lead you unto the land which I promised you, a land of great and goodly cities which thou buildedst not, and houses full of all good things which thou filledst not, and cisterns hewn out which thou hewedst not, and vineyards and olive-trees which thou plantedst not, and thou shalt eat and be full " (Deut. vi. 10, 11).

Once there, what did the Hebrews do in this promised land ? What sort of economic organization did they establish ? We cannot, of course, speak as to the details,[586] but one or two things we may imagine. Probably, as we have seen, the powerful and mighty among them after having conquered large tracts of land instituted a sort of feudal society. Part of the produce of the land they took for themselves, either by way of rent in kind, by farming it out to tax-collectors, or by means of the credit nexus. In any case, a large number of Hebrews lived in the towns, receiving rent or interest from the subject population who worked on the soil, either as "colonists," or "free peasants," or whatever term was used in the Orient for this class. Some of the conquering tribes may have become impoverished and themselves sunk to the level of unfree farmers, but they were hardly the influential ones. This position was held by those who inhabited the West Jordan lands, principally Judah, sections of Simeon and Levi and others. In those districts cattle farming only was possible : " Judah's teeth are white with milk." Other tribes, such as Reuben and Gad, remained east of the Jordan as semi-nomads, rearing cattle, and half the tribe of Manasseh crossed the Jordan to return thither. But all the tribes alike must have been impregnated with the nomadic spirit. Were this not the case, it would be exceedingly difficult to understand the rise and growth of the Jewish religious system.

It should not be forgotten that the Holy Scriptures of the Jews in which their religion is embodied, especially the Pentateuch, is the literature of a nomadic people. Their God, who triumphs over the false gods, is a desert and pastoral divinity. The traditions of the nomad state were maintained by Ezra and Nehemiah in the conscious re-establishment of the Jehovah cult, in doing which they paid no heed to the intervening period of agriculture. The Priestly Code "takes care not to mention the settled life in Canaan. . . it strictly limits itself to the wanderings in the wilderness, and in all seriousness wants to be regarded as a desert Code." [587] Open the historical books or the majority of the Prophets, that desert choir, include the Psalms also, and you everywhere find metaphors and similes taken from shepherd life. Only occasionally do you meet with the peasant " sitting contentedly at the door of his house in the shade of the fig-tree." Jehovah is the good Shepherd (Psa. 23) who will gather the remnants of Israel "as a flock in the midst of their pasture" (Micah ii. 12). And what does the Sabbatical year mean but that you cease being a peasant for the time being, and become an Israelite of the old sort? Israel never quite gave up its division into families and clans ; it was always composed of tribes, like most shepherd peoples. There seems to be little doubt that even as late as the 5th century B.C. there must have been a strong dash of the nomads, certainly in the ruling classes, but probably also in the great mass of the people. Else how would it have been possible to saddle them for any length of time with a nomadic religion ?

It may be asked, Were not the nomad tendencies of those days perchance a harking back to an earlier state ? Did not perhaps the old wandering instincts, which in the previous centuries had been lulled to sleep, awake again under the influences of the Exile ? It is quite likely, and what is more, the vicissitudes of the Jewish people since the Babylonian Exile could not but arouse any slumbering desert and nomad feelings within them. On this point I would lay especial stress. Hence, even if we were inclined to assume that the Children of Israel lived a settled life for five hundred years after the conquest of Canaan, it is perfectly clear that all the powers on earth seemed to have conspired together not to allow this state to become permanent. Scarcely had the plant taken root (so far as it could in so hot a country) than it was pulled up. The Jew's inherent " Nomadism " or " Saharaism " (if I may coin the words) was always kept alive through selection or adaptation. Throughout the centuries, therefore, Israel has remained a desert and nomadic people.

There is nothing new in this conclusion. But one does not establish it without some scruple of conscience. Why ? Because anti-Semitic pamphleteers rudely pounce upon it and make capital out of it for their abuse. That, of course, can be no reason for doubting its truth, or neglecting to take cognizance of it as an explanation of Jewish characteristics. What should be done to oppose the prejudiced scribblers is to analyse the problem most carefully, and present an illuminating view of its importance. Up to the present little has been achieved in this direction ; what has been done has been childish and spitefully distorted. No wonder that the idea that the Jew has always been a nomad has been received with scorn and jest by some people. It would have been much more to the point if these same people had been able to prove that it was wrong. This has never yet been seriously attempted. The chain of reasoning which runs : Agriculture was practised in Palestine in olden times ; the Jews lived in Palestine then ; therefore the Jews were agriculturists, is on the face of it a little weak. And another point. The term nomad is not meant to imply obloquy or disgrace. At most, objection may be taken to the robbing. But why should there be any dishonour attached to a brave Bedouin tribe which, under such a doughty leader as, say, King David, lived on plunder? Why should they appear less worthy, or call forth less sympathy, than an agricultural tribe of negroes somewhere in the wilds of Africa? It is obvious, of course, that when I use the term "nomad" as applied to later Jewish history, I want it to bear not its secondary meaning, which it has acquired in the lapse of time, but its original connotation in all its pristine strength.

Having cleared the air a little, let us now attempt to prove that our conclusion is true. Throughout the centuries Israel has remained a desert and nomadic people, either by the process of selection or of adaptation.

We have already mentioned the possible effect of the Exile in calling forth slumbering nomadic instincts. In reality, if the truth be told, we can form no clear conception of what the Exile meant, neither of the journey into it, nor of the return home. It only seems possible on the assumption that the Jews then were still nomads or semi-nomads. One can scarcely conceive the conquest of an agricultural people; whereas the forcible transplanting of nomad tribes is not unknown to-day.[588] Moreover, the assumption seems to be supported by the story of the Captivity. "And he carried away all Jerusalem and all the princes and all the mighty men of valour, even ten thousand captives, and all the craftsmen and the smiths; none remained save the poorest sort of the people of the land." And after the second expedition of the Babylonians, "the captain of the guard left of the poorest of the land to be vine-dressers and husbandmen" (2 Kings xxiv.

14 and xxv. 12). Jeremiah's version of the story agrees with this (Jer. xxxix. 10).

Whoever the exiles may have been, it is pretty certain that the actual agriculturists were not among them. These remained behind even after the second batch of exiles had been carried away captive. The passage in Jeremiah would seem to lend probability to my view that the soil was tilled by unfree villeins who, when their lords were led to Babylon, became independent husbandmen. It is not assuming too much to regard these men as the descendants of the original inhabitants whom the Hebrews had conquered. From the age of the Captivity, therefore, the population of Judæa had a thinner stream of Jewish blood in their veins than the Babylonian exiles, who were more or less the Jewish aristocracy, the cream of the people, as it were. This was indeed the view that obtained currency in later times. Even in Judæa itself it was admitted that the Babylonian Jews were of the very best stock, and an old Jewish saying helped to confirm the belief. " The Jews in the Roman Diaspora compared as to their descent with those in Judæa are like the mixed dough to the pure flour, but Judæa itself is only dough compared with Babylon." [589] And R. Ezekiel (220–299) excuses that good man, Ezra, for having returned to Palestine by saying that he took the families of doubtful origin away with him, and so left those that remained free from the danger of mixing with them (!). [590]

We come then to this conclusion. The Exile was a kind of selective process whereby the best elements of Jewry, never favourable to an economy of settled life, were forced to revive the inherent nomad instincts within them, and to gain their livelihood as townsmen, *i.e.*, traders. This does not mean that none of them became husbandmen. Far from it. The Babylonian

Talmud certainly makes it appear that some devoted themselves to agriculture, but the conditions must have been those prevalent in Palestine, where an aristocracy of wealth lived in the towns on the work of (non-Jewish?) peasants. Such at any rate is the impression of the typical state of affairs. But there were exceptions too. Do we not read of many an ancient Rabbi who himself walked behind the plough? What is of consequence, however, is that the prevailing conditions in the Exile were by no means exceptional. On the contrary, they were normal. Even before the Exile many Jews had settled in Egypt and other lands in a kind of voluntary Diaspora. Those who left Palestine were no doubt the men in whom the old nomadic instincts were not yet quite dead, and their self-imposed exile only called them forth the more. We never find these wandering Jews, be their origin Judæa or Palestine, establishing agricultural colonies or independent settlements of any sort, as most other emigrants did. But what do we find? That Jewish settlers scattered themselves in all corners of the inhabited globe among foreign nations, preferably in the large towns, where they sought their livelihood.591 We never hear of their return to their native hearth after having saved up sufficient money to keep them in affluence, as the Swiss, Hungarian or Italian emigrants do to-day. The only bonds that bound them with home were religious. If they ever do go back, it is only at the annual Passover pilgrimage, like real nomads that they are.

Little by little Palestine ceased to be the centre of Jewish life, and Jews became more and more scattered. Even as late as the destruction of the Second Temple (70 A.D.), the Jews in the Diaspora outnumbered those in Judæa. Perhaps there was some reason for this. That the country, even when it was most densely populated, could maintain more than a million, or a million and a half souls is scarcely likely. (To-day the inhabitants number at most 650,000.) As for Judæa, it had no more than 225,000 inhabitants, and Jerusalem no more than 25,000.592 There certainly was a larger number outside Palestine already at the commencement of the Common Era. In the Egypt of the Ptolemies it is said that out of a total population of seven or eight millions, one million were Jews.593 Nor was Egypt unique in this respect. It would have been difficult indeed to name one spot which, in the words of Strabo quoted by Josephus, was not inhabited and dominated (!) by Jews. Philo gives a list of countries that had a Jewish population in his day, and adds that they were settled in numerous cities of Europe, Asia, Lybia, on the mainland and on islands, on the coast and inland. We hear the same thing from a Sibylline Oracle, composed towards the end of the 2nd century, 594 while Jerome informs us that they were to be found "from sea to sea, from the British to the Atlantic Oceans, from the West to the South, from the North to the East, the world through." 595 How densely packed they were in the Rome of the early Empire may be gathered from the account of the visit of King Herod to the capital of the Cæsars, wherein we are told that no less than 8000 Jews resident in Rome accompanied him to Augustus. Again, in the year 19 A.D., 4000 freedmen of military age who "professed the Egyptian and Jewish superstition" were sentenced to be deported to Sardinia.596

But enough. No matter how many Jews were in the Diaspora in the pre-Christian age, so much is certain, that when the Second Temple fell, Israel was already scattered over the face of the earth.597 Nor did the ant-heap become quiescent in the Middle Ages ;

for Jewish wanderings continued apace. That, too, is certain.

What direction did the wanderings take ? About the end of the 5th century Babylon was emptied, at first slowly and then with speed, the Jews migrating to all points of the globe—to Arabia, India and Europe. Again in the 13th century streams of emigrants from England, France and Germany journeyed partly to the Pyrenean Peninsula, where there was already a large number of Jews from Palestine and Babylon, and partly to the kingdoms of Eastern Europe, which were likewise not without their Jewish inhabitants, who had settled there as far back as the 8th century, having arrived from the Byzantine Empire *via* the Black Sea. Then, towards the end of the Middle Ages, Spain and Portugal on the one hand and Russia and Poland on the other were the two great basins outside the Orient wherein the Jews had settled. From each of these the wandering commenced afresh ; we have already seen what course it took. The Spanish Jews first, then, after the Cossack pogroms in the 17th century, the Russian Jews began to disperse over the earth. This process of emigration from Russia and Poland was a steady one, until towards the end of the 19th century there was a volcanic eruption and hundreds of thousands sought a refuge in the New World.598

So this people was driven from place to place—tribe of the wandering foot whose fate has been so touchingly expressed in the legend of the Wandering Jew.599 The constant insecurity of their position made it impossible for them to think of settling down on the soil. As a matter of fact, however, they seldom had any inclination that way. All that we know of Jewish life in the Diaspora points to the conclusion that only an insignificant number of Jews devoted themselves to agriculture even in those lands where no difficulties were placed in their path. Perhaps Poland in the 16th century is the best instance. There they appear to have taken up farming. But even in Poland they showed a preference for city life. For every 500 Christian merchants in the Polish towns of the period there were to be found 3200 Jewish merchants.[600]

Yes, they became town-dwellers—whether voluntarily or by stress of circumstance is of no consequence—and town-dwellers they have remained. More than half the Jews of the world to-day are to be found in cities with over 50,000 inhabitants. In Germany this applies to about 43.6 per cent. of the Jews (1900), in Italy, Switzerland, Holland and Denmark to about four-fifths, and to all the Jews of England and the United States.

Now the modern city is nothing else but a great desert, as far removed from the warm earth as the desert is, and like it forcing its inhabitants to become nomads. The old nomadic instincts have thus through the centuries been called forth in the Jew by the process of adapting himself to his environment, while the principle of selection has only tended to strengthen those instincts. It is clear that in the constant changes to which the Jews were subjected, not those among them that had an inclination to the comfortable, settled life of the farmer were the ones likely to survive, but rather those in whom the nomadic instincts were strong.

This hot-blooded, restless people that had wandered not forty, but four thousand years in the wilderness came at last to its Canaan, to its promised land, where it should be able to repose from all its travels—it came to the Northern countries, meeting nations there who, while the Jews were hurrying from one oasis to another, had dwelt on their soil and smelt of the earth, who differed from the Jews as a horse of the Ardennes differs from a fiery Arab charger.

It will soon be of little moment whether the nations of Northern, Central and Eastern Europe are called Aryans or by some other name. The latest researches, it is true, would make it appear that most of them were indeed Aryans.[601] But the name tells us nothing. What is of importance is that they were all peoples from the cold North, and never able to acclimatize themselves in the warm lands of the South.[602] To consider them as Aryans is misleading. For then we shall have to include the dark Indian too, and obviously the fair, blue-eyed Europeans have little in common with him, except perhaps their language. In other respects they have peculiarities all their own. What these are may easily be seen by looking at those peoples as they are to-day, and if we had to characterize them in one word which should be in contrast to desert it would be forest. Forest and desert are indeed the two great opposites which sum up differences in countries and their inhabitants. Forests are of the North—those Northern forests with the murmur of their brooks, where the mist clings fast to the tree-trunks and the toads have their habitation " in the dank moss and the wet stones," where in winter the faint sunlight glistens on the rime and in summer the song of birds is everywhere. To be sure, there were forests on Lebanon's height, as there are forests to-day in the South of Italy. But who that has set foot in a Southern forest will not at once perceive that it has small affinity with the forests of the North, will not at once realize that " even in Italy the forest tells the heart and the eye something very different from the Alpine forest, or that on the Baltic shore ? The South Italian forest is full of harmonies, permeated with clear light and ineffable blue, pliant and yet vigorous in its aiming skyward and in its bending before the moaning wind ; it seems a sacred grove " (Hehn). But our Northern forests—they have a charm and a mystery about them at once intimate and fearful. Desert and forest, sand and marsh—those are the great opposites, depending in the long run on differences in the moisture of the air, and so creating dissimilar environments for the activities of man. In the one case the Fata Morgana is Nature's symbol, in the other the cloud of mist.

In olden times the characteristics of the Northern climes were even more strongly marked than to-day. The Romans' picture of Germany shows us a rude land, covered with bogs and dense forests, a land of leaden skies, with a misty and moist atmosphere, whose winters are long and wildly stormy. For thousands of years peoples and races (our ancestors) dwelt in the damp woods, the bogs, the mists, the ice and the snow and the rain. They hewed down the woods, made the land habitable and pitched their tents where axe and plough had gained for them a strip of the wilds. From the very first they seemed to be rooted in the soil ; from the very first it would seem that tillage was never quite absent. But even if we try to imagine these Northern folk as " nomads," theirs is a very different kind of life from that of a Bedouin tribe. We feel that they are more tied to the hearth than even an agricultural people in an oasis-land. The Northerners are settlers even when they only breed cattle ; the Bedouins are always nomads, even though they till the soil.

This is so because man is brought into closer touch with Nature in the North than in the hot countries. Man is part and parcel of Nature even if he only beats the woods as a huntsman, or as a shepherd breaks a path through the thickets for his flocks. I am inclined to say, even at the risk of being ridiculed as a modern mystic, that in the North there are between Nature and even the most prosaic of men tender bonds of love and friendship, unknown to the Southerner. In the South, as has been rightly observed, man regards Nature only as an instrument in the work of civilization. Even when he is a tiller of the soil, he is a stranger to Nature. In the South there is no country life, no living in and with Nature, no attachment to bush and tree, heath and meadow, wild creature and free bird.

Is it not clear that these varying and varied environments must produce different results, must influence men in different ways? Would it be too much to assume that the Jewish characteristics as we have seen them have been affected by, nay, have even received their peculiar impress from the thousands of years of wandering in the wilderness? The answer of course is yes, and if in the following pages I try to prove it, I must nevertheless admit that the present state of our knowledge of biology is inadequate to show *how* environment has bearing on the anatomical and physiological character of man, and therefore also on his psychical disposition. The direction which our inquiries under this head should take has been laid down by Juan Huarte de San Juan, that wise old 16th-century Spanish physician whom I have already mentioned, in his splendid book, *Examen de ingenios*, in which he makes a serious attempt (the first of its kind) to give a biological and psychological explanation of Jewish characteristics by referring to the vicissitudes of the Jewish people. The ideas of this profound thinker, who treated of some of the problems of human selection in a manner which for that period was certainly remarkable, appear to me to be worth saving from an undeserved oblivion, and I shall here give them in outline.[603]

Huarte mentions four causes which contributed to make

the Jews what they are : (1) A hot climate. (2) An unfruitful soil. (3) The peculiar food of the people during their forty years' wandering in the wilderness : they subsisted on Manna ; the water they drank was exceedingly pure, and the air they breathed very rare. In such circumstances there was a tendency (as Aristotle had already pointed out) for children to be born who were keen of intellect (*hombre de muy agudo ingenio*). (4) " When the Children of Israel entered into possession of the Promised Land they were faced with so many difficulties, scarcity, hostile raids, conquests and tribulations of all sorts, that the misery of it had the effect of adding to their intellectual genius a fiery, dry and parched temperament. . . . Continual melancholy and a never-ending wretchedness together resulted in collecting the blood in the brain, the liver and the heart, and a process of blood consuming and burning ensued. . . . This produced much burnt black gall (*melancolia por adustion*). Of this almost all the Jews still have a great deal and it results . . . in craft, cunning and spite (*solercia, astucia, versacia, malicia*)." The author then proceeds to answer the objection, that in the three thousand years since their feeding on Manna the Jews very probably lost the characteristics they then acquired, by saying that once certain tendencies enter into the system they become second nature and are passed on for many generations. He is ready to admit, however, that possibly the Jews are not quite as sagacious as they used to be.

Into the depths to which the Madrid physician descends I cannot take the reader. We should not find anything but unproved theories there. We shall therefore remain above ground and content ourselves with noting the connexion between Jewish psychological qualities and the vicissitudes of the Jewish people.

143. A. Levy, "Notes sur l'histoire des Juifs en Saxe," in *R.E.J.*, vol. 26 (1898), p. 259. For Berend (Behrend) Lehmann, *alias* Jisachar Berman, see B. H. Auerbach, *Geschichte der israelitischen Gemeinde Halberstadt* (1866), p. 43; for his son Lehmann Berend, see p. 85.

144. Auerbach, *loc. cit.*, p. 82 (for Hanover); see also S. Haenle [note 123], pp. 64, 70, 89; for more cases of Hofjuden, see L. Müller, "Aus fünf Jahrhunderten," in the *Zeitschrift des historischen Vereins für Schwaben und Neuburg*, vol. 26 (1899), p. 142.

145. F. von Mensi, p. 409.

146. *Memoiren der Glückel von Hameln* [published in the original Yiddish by D. Kaufmann (1896)], German translation (privately printed) in 1910, p. 240.

147. M. Zimmermann, *Josef Süss Oppenheimer, ein Finanzmann des 18ᵗᵉⁿ Jahrhunderts* (1874).

148. Address by Louis Marshall in *The 250th Anniversary of the Settlement of the Jews in the U.S.*, p. 102.

149. H. Friedenwald [note 127], p. 63.

150. W. Graham Sumner, *The Financiers and the Finances of the American Revolution*, 2 vols. (1891).

CHAPTER VI

151. For a legal consideration of the question, see Brunner, *Endemanns Handbuch*, vol. 2, p. 147, and Goldschmidt, *Universalgeschichte des Handelsrechts* (1891), p. 386. Cf. also Knies, *Der Credit* (1876), p. 190.

152. I give the "credit relationship" its most extended meaning in the sense that you create duties between persons by the one giving an economic value to the other and the second promising a *quid pro quo* in the future.

153. Cf. F. A. Biener, *Wechselrechtliche Abhandlungen* (1859), p. 145.

154. The view of Kuntze and others. See Goldschmidt [note 151], p. 408.

155. Goldschmidt, *loc. cit.*, p. 410, who puts the question in the form of a query, leaving the answer vague. See on the other hand A. Wahl, *Traité théor. et pratique des titres au porteur* (1891), vol. 1, p. 15.

156. Cf. Kuntze, "Zur Geschichte der Staatspapiere auf den Inhaber," in the *Zeitschrift für das ges. Handelsrecht*, vol. 5, p. 198 ; the same writer's *Inhaber Papiere* (1857), pp. 58, 63 ; Goldschmidt [note 151], pp. 448–9 ; Sieveking in *Schmollers Jahrbuch* (1902) ; and above all, G. Schaps, *Zur Geschichte des Wechselindossaments* (1892), p. 86. Cf. also Biener [note 153], pp. 121, 137.

157. Goldschmidt, p. 452 ; Schaps, p. 92.

158. The text is given in D. Kaufmann's article in the *J.Q.R.*, vol. 13 (1901), p. 320, "Die Vertreibung der Marranen aus Venedig im Jahre 1550."

159. Graetz, vol. 8, p. 354 ; vol. 9, p. 328.

160. So far as I am aware, this question has never yet been asked : What part did the Jews play in the Genoese fairs ? It will be most difficult to give a satisfactory answer, because the Jews in Genoa were forced, especially after the Edict of Expulsion in 1550, to keep secret their identity. Probably also they changed their names and made a pretence of accepting Christianity. Nevertheless, it would be worth while to make the attempt. Anyhow, we have here one instance where in the post-mediæval period a great financial and credit system was developed without the clear proof of Jewish influence. It may be, of course, that the proof has slipped my observation ; in that case I should be glad to have my attention drawn to it.

The best account of the Genoese fairs will be found in Ehrenberg's *Zeitalter der Fugger*, vol. 2, p. 222, and Endemann, *Studien in der römisch-kanonischen Wirtschafts- und Rechtslehre*, vol. 1 (1874), p. 156. Endemann bases his conclusions chiefly on Scaccia and R. de Turris, while Ehrenberg also relied on documents in the Fugger archives.

161. Possibly earlier, in the case of the Company of the Pairiers, to whom was transferred in the 12th century the mill in Toulouse, du Basacle, by means of securities (*uchaux* or *saches*). Cf. Edmund Guillard, *Les opérations de Bourse* (1875), p. 15.

162. Cf. K. Lehmann, *Die geschichtliche Entwickelung des Aktienrechts* (1895).

163. J. P. Ricard, *Le Négoce d'Amsterdam* (1723), pp. 397–400.

164. This is the conclusion arrived at by André E. Sayous, " Le fractionnement du capital social de la Compagnie néerland

des Indes orientales," in *Nouv. Rev. Historique du droit franç. et étrangers*, vol. 25 (1901), pp. 621, 625.

165. Cf. Endemann, *Studien* [note 160], vol. 1, p. 457.

166. See instances—1422 in Palermo and 1606 in Bologna—in Goldschmidt, p. 322.

167. The most important collection of documents concerning the history of banking in Venice is still Elia Lattes' *La libertà delle banche e Venezia dal secolo xiii al xvii secondo i documenti inediti del R. Archivio dei Frari ec.* (1869). The subject has been dealt with by Ferrara, "Gli antichi banchi di Venezia" in *Nuova Antologia*, vol. xvi. ; E. Nasse, "Das venetianische Bankwesen in 14, 15, und 16 Jahrhundert," in the *Jahrbuch für Nationalökonomie*, vol. 34, pp. 329, 338. To show the share of the Jews in Venetian banking would be a welcome piece of work. But it would be most difficult of accomplishment because, so far as I can judge, the Jews in Venice already in the 15th century were the most part New Christians, often holding high offices and having Christian names.

168. Macleod, *Dictionary of Political Economy*, art. "Bank of Venice" (? authorities), quoted by A. Andréades, *History of the Bank of England* (1909), p. 28.

169. "Gallicioli Memorie Venete," ii., No. 874, in Graetz, vol. 6, p. 284.

170. S. Luzzato, *Dis. circa il stato degli Hebrei in Venezia* (1638), ch. 1, and pp. 9*a*, 29*a*. The figures need not be taken too seriously ; they are only an estimate.

171. See, for instance, D. Manuel Calmeiro, *Historia de la economia politica en España*, vol. 1, p. 411 ; vol. 2, p. 497.

171A. See A. Andréades, *History of the Bank of England* (1909), p. 28. That will certainly have to be the conclusion if importance is attached to the scheme (1658) of Samuel Lambe (printed in *Somer's Tracts*, vol. vi). Andréades actually dates the first idea of the Bank from Lambe's scheme. There was a scheme previous to that—Balthasar Gerbier's in 1651, and between that year and 1658 Cromwell had allowed the Jews to settle in this country. For my own part I cannot admit "the superiority" of Lambe's scheme. But other writers also lay stress on the very great share of the Jews in the establishment of the Bank of England.

172. Cf. F. von Mensi [note 125], p. 34.

173. Ad. Beer, *Das Staatsschuldenwesen und die Ordnung de Staatshaushalts unter Maria Theresia* (1894), p. 13.

174. For instances of public debt bonds, see Walter Däbritz, *Die Staatsschulden Sachsens in der Zeit von* 1763 *bis* 1837, Doctoral Dissertation (1906), pp. 14, 55.

175. Also, E. von Philippovich, *Die Bank von England* (1885), p. 26.

176. Also, Ehrenberg, *Fugger* [note 160], vol. 2, pp. 141, 299.

176A. Witness a pamphlet little known generally (even Däbritz [note 174] has overlooked it), to which I should like to call attention. It has a very long title : "Ephraim justifié. Mémoire historique et raisonné sur l'Etat passé, présent et futur des finances de Saxe.   Avec le parallèle de l'Oeconomie prussienne et de l'Oeconomie saxonne.   Ouvrage utile aux Créanciers et Correspondans, aux Amis et aux Ennemis de la Prusse et de la Saxe. Adressé par le Juif Ephraim de Berlin à son Cousin Manassés d'Amsterdam.   Erlangen.   A l'enseigne de 'Tout est dit.'" 1785.

177. Cf. (Luzac) *Richesse de la Hollande*, vol. 2 (1778), p. 200. Also vol. 1, p. 366.   Luzac, besides his own personal experiences, must have also used Fermin, *Tableau de Surinam* (1778).

178. Chief among them Kuntze, *Die Lehre von den Inhaberpapieren* (1857), p. 48, which is still unsurpassed.   We may mention besides, Albert Wahl, *Traité théorique et pratique des titres au porteur français et étrangers*, 2 vols. (1891).

179–180. The best history of mediæval credit instruments is that of H. Brunner, *Das französische Inhaberpapier* (1879).   Cf. also his "Zur Geschichte des Inhaberpapiers in Deutschland," in the *Zeitschrift für das gesammte Handelsrecht*, vols. 21 and 23.

181. For Holland, see F. Hecht, *Geschichte der Inhaberpapier in den Niederlanden* (1869), p. 4.

182. By the way, it is interesting to note that credit instruments have been said to be of Hellenic origin.   Cf. Goldschmidt, "Inhaber- Order- und exekutorische Urkunden im Klassischen Altertum," in *Zeitschrift für Rechtsgeschichte Roms*, vol. 10 (1889), p. 352.

183. But Goldschmidt's view is not generally accepted.   Cf. Benedict Frese, *Aus dem gräko-ägyptischen Rechtsleben* (1909), p. 26.

184. Another criticism of Goldschmidt's theory may be found in H. Brunner, "Forschungen zur Geschichte des deutschen und französischen Rechts," in his *Gesammelte Aufsätze* (1894), p. 604.

185. Brunner also deals with the same problem in his *Französische Inhaberpapier*, pp. 28, 57.

186. Made casually by Kuntze, but rejected by Goldschmidt in the *Zeitschrift für Rechtsgeschichte*, vol. 10, p. 355.

187. Also rejected by Salvioli, *I titoli al portatore nella storia del diritto italiano* (1883).

188. Cf. L. Auerbach, *Das judische Obligationenrecht*, vol. 1 (1871), p. 270. Other passages from rabbinic literature are given in Hirsch B. Fassel, *Das mosaisch-rabbinische Zivilrecht*, vol. 2, Part 3 (1854), § 1390; Frankel, *Der gerichtliche Beweis nach mosaischem Recht* (1846), p. 386; Saalschütz, *Mosaisches Recht*, 2 vols. (1848), p. 862.

189. For the Mamre, cf. L. L'Estocq, *Exercitatio de indole et jure instrumenti Judæis usitati cui nomen " Mamre " est* (1755), § vii; J. M. G. Besekes, *Thes. jur. Camb.*, Part II (1783), pp. 1169, 1176; P. Bloch, *Der Mamran, der judisch-polnische Wechselbrief*.

190. Ehrenberg's *Fugger* [note 160], vol. 2, p. 141.

191. Brunner [note 180], p. 69.

192. Schaps [note 156], p. 121.

193. Cf. F. Hecht [note 181], p. 44.

194. Hecht, p. 96.

195. Däbritz [note 174], p. 53.

196. Kuntze [note 178], p. 85.

197. Straccha, *Tract. de assicur.* (1568).

198. A. Wahl [note 155], vol. 1, pp. 15, 84.

199. Hecht [note 181], p. 37.

200. Cf. J. H. Bender, *Der Verkehr mit Staatspapieren* (2 ed., 1830), p. 167.

200A. "Ex diversis animi motibus in unum consentiunt, id est in unam sententiam decurrunt " (Ulp., L. I, § 3, *D. de pact.*, 2, 14).

201. Cf. Goldschmidt [note 151], p. 393.

202. I am indebted for what follows above all to L. Auerbach [note 188], vol. 1, pp. 163, 251, 513. This work (unfortunately uncompleted) is written in a most suggestive fashion and deserves to be widely known. For it is one of the best accounts of Talmudic law in existence. Of much less importance, yet useful nevertheless, are the works of Saalschütz [note 188]; H. B. Fassel [note 188]; J. J. M. Rabbinowicz, *Législation du Talmud,*

vol. 3 (1878) ; Frankel [note 188].   On the basis of Gold-schmidt's translation of the Talmud, J. Kohler attempted a " Darstellung des talmudischen Rechts " in *Zeitschrift für vergleichende Rechtswissenschaft*, vol. 20 (1908), pp. 161–264.   Cf. the criticism of V. Aptowitzer in the *Monatschrift* (1908), pp. 37–56.

203. Otto Stobbe, *Die Juden in Deutschland während des mittelalters* (1866), pp. 119, 242 ; Sachsenspiegel, III, 7, § 4.

204. Goldschmidt [note 151], p. 111.

205. (Isaac de Pinto) *Traité de la circulation du crédit* (1771), pp. 64, 67–68.   Cf. also E. Guillard [note 161], p. 534.

206. See also Däbritz [note 174], p. 18, for illustrations.

207. Ehrenberg, *Fugger*, vol. 2, p. 244.   We owe most of what we know about the history of the Stock Exchanges to Ehrenberg.

208. Cf. note 21.

209. Van Hemert, *Lectuur voor het ontbijt en de Theetafel*, VII^{de}. Stuk, p. 118, quoted by Koenen [note 12], p. 212.

210. H. Stephanus, *Francofordiense Emporium sive Francofordienses Nundinæ* (1574), p. 24.

211. Quoted by Ehrenberg, *Fugger*, vol. 2, p. 248.

212. *Memoirs*, p. 297.

213. Given by M. Grunwald [note 31], p. 21.

214. S. Haenle [note 123], p. 173.

215. *Die Juden in Österreich*, vol. 2 (1842), p. 41.

216. In a report of the Sous-Intendant, M. de Courson, dated 11 June, 1718, quoted by Malvezin [note 4].

217. E. Meyer, " Die Literatur für und wider die Juden in Schweden im Jahre 1815," in *Monatschrift*, vol. 57 (1907), p. 522.

218. H. Sieveking, " Die Kapitalistische Entwickelung in den italienischen Städten des Mittelalters," in the *Vierteljahrsschrift für Soziale- und Wirtschaftsgeschichte*, vol. 7, p. 85.

219. H. Sieveking, *Genueser Finanzwesen*, vol. i. (1898), pp. 82, 175.

220. Saravia della Calle, " Institutione de' Mercanti," in *Compendio utilissimo di quelle cose le quali a Nobili e Christiani mercanti appartengono* (1561), p. 42.

221. Art. " Börsenwesen " in *Handwörterbuch der Staatswissenschaften*.

222. The most reliable sources for the history of Stock Exchange dealing in Amsterdam in the first decades of the

17th century are the Plakate of the States General, which prohibit this sort of business. Reference should also be made to the controversial pamphlets of the period on this topic, more especially those written by the opponent of stock and share dealing, Nicolas Muys van Holy. See Laspeyres, *Geschichte der volkswirtschaftlichen Anschauungen* (1863). Not to be omitted is also de la Vega's book, about which more in due course. For the subsequent period there is much valuable material in books on Commerce, notably J. P. Ricard, *Le négoce a'Amsterdam* (1723), from whom later writers quote. The works of Joseph de Pinto dating from the second half of the 18th century [note 205], are also very useful. Of recent books the following may be mentioned : G. C. Klerk de Reus [note 53], S. van Brakel, *De Holland. Hand. Comp. der xvii. eeuv* (1908).

223. In the periodical *De Koopman*, vol. 2, pp. 429, 439, quoted by Ehrenberg, *Fugger*, vol. 2, p. 333.

224. *De la Circulation* [note 205], p. 84.

225. [See note 87.]

226. [See note 52.]

227. Ehrenberg, *Fugger*, vol. 2, p. 336, gives a fairly lengthy extract from this remarkable book.

228. *Extrait d'un mémoire présenté en* 1698, from the Archives of the French Foreign Office, published in the *Revue historique*, vol. 44 (1895). I am indebted to my friend André E. Sayous, of Paris, for having called my attention to this article.

229. "The Anatomy of Exchange Alley, or a System of Stock-jobbing" (1719). Printed in J. Francis's *Stock Exchange* (1849), Appendix.

230. Art. "Brokers" in *Jewish Encycl.*

231. J. Picciotto [note 18], p. 58.

232. *Universal Dictionary of Trade and Commerce*, vol. 2 (1755), p. 554.

233. Tovey, *Anglia Judaica*, p. 297.

234. As would appear from a complaint of the Christian merchants, of the year 1685, mentioned by Ehrenberg, *Fugger*, vol. 2, p. 248.

235. M. Grunwald [note 69], p. 6.

236. Postlethwayt, *Dictionary*, vol. 1, p. 95.

237. Joseph Jacobs, "Typical Character of Anglo-Jewish History," in *J.Q.R.*, vol. 10 (1898), p. 230.

238. Ranke, *Französische Geschichte*, vol. 4³ , p. 399.

239. Mélon, *Essai pol. sur le commerce* (1734), éd. Davie, p. 685.

240. See Ehrenberg, *Fugger*, vol. 2, p. 142.

241. (Du Hautchamp) *Histoire du système des Finances sous la minorité de Louis XV*, vol. 1 (1739), p. 184.

242. Oscar de Vallée, *Les Manieurs d'argent* (1858), p. 41.

243. P. A. Cochut, *Law, son système et son époque* (1853), p. 33.

244. E. Drumont, *La France Juive* (1904), vol. 1, p. 259.

245. All the figures are from *Von den Gilde-Dienern Friedrich Wilhelm Arendt und Abraham Charles Rousset herausgegebenen Verzeichnissen . . . der gegenwärtigen Aelter-Manner*, etc. (1801).

245A. In the *Hamburger Münz- und Medaillenvergnügen* (1753), p. 143, No. 4, there is a coin struck in commemoration of the trade in stocks and shares.

245B. Raumburger, in the preface to his *Justitia selecta Gent. Eur. in Cambiis*, etc.

246. Kiesselbech [note 32], p. 24.

247. The case is mentioned and discussed by von Gönner, *Von Staatsschulden, deren Tilgungsanstalten und vom Handel mit Staatspapieren* (1826), § 30.

248. *Dictionary*, vol. 2, p. 553. Cf. also the very informing article, " Monied Interest," p. 284.

249. See articles "Monied Interest" and "Paper Credit" in Postlethwayt, vol. 2, pp. 284 and 404.

250. D. Hume, *Essays*, vol. 2 (1793), p. 110.

251. Adam Smith, *Wealth of Nations*, ch. 3.

252. Von Gönner [note 247], § 31.

253. Pinto [note 205], pp. 310–11.

254. Ehrenberg, *Fugger*, vol. 2, p. 299.

255. I must content myself with mentioning the following three works which appear to me to be the best : *Das Haus Rothschild. Seine Geschichte und seine Geschäfte*, 2 Parts (1857) ; John Reeves, *The Rothschilds : the Financial Rulers of Nations* (1887) ; R. Ehrenberg, *Grosse Vermögen*, etc., vol. 1, " Die Fugger-Rothschild-Krupp " (2nd ed., 1905).

256. J. H. Bender, *Der Verkehr mit Staatspapieren* (2nd ed., 1830), p. 145.

257. *E.g.*, von Gönner [note 247], p. 60 ; Bender, p. 142.

258. *Das Haus Rothschild*, vol. 2, p. 216.

259. A. Crump, *The Theory of Stock Exchange* (1873). Reprinted 1903, p. 100.

260. Von Mensi [note 125], p. 54.

261. Ad. Beer [note 173], p. 43.

262. J. H. Bender [note 256], p. 5.

263. J. Francis, *Stock Exchange*, p. 161.

264. *Das Haus Rothschild*, vol. 2 (1857), p. 85.

265. The best books on this period in Germany are, despite their prejudice and one-sidedness, Otto Glagau's *Der Börsen- und Gründungsschwindel in Berlin* (1876) and *Der Börsen- und Gründungsschwindel in Deutschland* (1877). These books are particularly useful for the short historical sketches of the different companies, giving the names of the founders and the first directors. Cf. also the annual issues of Saling's *Börsenpapieren*, and Rudolf Meyer, *Die Aktiengesellschaften*, 1872-3 (which, however, deal only with banks). The figures given in the text were supplied by Mr. Arthur Loewenstein, at my request.

266. M. Wirth, *Geschichte der Handelskrisen* (3rd ed., 1883), p. 184.

267. Riesser, *Entwicklungsgeschichte der deutschen Grossbanken* (1905), p. 48.

268. For a glorification of this policy see J. E. Kuntze [note 178], p. 23.

269. A. Beer [note 173], p. 35.

270. C. Hegemann, *De Entwickelung des französischen Grossbankbetriebes* (1908), p. 9.

271. Books of reference are given fully in J. Plenge, *Gründung und Geschichte des Crédit mobilier* (1903).

272. Model-Loeb, *Die Grossen Berliner Effectenbanken* (1895), p. 43—an excellent book, from which the information in the text is taken in so far as it is not my own personal knowledge.

273. Cf. R. Ehrenberg, *Fondsspekulation* (1883), and Adolf Weber, *Depositenbanken und Spekulationsbanken* (1902).

274. See for instance A. Gomoll, *Die Kapitalistische Mausefalle* (1908). Despite its curious title the book deals seriously with Stock Exchange speculations and is one of the best pieces of work recently published.

275. Mostly from local histories, too numerous to mention here.

CHAPTER VII

276. König [see note 122], p. 97.

277. " Zur Geschichte der Juden in Danzig," in *Monatschrift*, vol. 6 (1857), p. 243.

278. M. Güdemann, " Zur Geschichte der Juden in Magdeburg," in *Monatschrift*, vol. 14 (1865), p. 370.

279. Quoted by Liebe [note 121], pp. 91–2.

280. Regesten, in Hugo Barbeck's *Geschichte der Juden in Nürnberg und Fürth* (1878), p. 68.

281. See, for instance, the conduct of the Berlin Retailers' Gild as related in Geiger's *Geschichte der Juden in Berlin*, vol. 2 (1871), pp. 24, 31.

282. Josiah Child, *Discourse on Trade*, 4th ed., p. 152. Child reports the prevailing opinion without saying one word by way of criticism. But he does make it clear that the accusation levelled against the Jews is no crime at all.

283. See extracts from the polemical pamphlets of the period in Hyamson, p. 274.

284. Given in Léon Brunschvicg, " Les Juifs en Bretagne au 18 sc.," in *R.E.J.*, vol. 33 (1876), pp. 88, 111.

285. " Les Juifs et les Communautés d'Arts et Métiers," in *R.E.J.*, vol. 36, p. 75.

286. M. Maignial, *La question juive en France en* 1789 (1903), contains a great deal of material from which the prevailing feeling among French merchants against the Jews in the 17th and 18th centuries becomes apparent.

287. " L'admission de cette espèce d'hommes ne peut être que très dangereuse. On peut les comparer à des guêpes qui ne s'introduisent dans les ruches que pour tuer les abeilles, leur ouvrir le ventre et en tirer le miel qui est dans leurs entrailles : tels sont les juifs."—Requête des marchands et négociants de Paris contre l'admission des Juifs (1777), p. 14, quoted by Maignial [note 11], p. 92.

288. Maignial, p. 92.

289. The opinion of Wegelin is given by Ernst Meyer, [note 217], pp. 513, 522.

290. Czacki, *Rosprava o Zydach*, p. 82 ; cf. Graetz, vol. 9, p. 443. Almost word for word the same cry is heard from Rumania, cf. Verax, *La Roumanie et les Juifs* (1903).

291. Philander von Sittewaldt [see note 124].

292. Georg Paul Hönn, *Betrugs-Lexicon, worinnen die meisten Betrügereyen in allen Ständen nebst denen darwider guten Theils aienenden Mitteln endeckt*, Dritte Edition (1724).

293. *Allgemeine Schatzkammer der Kaufmannschaft oder vollständiges Lexikon aller Handlungen und Gewerbe*, vol. 2 (1741), p. 1158.

294. *Charakteristik von Berlin. Stimme eines Kosmopoliten in der Wüste* (1784), p. 203.

295. J. Savary (Œuvre posthume, continué . . . par Phil-Louis Savary), *Dictionnaire universel de Commerce*, vol. 2 (1726), p. 447.

296. *Allgemeine Schatzkammer* [note 293], vol. 1 (1741), p. 17.

297. *Allgemeine Schatzkammer*, vol. 3 (1742), p. 1325.

298. This is only the expression of the mediæval view. It is excellently well discussed in R. Eberstadt, *Französische Gewerberecht* (1899), p. 378.

299. D. Defoe, *The Complete English Tradesman*, 1st ed., 1726. I have used the 2nd edition in 1 vol. (1727), and the 5th edition in 2 vols. (1745), published after the author's death. The passage cited in the text is from the 1st ed., p. 82.

300. *Allgemeine Schatzkammer* [note 293], vol. 3, p. 148.

301. Ditto, vol. 4, p. 677.

302. Ditto, vol. 3, p. 1325.

303. Ditto, vol. 3, p. 1326.

304. Ditto, vol. 1, p. 1392—" Sächsischen Krämer-Ordnungen " of 1672, 1682, and 1692, § 18.

305. See the highly instructive Letter (No. 19 in the 2nd ed., corresponding to No. 22 in the 5th) "Of fine shops and fine shews."

306. Jules de Bock, *Le Journal à travers les âges* (1907), p. 30, quoted in F. Kellen, *Studien über das Zeitungswesen* (1907), p. 253.

307. Much useful information, especially as regards England, will be found in Henry Sampson's *History of Advertising from the Earliest Times* (1875), pp. 76, 83.

308. M. Postlethwayt, *A Universal Dictionary of Trade and Commerce*, 2 vols. (1741), 2nd ed. (1757), vol. 1, p. 22. Postlethwayt calls his work a translation of Savary's *Lexicon*, but in reality there are so many additions in it that it may be regarded as original. It should be mentioned by the way that the work is an invaluable source of information concerning economic conditions in England in the 18th century.

309. Savary, *Dict. du Commerce* (1726), Suppl. 1732.

310. P. Datz, *Histoire de la Publicité* (1894), p. 161, contains a facsimile of the whole of the first issue of *Les Petites Affiches*.

311. *Allgemeine Schatzkammer* [note 293], vol. 4, p. 677.

312. *The Complete English Tradesman* [note 299], vol. 5², p. 163.

313. Cf. G. Martin, *La grande industrie sous Louis XV* (1900), p. 247.

314. Josiah Child, *A New Discourse of Trade*, 4th ed., p. 159.

315. Such teaching is met with as early as the later 16th century. Saravia della Calle, whom I regard as of supreme importance in the history of the theory of just price, goes so far as to deduce it from the relationship of supply and demand. His work, together with those of Venuti and Fabiano, is printed in the *Compendio utilissimo* [note 220].

316. (Mercier) *Tableau de Paris*, vol. 11 (1788), p. 40.

317. "A Paris on court, on se presse parce qu'on y est oisif; ici l'on marche posément, parce que l'on y est occupé." Quoted by J. Godard, *L'Ouvrier en Soie*, vol. 1 (1899), pp. 38-9.

318. Memoirs of the Rev. James Fraser, written by himself. *Selected Biographies*, vol. 2, p. 280; Durham's *Law Unsealed*, p. 324, quoted by Buckle, *History of Civilization*, vol. 2, p. 377.

319. Durham's *Exposition of the Song of Solomon*, quoted by Buckle, *loc. cit.*

320. *Allgemeine Schatzkammer* [note 293], vol. 4 (1742), p. 666.

321. See, for instance, Mercier, *Tableau de Paris*, vol. 2, p. 71.

322. Samuel Lambe, in his scheme for a national bank [see note 171A] speaks of the low commercial morality of English merchants as compared with the reliability of (say) the Dutch.

323. Owen Felltham in his *Observations* (1652), quoted by Douglas Campbell, *The Puritan in Holland, England, and America*, vol. 2 (1892), p. 327.

324. This accusation was levelled against the Jews from the early mediæval period down almost to this very day. Cf. G. Caro, *Sozial- und Wirtschaftsgeschichte der Juden*, vol. 1 (1908), p. 222; Bloch [note 23], p. 12; article "Juden," in *Allgemeine Schatzkammer* [note 293]; von Justi, *Staatswirtschaft*, vol. 1 (1758), p. 150. For Germany more especially, see Liebe, *Das Judenthum in der deutschen Vergangenheit* (1903).

325. According to a Minute Book of the Portuguese community in Hamburg—A. Feilchenfeld, "Die älteste Geschichte der deutschen Juden in Hamburg," in *Monatschrift*, vol. 43 (1899), p. 279.

326. Geyler von Kaiserberg's sermon on the 93rd "Narrengeschwärm," in S. Brandt's *Narrenschiff* (to be found in the collection called *Das Kloster*, vol. 1, p. 722, published by J. Scheible). Cf. Oskar Franke, *Der Jude in den deutschen Dichtungen des 15, 16, und 17 Jahrhunderts* (1905), especially section 4.

327. Quoted by A. M. Dyer [note 86], p. 44.

328. Will. Ussellinx, quoted by Jameson, in *Transactions* of the Jewish Historical Society of America, vol. 1, p. 42. For Usselinx, see E. Laspeyres, *Volkswirtschaftliche Ansichten der Niederlande* (1863), p. 59.

329. Savary [note 295], vol. 2, p. 449.

330. See *Transactions* of the Jewish Historical Society of America, vol. 3, p. 44.

331. Josiah Child, *Discourse on Trade*, 4th ed., p. 152.

332. Cf. R. Ehrenberg, *Grosse Vermögen*, 2nd ed., p. 147.

333. *Annalen der Juden* [note 122], pp. 106–17.

334. Liebe, *Das Judentum*, p. 34.

335. Risbeck [note 10]. Cf. also Scheube [note 10], p. 393.

336. *Uber das Verhältniss der Juden zu den Christen in den deutschen Handelsstädten* (1818), pp. 171, 252, 270, 272.

337. See *R.E.J.*, vol. 33, p. 111.

337A. H. Bodemeyer, *Die Juden. Ein Beitrag zur Hannoverschen Rechtsgeschichte* (1855), p. 68.

338. See Albert Wolf, "Etwas über jüdische Kunst und ältere jüdische Künstler," in *Mitteilungen zur jüdischen Volkskunde*, edited by M. Grunwald, vol. 1 (1905), p. 34.

339. See Ehrenberg, *Grosse Vermögen*, p. 147.

340. The documents are printed in Kracauer's "Beiträge zur Geschichte der Frankfurter Juden im 30 jährigen Kriege," in *Zeitschrift für die Geschichte der Juden in Deutschland*, vol. 3 (1899), p. 147. Cf. Schudt [note 14], vol. 2, p. 164.

341. *Annalen der Juden* [note 122], pp. 97, 106–17.

342. *Versuch über die jüdischen Bewohner der österreichischen Monarchie* (1804), p. 83. Contains much valuable material.

343. L. Holst, *Judentum in allen dessen Teilen aus einem staatswissenschaftlichen Standpunkte betrachtet* (1821), pp. 293–4.

344. " Les fripiers de Paris qui sont à la plus part Juifs," Noel du Fail, *Contes d'Eutrapel*, xxiv, quoted by G. Fagniez, *L'économie sociale de la France sous Henry IV* (1897), p. 217.

345. Mercier, *Tableau de Paris*, vol. 2, p. 253. In Breslau this method of attracting custom is not unknown, and is called "Ärmelausreissgeschäfte."

346. Romani, *Eines edlen Wallachen landwirtschaftliche Reise durch verschiedene Landschaften Europas*. Zweyter Theil (1776), p. 150. Cf. Schudt, vol. 2, p. 164.

347. *Über das Verhältniss*, etc. [note 336], p. 184.

348. Jules de Bock [note 306], p. 30.

349. Max J. Kohler [note 66].

350. Bloch [note 23], p. 30.

351. Hyamson, *Jews in England*, p. 274.

352. S. Kahn, " Les Juifs de Montpellier au 18 siècle," in *R.E.J.*, vol. 33 (1896), p. 290.

353. Leon Brunschvicg [note 284], p. 111.

354. " Requête des marchands," etc. [note 287], p. 234.

355. L. Kahn, *Les Juifs de Paris au XVIII sc.* [note 11], p. 71.

356. Justin Godard, *L'Ouvrier en Soie* (1899), p. 224.

357. For Wegelin's view, see note 289 (p. 522).

358. See note 290.

359. *Annalen* [note 122], p. 97.

360. F. Bothe, *Beiträge zur Wirtschafts-und Sozial-Geschichte der Reichstadt Frankfurt* (1906), p. 74.

361. *Bericht der Kriegs- und Domänenkammer über den wirtschaftlichen Niedergang des Herzogtums Magdeburg* (1710), quoted by Liebe, *Das Judentum*, p. 91.

362. Romani [note 346], p. 147.

363. In *Geschichte der Juden in der Reichstadt Augsburg* (1803), p. 42.

364. Von Mensi [note 125], p. 367.

365. *Allgemeine Schatzkammer* [note 293], vol. 2, p. 1158.

366. See note 328.

367. See note 321.

368. See note 322.

369. *R.E.J.*, vol. 33, p. 111 [cf. note 352].

370. *Le cri du citoyen contre les juifs de Metz* (18 sc.), quoted by Maignial [note 11].

371. See Bothe [note 360], p. 74.

372. See note 323. "Cette nation ne fait fabriquer que des étoffes inférieures et de mauvaise qualité."

373. Quoted by Liebe, *Das Judentum*, p. 91.

374. N. Roubin, "La vie commerciale des juifs contadines en Languedoc," in *R.E.J.*, vols. 34, 35, and 36.

375. [See note 336] p. 254.

376. Note 361.

377. *Juden, sind sie der Handlung schädlich?* (1803), p. 25.

378. Graetz, vol. 9, p. 445.

379. Romani [note 346], p. 148.

380. I am indebted to Mr. Josef Reizman for kindly calling my attention to this passage.

381. Child, *Discourse on Trade*, p. 152.

382. Hysamson, p. 274.

383. *R.E.J.*, vol. 33, p. 290.

384. L. Holst [note 343], p. 290.

385. See note 336, p. 239.

386. Holst [note 343], p. 288.

387. *R.E.J.*, vol. 36.

388. *R.E.J.*, vol. 33, p. 289.

389. *Annalen* [note 122], p. 90.

390. From a Memorandum, dated January 9, 1786, of the Hungarian Court Chancery ; again I am indebted to Mr. Josef Reizman.

391. Königlichen Staatsarchiv (Mr. Ludwig Davidsohn informed me of it).

392. "In the U.S.A. the most striking characteristic of Jewish commerce is found in the large number of department stores held by Jewish firms." Art. "Commerce," in *Jewish Encycl.* (vol. 4, p. 192).

393. See the lists of firms in J. Hirsch, *Das Warenhaus in Westdeutschland* (1910).

394. See note 377, p. 33.

395. Henry Sampson, *A History of Advertising* (1875), p. 68.

CHAPTER IX

396. For a fuller account of the subject of this chapter, see an article of mine, "Der Kapitalistische Unternehmer," in *Archiv für soziale Wissenschaft und Soziale Politik*, vol. 29.

CHAPTER X

397. M. Kayserling [note 76], p. 708.

398. An account of the Jewish world-famed firms of his time is given by Manasseh ben Israel in his Humble Address to Cromwell [note 52]. The story of the single families may be found in the *Jewish Encyclopedia*, which is specially good for biographies.

399. "Lettres écrites de la Suisse, d'Italie," etc., in *Encycl. méth. Manuf.* [note 39], vol. 1, p. 407. Cf. the opinion of Jovet, quoted by Schudt, *Jüdische Merkwürdigkeiten*, vol. 1, p. 228.

400. The *Spectator*, No. 495.

401. *Revue Historique*, vol. 44 (1890).

402. Graetz, vol. 5, p. 323.

403. These instances of Jewish diplomatists are generally known. The number could easily be added to. Any one specially interested in this question should refer to Graetz, where abundant material will be found (*e.g.*, vol. 6, pp. 85, 224 ; vol. 8. ch. 9, etc.).

404. M. Kayserling, *Christopher Columbus* (1894), p. 106.

405. H. J. Koenen [note 12], p. 206.

406. Edmund Bonaffé, *Dictionnaire des amateurs français au XVII siècle* (1881), p. 191.

407. Friedländer, *Sittengeschichte Roms*, vol. 3, p. 577.

408. (v. Kortum) *Über Judentum und Juden* (1795), p. 165.

409. Ditto, p. 90.

410. *R.E.J.*, vol. 23 (1891), p. 90.

411. M. de Maulde, *Les juifs dans les Etats français du Saint-Siège* (1886). The legal position of the Jews generally is treated fully in the current Jewish histories, most of which are in reality nothing more than the history of the legal position of the Jews. Indeed, a goodly number of their authors imagine they are writing economic history when all the time it is just legal history they are dealing with. For records, consult the article "Juden" in Krünitz (vol. 31) and Schudt, *Jüdische Merkwürdigkeiten* (specially for Frankfort). For France, see Halphen, *Recueil des lois, etc.*, concernant les Israëlites (1851) ; for Prussia, L. von Rönne and Heinrich Simon, *Die früheren und gegenwärtigen Verhältnisse der Juden in den sämtlichen Landesteilen des preussischen Staates* (1843). All the laws quoted in

the text I have taken from this collection. A. Michaelis, *Die Rechtsverhältnisse der Juden in Preussen seit dem Beginn des 19 Jahrhunderts: Gesetze, Erlasse, Verordnungen, Entscheidungen* (1910).

412. Cf. B. Bento Carqueja [note 128], pp. 73, 82, 91.

413. Wagenaar, *Beschrijving van Amsterdam*, quoted by Koenen [note 12], p. 142. Further, for the wealth of the Dutch Jews (greatly exaggerated) see Schudt, vol. 1 (1714), p. 277 ; vol. 4 (1717), p. 208. Cf. M. Mission, *Reise nach Italien* (1713), p. 43. Of newer books, M. Henriquez Pimentel [note 12], p. 34.

414. *Memoiren*, p. 134.

415. Savary, *Dict.*, vol. 2 (1726), p. 448.

416. Lucien Wolf, *The Jewry of the Restoration*, 1660–1664, p. 11.

417. See H. Reils, "Beiträge zur ältesten Geschichte der Juden in Hamburg," in *Zeitschrift des Vereins für hamburgische Geschichte*, vol. 2 (1847), pp. 357, 380, 405 ; and M. Grunwald [note 43], pp. 16, 26, 35.

418. In M. Grunwald's *Hamburgs deutsche Juden*, pp. 20, 191.

419. F. Bothe, *Die Entwickelung der direkten Besteuerung der Reichsstadt Frankfurt* (1906), p. 166, Tables 10 and 15.

420. Kracauer [note 340], p. 341.

421. Alexander Dietz, *Stammbuch der Frankfurter Juden* (1907), p. 408.

422. L. Geiger, *Geschichte der Juden in Berlin* (1871), vol. 1, p. 43.

CHAPTER XI

423. M. Lazarus, *Ethik des Judentums* (1904), pp. 67, 85, etc. [There is an English edition of this book issued by the Jewish Publication Society of America.]

424. Hermann Cohen, "Das Problem der jüdischen Sittenlehre. Eine Kritik (adverse) von Lazarus' Ethik des Judentums," in *Monatschrift*, vol. 43, p. 385.

425. *Orach Chajim*, § 8.

426. Quoted by F. Weber, *Altsynagogale Theologie* (1880), p. 273.

427. J. Wellhausen, *Israelitische und jüdische Geschichte*, p. 340.

428. Graetz, vol. 4, p. 411. Graetz also has an excellent appreciation of the Talmud (one-sided of course, and optimistic), and its influence in Judaism.

429. J. Fromer, *Vom Ghetto zur modernen Kultur* (1906), p. 247.

430. M. Kayserling, *Columbus* (1894), ch. vi.

431. *Das Haus Rothschild*, vol. 1 (1857), p. 186.

432. This is not the place to enter into an account of the results of Biblical criticism. All I can do here is to mention a few books that may serve as an introduction to the subject : Zittel, *Die Entstehung der Bibel* (5th ed., 1891) ; for the history of the Pentateuch, Adalbert Merx, *Die Bücher Moses und Josua* (1907), and Ed. Meyer, *Die Entstehung des Judentums* (1896).

433. W. Frankenberg, " Die Sprüche, übersetzt und erläutert," in *Handkommentar zum Alten Testament*, herausgegeben von D. W. Nowack. On p. 16 there is a list of books for the Wisdom Literature. See also Henri Traband, *La loi mosaïque, ses origines et son développement* (1903), p. 77.

434. Cf. M. Friedländer, *Geschichte der jüdischen Apologetik* (1903).

435. Books about the Talmud form a small library in themselves. I can only mention one or two to serve as an introduction to the subject. The best is H. L. Strack's *Einleitung in den Talmud* (4th ed., 1908), which also contains a pretty full bibliography. For Talmudic Ethics, see Salo Stein's *Materialien zur Ethik des Talmud* (1904). Talmudic scholars, however, do not apprize this book very highly. A more recent book is by J. Fromer, who has occupied himself with Talmudic and later Jewish literature. See his *Die Organization des Judentums* 1908), which is intended to serve as an Introduction to a big Encyclopedic Dictionary of the Talmud, which Fromer has planned. Another book which deals with the sources is E. Schürer, *Geschichte des jüdischen Volkes im Zeitalter Jesu Christi*, in 3 vols. The first (2nd ed., 1890) in §3 contains an extensive bibliography. In addition, the standard Jewish histories, especially Graetz, deal with this aspect of Jewish literature.

To comprehend the spirit of the Talmud it is necessary to read the text itself. There is a German translation (almost complete) by Lazarus Goldschmidt. The Talmud has this characteristic : that although the sections follow each other in some fixed order, yet not one of them is strictly limited as regards its subject matter. They all deal with practically the whole field of Talmudic subjects. Hence by studying one or more of the (63) Tractates, it is comparatively easy to obtain a fair notion of the contents of the whole, and certainly, to find one's way about in the great sea. Specially to be recommended is the Tractate *Baba Mezia* and its two sister tractates [*Baba Kama* and *Baba Bathra*]. There is a good edition of *Baba Mezia*, with an introduction and a translation by Dr. Sammter (1876).

A special branch of Talmudic literature is composed of the so-called "Minor Tractates," usually found in an appendix to the Talmud, though often published separately. These are *Derech Erez Rabba* (3rd century), *Aboth*, *Aboth de R. Nathan*, *Derech Erez Zutta* (9th century, according to Zunz). Zunz calls them Ethical *Hagadoth* because of their obvious intention of teaching practical wisdom. They have had no small influence on the development of the Jewish people and are therefore of great interest to us here. Next to the Bible, these tractates enjoyed a widespread popularity. They formed the principal reading of the layman, unacquainted with the Talmud. They were (are) found in Prayer Books and devotional literature. Some of them have been issued in German translations. *R. Nathan's System der Ethik und Moral*, translated by Kaim Pollock (1905). *Derech Erez Zutta*, translated by A. Tawrogi (1885). *Derech Erez Rabba*, translated by M. Goldberg (1888). We must also mention the *Tosephta*, which contains the teaching not included in the *Mishna*. This also dates from the period of the *Tanaim* and is arranged like the *Mishna*.

Finally, a word as to the Rabbinical commentaries or *Midrashim*, which are partly *halachic* [*i.e.*, legal] and partly *hagadic* [*i.e.*, moral and edifying]. The oldest of them, mostly *halachic*, are *Mechilta* (on Exodus), *Siphra* (on Leviticus), and *Siphre* (on Numbers and Deuteronomy).

The *Targumim* are the Aramaic translations of the O.T.

436. There is no good translation of the *Shulchan Aruch*. The only available one is by Löwe (1837), which is incomplete and one-sided. On the other hand, the *Orach Chajim* and the *Jore Deah* have been published in a German dress by Rabbi P. Lederer (1906 and 1900), but not in a complete form.

As for works on the *Shulchan Aruch*, they are mostly of the nature of apologetic pamphlets. Anti-Semites have turned to the *S. A.* for material to attack Jews and Judaism ; and Jewish scholars have naturally replied. We may mention, for instance, A. Lewin, *Der Judenspiegel des Dr. Justus* (1884), and D. Hoffmann, *Der Schulchan Aruch und die Rabbiner über das Verhältniss der Juden zu Andersgläubigen* (1885). Thus there is no subjective treatment of the *Shulchan Aruch*, though it deserves as thorough a consideration as the Talmud. The only strictly scientific book with which I am acquainted and which should be mentioned in this connexion is S. Bäck's *Die religionsgeschichtliche Literatur der Juden in dem Zeitraume vom* 15–18 *Jahrhundert* (1893), reprinted from Winter and Wünsche, *Die jüdische Literatur seit Abschluss des Kanons*, vol. 2. But Bäck's book is not big and his treatment therefore can only be of the nature of a sketch.

437. Paul Volz, *Jüdische Eschatologie von Daniel bis Akiba* (1903).

438. Fürst, *Untersuchungen über den Kanon des Alten Testaments nach den Uberlieferungen in Talmud und Midrasch* (1868).

439. L. Stern, *Die Vorschriften der Thora, welche Israel in der Zerstreuung zu beobachten hat. Ein Lehrbuch der Religion für Schule und Familie* (4th ed., 1904), p. 28. This book, which may be looked upon as a type, gives the view current in strictly orthodox circles.

440. Cf. Rabbi S. Mandl, *Das Wesen des Judentums* (1904), p. 14. Mandl relies on J. Gutmann, *Uber Dogmenbildung und Judentum* (1894). Cf. also S. Schechter, " The Dogmas of Judaism," in *J.Q.R.*, vol. 1 (1889), pp. 48, 115. As is well known, Moses Mendelssohn was the first to express (in his *Jerusalem*) the idea that Judaism has no dogmas, with some degree of insistence.

440A. The best that I am acquainted with is Ferdinand Weber's *System der altsynagogalen palästinensischen Theologie aus Targum, Midrash und Talmud* (1880). [Cf. note 426.]

441. Stern [note 439], p. 5.

442. Döllinger, *Heidentum und Judentum* (1857), p. 634.

443. Rutilius Namatianus, " De reditu suo," in Reinach's *Textes d'auteurs grecs et romains relatifs au judaisme*, vol. 1 (1895), p. 358.

444. Stern [note 439], p. 49 ; S. R. Hirsch, *Versuche über Jissroëls Pflichten in der Zerstreuung* (4th ed., 1909), § 711.

445. Cf. Weber [note 440A], p. 49. Weber has worked out this idea of contract in Judaism better than any other writer. The treatment in the text owes much to him, as will be apparent. I have also utilized his references. In this particular instance, cf. *Sifre*, 12*b*, *Wajjikra Rabba*, c. 31.

446. *Aboth*, II, near the beginning.

447. Cf. Weber [note 440A], pp. 270, 272.

448. Ditto, p. 292.

449. R. Joseph Albo, *Ikkarim*, a book on the principles of Judaism, dating from the 15th century. W. and L. Schlesinger have issued a German translation [of the Hebrew] (1844). This particular problem is dealt with in ch. 46.

450. S. R. Hirsch [note 444], ch. 13, especially §§ 100 and 105.

451. J. F. Schröder, *Talmudisch-rabbinisches Judentum* (1851), p. 47.

452. Graetz, vol. 2, p. 203 and note 14 ; J. Bergmann, *Jüdische Apologetik im neutestamentlichen Zeitalter* (1908), p. 120. For the spirit of ancient Judaism, see Wellhausen [note 427], ch. 15.

453. H. Deutsch, *Die Sprüche Salomons nach der Auffassung in Talmud und Midrasch* (1885).

454. J. F. Bruch, *Weisheitslehre der Hebräer* (1851), p. 135.

455. Rabbi S. Schiffer, *Das Buch Kohelet. Nach der Auffassung der Weisen des Talmud und Midrasch* (1884).

456. Cf. Graetz, vol. 4, p. 233 ; Wellhausen [note 427], pp. 250, 339 ; and also the well-known works of Müller, Schürer, and Marti.

457. Mandl [note 440], p. 14.

458. S. R. Hirsch [note 444], § 448.

459. A number of similar extracts from Talmudic literature will be found in S. Schaffer, *Das Recht und seine Stellung zur Moral nach talmudischer Sitten- und Rechtslehre* (1889), p. 28.

460. M. Lazarus [note 423], p. 22. Lazarus has worked out the idea that to be holy means to overcome your passions, exceedingly well, though he approaches very closely to Kant's system of Ethics.

461. *Kiddushin*, 30*b*, *Baba Bathra*, 16*a*.

462. Cf. Schaffer [note 459], p. 54.

463. Cf. Fassel, *Tugend- und Rechtslehre des Talmud* (1848), p. 38.

464. Albo's *Ikkarim* [note 449], ch. 24, deals fully with this.

465. Cf. S. Bäck [note 436], Preface.

466. Cf. also M. Lazarus [note 423], p. 20.

467. Stern [note 439], p. 126.

468. *Aboth de R. Nathan*, xxi. 5 [also *Aboth*, III, 14].

469. G. F. Oehler, *Theologie des A.T.* (3rd ed., 1891), p. 878.

470. Lazarus [note 423], p. 40.

471. *Aboth de R. Nathan*, xvi. 6.

471A. Cf. Eccles. 1, 8 ; Prov. x. 8 ; x. 10 ; x. 31 ; xiv. 23 ; xvii. 27, 28 ; xviii. 7, 21 ; xxi. 23 ; Ecclus. iv. 34 (29) ; v. 15 (13) ; ix. 25 (18) ; xix. 20, 22.

472. Stern [note 439], No. 127*a*.

473. Cf. also Prov. xii. 27 ; xiii. 11 ; xviii. 19 ; xxi. 20. For further passages in praise of labour, cf. L. K. Amitai, *La sociologie selon la législation juive* (1905), p. 90.

474. Hirsch [note 444], § 448.

475. Ditto, § 463.

476. Stern [note 439], p. 239.

477. Hirsch [note 444], § 443, almost identically expressed by Stern [note 439], Nos. 125, 126.

478. J. Fromer [note 429], p. 25.

479. *Iggeret ha-Kodesh*, first published in 1556 ; translated into Latin by Gaffareli ; cf. Graetz, vol. 7, p. 46.

480. Hirsch [note 444], § 263. Cf. also § 264, § 267.

481. The figures are taken from Hugo Nathansohn, " Die unehelichen Geburten bei den Juden," in *Z.D.S.J.*, vol. 6, (1910), p. 102.

482. We may mention as one of the foremost authorities S. Freud. See his *Sammlung kleiner Schriften zur Neurosenlehre* (2nd series, 1909).

483. See Dr. Hoppe, " Die Kriminalität der Juden und der Alkohol," in *Z.D.S.J.*, vol. 3 (1907), p. 38 ; H. L. Eisenstädt, " Die Renaissance der jüdischen Sozialhygiene," in *Archiv für Rassen- und Gesellschaftsbiologie*, vol. 5 (1908), p. 714 ; L. Cheinisse, " Die Rassenpathologie und der Alkoholismus bei den Juden," in *Z.D.S.J.*, vol. 6 (1910), p. 1. It can be proved with great certainty that the Jew's freedom from the evil effects of alcohol (as also from syphilis) is due to his religion.

484. Wellhausen [note 427], p. 119.

485. Cicero, *Pro Flacco*, ch. 28.

486. Mommsen, *Römische Geschichte*, vol. 5, p. 545.

487. The passages may be found in Felix Stähelin, *Der Antisemitismus des Altertums* (1905). Cf. Reinach [note 443].

488. J. Bergmann [note 452], p. 157.

489. Graetz, vol. 5, p. 73.

490. Graetz, vol. 5, p. 321.

491. Graetz, vol. 6, pp. 140, 161.

492. A comprehensive account of laws on interest in the old Jewish legal system will be found in J. Heicl, *Das alttestamentliche Zinsverbot* (*Biblische Studien*, herausgegeben von O. Bardenhewer, vol. 12, No. 4, 1907).

493. Cf. a collection of "Responsa" by Hoffmann, in *Schmollers Forschungen*, vol. 152.

494. Cf. Fassel [note 463], p. 193; E. Grünebaum, *Die Sittenlehre der Juden andern Bekenntnissen gegenüber* (2nd ed., 1878), p. 414; the same writer's "Der Fremde nach rabbinischen Begriffen," in *Geigers jüdische Zeitschrift*, vols. 9 and 10; D. Hoffmann [note 436], p. 129; Lazarus [note 423], § 144. Lazarus is curiously incomplete. What he says in his third chapter about the duty of Israel towards non-Jews does his heart all credit, but it is hardly in accord with historic truth.

494A. Cf. *Choshen Mishpat*, §§ 188, 194, 227, 231, 259, 266, 272, 283, 348, 389, etc.

495. "When he appears before the divine Judge, the first question that man is asked is, Have you been straightforward and honest in business?" *Sabbath*, 31a. This Talmudic quotation is the motto of a little book (privately printed) dealing with passages concerning honesty, *Das Biblisch-rabbinische Handelsgesetz*, by Rabbi Stark.

495A. *Choshen Mishpat*, § 231. The passage given in the text is from § 227.

496. Graetz, vol. 10, pp. 62, 81.

496A. *Choshen Mishpat*, § 227; *Baba Mezia*, 49b.

496B. In addition, see John G. Dow, "Hebrew and Puritan," in *J.Q.R.*, vol. 3 (1891), p. 52.

497. Graetz, vol. 9, pp. 86, 213; vol. 10, p. 87; Hyamson, p. 164; *J.Q.R.*, vol. 3, p. 61.

CHAPTER XII

498. Cf. also R. S. Woodworth, "Racial Differences in Mental Traits," in *Bulletin mensuel des Institut Solvay* (1910), No. 21.

499. Anatole Leroy-Beaulieu, *Israël chez les nations* (1893), p. 289.

500. Cf. H. St. Chamberlain, *Die Grundlagen des* 19 *Jahrhunderts* (3rd ed., 1901), p. 457. [An English edition of this book is now to be had.]

501. I cannot here enter into a disquisition of the various meanings attached to the terms People, Nation, Nationality. The reader will find all that he needs in that excellent study of F. J. Neumann, *Volk und Nation* (1888). See, too, Otto Bauer, *Die Nationalitätenfrage und die Sozialdemokratie* (1907); F. Rosenblüth, *Zur Begriffsbestimmung von Volk und Nation* (1910).

502. A. Jellinek, *Der jüdische Stamm in Sprichwörtern* (2nd series, 1882), pp. 18, 91.

503. J. Zollschan, *Das Rassenproblem unter besonderer Berücksichtigung der theoretischen Grundlagen der jüdischen Rassenfrage* (1910), p. 298.

504. Jellinek [note 502], (3rd series, 1885), p. 39.

505. Juan Huarte de San Juan, *Examen de ingenios para las Sciencias.* Pomplona (1575), (Biblioteca de autores Españoles, lxv, p. 469).

506. Jellinek [note 502]. This book by the well-known Rabbi of Vienna is one of the very best that has been written on the Jewish spirit. Good, too, is the booklet of D. Chwolson, *Die semitischen Völker* (1872), which criticizes Renan's *Histoire générale et système comparé de langues Sémitique* (1855). A third writer who in my opinion has looked deep into the Jewish soul is Karl Marx, in his *Judenfrage* (1844). What has been said about the Jewish spirit since these men (all Jews !) wrote is either a repetition of what they said or a distortion of the truth.

507. For Jews as mathematicians, see M. Steinschneider in *Monatschrift*, vols. 49–51 (1905–7).

508. For Jews as physicians, see M. Kayserling, "Zur Geschichte der jüdischen Aerzte," in *Monatschrift*, vols. 8 (1859) and 17 (1868).

509. Zollschan [note 503], p. 159.

510. C. Lassen, *Indische Altertumskunde*, vol. 1 (1847), p. 414.

511. "Une certaine gravité orgueilleuse et un fierté noble fait le caractère distinctif de cette nation," Pinto, "Reflexions," etc., in the *Lettres de quelques juijs*, vol. 1, p. 19.

512. J. M. Jost, *Geschichte des Judentums und seiner Sekten*, vol. 3 (1859), p. 207.

513. *Derech Erez Zutta*, ch. viii.

514. *Megilla*, 16.

515. *Midrash Rabba* to Genesis, 1, 44.

516. "Développer une chose qui existe en germe, perfectionner ce qui est, exprimer tout ce qui tient dans une idée qu'il n'aurait pas trouvée seul."—M. Murel, *L'esprit juif* (1901), p. 40.

517. K. Knies, *Credit*, vol. 1, p. 240 ; vol. 2, p. 169.

CHAPTER XIII

518. F. Martius, "Die Bedeutung der Vererbung für Krankheitsenstehung und Rassenerhaltung," in *Archiv für Rass. und Ges. Biologie*, vol. 7 (1910), p. 477.

519. Some of the most important of recent works on the ethnology and anthropology of the Jews are the following : von Luschan, "Die anthropologische Stellung der Juden," in *Korrespondenzblatt für Anthropologie*, vol. 23 (1892) ; Judt, *Die Juden als Rasse* (1903). On the historic side, much light has been thrown on the problem by Ed. Meyer, *Die Israeliten und ihre Nachbarstämme* (1906). Side by side with this excellent book may be placed one somewhat older, A. Bertholet, *Die Stellung der Israeliten und der Juden zu den Fremden* (1896). That the whole literature on Babylonia must be mentioned here goes without saying, *i.e.*, the works of Winkler, Jeremias, and others. Recently there appeared a book by W. Erbt, *Die Hebräer. Kanaan im Zeitalter der hebraischen Wanderung und hebraischen Staatengründung* (1906).

520. H. V. Hilprecht, *The Babylonian Expedition of the University of Pennsylvania*. Series A, Cuneiform Texts, vol. 9 (1898), p. 28 ; the same author's *Explorations in Bible Lands during the 19th Century* (1903), p. 409.

521. Cf. von Luschan, "Zur phys. Anthropologie der Juden," in *Z.D.S.J.*, vol. 1 (1905), p. 1.

522. The chief exponent of this theory is Ludwig Wilser, who has set forth his view in numerous articles, and at great length in his book, *Die Germanen* (1903). His chief opponent is Zollschan [note 503], p. 24.

523. Mommsen, *Römische Geschichte*, vol. 5, p. 549.

524. Graetz, vol. 5, pp. 188, 330, 370.

525. Graetz, vol. 7, p. 63.

526. All these instances in Lindo [see note 128], p. 10.

527. In his criticism of Hoeniger, who holds the view expressed in the text as applicable to Cologne. Others who have supported Brann are Lau, Keussen, and A. Kober, *Studie zur mittelalterlichen Geschichte der Juden in Köln am Rhine* (1903), p. 13.

528. Maurice Fishberg, "Zur Frage der Herkunft des blonden Elements im Judentum" in *Z.D.S.J.*, vol. 3 (1907), pp. 7, 25. A contrary view in the same journal, vol. 3, p. 92, is Elias Auerbach's "Bemerkungen zu Fishbergs Theorie," etc.

529. Cf. F. Sofer, "Über die Plastizität der menschlichen Rassen," in *Archiv für Rass. und Ges. Biologie*, vol. 5 (1908), p. 666; E. Auerbach, "Die jüdische Rassenfrage," in the same journal, vol. 4, p. 359; also vol. 4, p. 370, where von Luschan expounds an almost identical view. Cf. also Zollschan [note 503], pp. 125, 134, etc.

530. See the results in Judt [note 519]. Cf. also A. D. Elkind, *Die Juden. Eine vergleichend-anthropologische Untersuchung* (1903). I know the book only from the review by Weinberg in *Archiv für Rass. und Ges. Biologie*, vol. 1 (1904), p. 915. Cf. also Elkind's "Anthropologische Untersuchungen über die russ.-polnischen Juden," in *Z.S.D.J.*, vol. 2 (1906), pp. 49, 65, and his other essay in vol. 4 (1908), p. 28; Leo Sofer, "Zur Anthropologische Stellung der Juden," in *Pol. anthrop. Revue*, vol. 7 (cf. review of this in *Z.S.D.F.*, vol. 4, p. 160). Cf. E. Auerbach [note 529], p. 332; Aron Sandler, *Anthropologie und Zionismus* (1904), though his results are not first-hand; Zollschan [note 503], pp. 125, 134, etc.

531. The theory of "racial differences" between Ashkenazim and Sephardim is supported by S. Weissenberg, "Das jüdische Rassenproblem," in *Z.D.S.J.*, vol. 1 (1905); M. Fishberg, "Beiträge zur phys. Anthropologie der nordafrikanischen Juden," ditto. Opponents of the view are most of the authors mentioned in note 530.

532. For an all-round consideration of this question see Leo Sofer, "Zur Biologie und Pathologie der jüdischen Rasse," in *Z.D.S.J.*, vol. 2 (1906), p. 85. For further views, see the issues of this learned journal. Cf. also *Archiv für Rass. und Ges. Biologie*, vol. 4 (1907), pp. 47, 149: Siegfried Rosenfeld, "Die Sterblichkeit der Juden in Wien und die Ursachen der jüdischen Mindersterblichkeit."

533. F. Hertz, *Moderne Rassen-Theorie* (1904), p. 56.

534. C. H. Stratz, *Was sind Juden? Eine ethnographisch-anthropologische Studie* (1903), p. 26.

535. Illustrations in Judt [note 519] and elsewhere. Cf. also L. Messerschmidt, *Die Hettiter* (1903).

536. Cf. Hans Friedenthal, *Über einen experimentalen Nachweis von Blutsverwandtschaft* (1900). Also appeared in the author's *Arbeiten aus dem Gebiete der experimentellen Physiologie* (1908).

537. Carl Bruck, " Die biologische Differenzierung von Affenarten und menschlichen Rassen durch spezifische Blutreaktion," reprinted from the *Berliner Klinischen Wochenschrift*, vol. 4 (1907), p. 371.

538. Von Luschan, " Offener Brief an Herrn Dr. Elias Auerbach," in *Archiv für Rassen und Ges. Biologie*, vol. 4 (1907), p. 371.

539. A. Ruppin, " Die Mischehe," in *Z.D.S.J.*, vol. 4, p. 18.

540. Mommsen, *Römische Geschichte*, vol. 5, p. 529.

541. M. Braunschweiger, *Die Lehrer der Mischna* (1890), p. 27.

542. Graetz, vol. 6, p. 22.

543. Graetz, vol. 6, p. 320.

544. Gregor. Ep. ix. 36, In Schipper, p. 16.

545. Herzfeld [note 591], p. 204.

545A. Herzfeld has perhaps dealt most fully with these questions. But besides many errors of textual interpretation he is also wrong as regards the dates of documents. He still maintains the chronology current before the age of criticism, and therefore places most of his sources in the pre-exilic period.

546. For the Talmudic period, see Herzfeld [note 591], p. 118, where over a hundred imports into Palestine are given.

547. A. Bertholet [see note 519], p. 2.

548. Cf. Büchsenschütz, *Besitz und Erwerb im griechischen Altertum* (1869), p. 443.

549. Friedländer [note 594], vol. 3, p. 571.

550. *Kiddushin*, 82b.

551. *Aboth de R. Nathan*, xxx. 6.

552. *Pesachim*, 113a.

553. *Pesachim*, 50b. Cf. also the articles " Welthandel " and " Handel " in J. Hamburger's *Real-Encyklopädie des Judentums* (1883, 1886) for more material under this heading.

398 THE JEWS AND MODERN CAPITALISM

554. A. Bertholet, "Deuteronomium" (1899), in Marti's *Kurz. Handkommentar zum A.T.* On the passage in the text, Bertholet remarks that it refers to a period in which Israel is scattered all over the globe as a people of traders, and is a force in the world because of its wealth. Bertholet informs me that he regards the passage xv. 4–6 as a later addition to the text, and because the words appear to point to an extensive distribution of Israel he would incline to assign them to the Greek period after Alexander.

But for myself I cannot believe that the Jews were then a scattered *commercial* people. In order to make quite sure that I had not overlooked important passages I wrote to Professor Bertholet to ask him on what grounds he based his opinion. In his reply he referred me to Prov. vii. 19; xii. 11; xiii. 11; xx. 21; xxiii. 4; xxiv. 27; xxviii. 19, 20, 22; Ecclus. xxvi. 29–xxvii. 2. These passages deal with the dangers of wealth, and I have already discussed them in another connexion. None of them, however, appear to me to point to trade on a large scale. Certainly Prov. vii. 19 *may* have reference to a travelling trader, but not necessarily. And when we are told of Tobit (to whom also Professor Bertholet referred) that he was King Enemessar's "agorastes" and as such had a comfortable income, does not that rather point to a feudal state of society? Again, Ananias, a merchant at the court of Adiabene (of whom Josephus tells), may have been a Hofjude. Of course, I do not deny that Jews participated in international trade. But I contend that this was not characteristic of them. What was characteristic was the business of lending, and of this it may be said, as Bertholet does, that Israel was then (in the period after Alexander) a power in the earth.

555. I am indebted to Professor Bertholet for calling my attention to this document.

556. E. Renan, *Les Apôtres* (1866), p. 289.

557. J. Wellhausen, *Medina vor dem Islam* (1889), p. 4.

558. Cf. Aronius, *Regesten zur Geschichte der Juden im fränkischen und deutschen Reiche bis zum Jahre* 1273 (1902), Nos. 45, 62.

559. Cf. Lindo [note 128], p. 73.

560. Statutes of Jewry, in Cunningham, *Growth of English Industry and Commerce*, vol. 1 (1905), p. 204.

561. Wassermann, "Die Entwickelung der jüdischen Bevölkerung in d. Provin. Posen," in *Z.D.S.J.*, vol. 6 (1910), p. 37.

562. F. Delitzsch, *Handel und Wandel in Altbabylon* (1910), p. 33. Cf. Heicl, *Alttestamentliches Zinsverbot* (1907), p. 32, and especially p. 54.

563. Weber, article " Agrargeschichte im Altertum," in *Handwörterbuch der Staatswissenschaften*. Cf. also Marquardt, *Römische Staatsverwaltung*, vol. 2, p. 55.

563A. In the years 1436 and 1437 a number of Jewish pawnbrokers were invited to Florence by the city council, in order to assist the poor who were in need of cash. Cf. M. Ciardemi, *Banchieri ebrei in Firenze nel secolo XV e XVI* (1907).

When the city of Ravenna was about to join itself to the Republic of Venice, one of the conditions of its adhesion was that wealthy Jews should be sent there to open a loan bank, so that the poverty of the population might be lessened. Cf. Graetz, vol. 8, p. 235.

" We have seen that the business of finance in the period up to 1420 was gradually increasing in the hands of the Jews of Rome ; from 1420 to 1550 circumstances were even more favourable, and hence we find a still greater growth. Indeed, it became customary for the Italian communes to make regular agreements with Jews concerning money-lending." Cf. Theiner, Cod. dipl. 3, 335, in Paul Rieger's *Geschichte der Juden in Rom* (1895), p. 14.

563B. A. Moreau de Jonnès, *Statistique des peuples de l'antiquité*, vol. 1 (1851), p. 98. For censuses in the Bible, cf. Max Waldstein in *Statistische Monatschrift*, Vienna (1881).

564. A. Jeremias, *Das alte Testament im Lichte des alten Orients* (2nd ed., 1906), p. 534.

565. F. Buhl, *Die sozialen Verhältnisse der Israeliten* (1899), pp. 88, 128.

566. Biographies of the Talmudic Rabbis are frequent enough. Cf. Strack [note 435] ; Graetz, in vol. 4 ; A. Sammter in the Appendix to his translation of *Baba Mezia* (1876) and M. Braunschweiger, *Die Lehrer der Mishna* (1890).

567. Mommsen, *Römische Geschichte*, vol. 5, p. 529.

568. The 58th Canon of the 4th Council of Toledo (633), quoted by Lindo [note 128], p. 14.

569. J. Wellhausen [note 557], vol. 4, p. 14.

570. Cf. Graetz, vol. 5, p. 345.

571. Cf. Graetz, vol. 5, pp. 11, 39, 50 ; also the passages in Schipper [note 544], pp. 20, 35 ; Aronius [note 558], Nos. 45, 62,

173, 206, 227, etc. How Caro [note 324], p. 83, arrives at the contrary conclusion it is not easy to perceive.

572. For the period up to the 12th century, see the references in Schipper [note 544], also my *Moderne Kapitalismus*, vol. 1.

573. K. F. W. Freiherr von Diebitsch, *Kosmopolitische, unparteiische Gedanken über Juden und Christen* (1804), p. 29.

574-585. I cannot give a complete bibliography of all the works on biology, anthropology, ethnology, etc. Only a few will be mentioned for the guidance of the reader.

The works of Moritz Wagner appear to me to be of great value : *Die Darwinsche Theorie und das Migrationsgesetz* (1868) ; *Über den Einfluss der geographischen Isolierung und Kolonienbildung auf die morphologische Veränderung der Organismen* (1871) ; *Die Enstehung der Arten durch räumliche Sonderung* (1889).

Ludwig Gumplovicz, *Der Rassenkampf* (1883) ; *Die soziologische Staatsidee* (2nd ed., 1901) ; Ward, *Reine Soziologie*, vol. 1 ; L. Woltmann, *Politische Anthropologie* (1903).

For the question of heredity, see H. E. Ziegler, *Die Vererbungslehre in der Biologie* (1905) ; W. Schallmeyer, *Vererbung und Auslese* (2nd ed., 1910) ; R. Sommer, *Familienforschung und Vererbungslehre* (1907) ; F. Martius, *Das pathologische Vererbungsproblem* (1909) ; J. Schultz, *Die Maschinentheorie des Lebens* (1909) ; W. Bölsche, *Das Liebesleben in der Natur* (1909).

CHAPTER XIV

586. For the social and economic conditions in ancient Palestine there are not many books to hand. Perhaps the best is F. Buhl's work [note 565]. A more recent book is Max Lohr's *Israels Kulturentwickelung* (1911).

587. Wellhausen, *Proleg.*, p. 10 ; cf. Budde, *The Nomadic Ideal in the O.T.* (1895).

588. F. Ratzel, *Völkerkunde*, vol. 3, p. 47.

589. *Kiddushin*, 71a. Cf. Graetz, vol. 4, p. 273.

590. Graetz, vol. 4, p. 321.

591. For a list of Biblical passages in support, see Herzfeld, *Handelsgeschichte der Juden des Altertums*, note 9.

592. For this estimation, see Buhl [note 565], p. 52.

593. Philo, *in Flaccum*, 6 (II, 523, Mangey), in Stähelin [note 487], p. 33.

594. L. Friedländer, *Sittengeschichte Roms*, vol. 3, p. 570.

595. Cassel, in the article "Juden" in Ersch and Gruber, p. 24.

596. Tacitus, *Annal.*, II, 85 ; Suetonius and Josephus mention only Jews.

597. The best accounts of the Diaspora will be found in Graetz, vol. 3, p. 90 ; Frankel, "Die Diaspora zur Zeit des zweiten Tempels," in *Monatschrift*, vol. 2, p. 309 ; Herzfeld [note 591], p. 200, and note 34.

598. An excellent example of Jewish migration within one particular country is furnished by the history of the Jews in the province of Posen. In 1849 there were 21 localities (out of a total of 131) with a population of 30 to 40 per cent. of Jews while in 4 there were 41 to 50 per cent. Jews, in 3 over 50 per cent. But in the last half century the Jewish population of the Posen province has shrunk considerably. Cf. E. von Bergmann, *Zur Geschichte der deutschen, polnischen und jüdischen Bevölkerung in der Provinz Posen* (1883) ; *Zwanzig Jahre deutscher Kulturarbeit* (1906) ; B. Breslauer, *Die Abwanderung der Juden aus der Provinz Posen* (1909). For the expulsion of the Jews from Vienna at the close of the 17th century cf. David Kaufmann, *Die letzte Vertreibung der Juden aus Wien und Niederösterreich ; ihre Vorgeschichte (1625–1670) und ihre Opfer* (1889).

599. L. Neubaur, *Die Sage vom ewigen Juden* (2nd ed., 1893).

600. According to Gratian, *Vita Joh. Commendoni*, II, c. 15 ; Victor von Karben, *De Vita et Moribus Judæorum* (1504) ; Graetz, vol. 9, p. 62.

601. J. Ranke, *Der Mensch*, vol. 2, p. 533.

602. Ratzel, *Völkerkunde*, vol. 3, p. 743.

603. Juan Huarte de San Juan [note 505], p. 409.

604. F. Delitzsch [note 562], p. 12.

605. A. Wahrmund, *Das Gesetz des Nomadentums* (1887), p. 16.

606. Ratzel [note 602], vol. 3, p. 56.

607. *Pesachim*, 87*b*. Cf. also 119*b*.

608. W. Erbt, *Die Hebräer* (1906), p. 166.

609. *Ephraim justifié* (1758). L'éditeur à Mr. André de Pinto, Juif Portugais, Citoyen et négociant d'Amsterdam.

610. Pinto, "Réflex. critiques sur le premier chap. du vii tome des œuvres de M. Voltaire (1762)," in the *Lettres de quelques juifs,* 5th ed., 1781), p. 10.

611. Graetz, vol. 11, p. 54.

612. "L'idée, où ils sont assez généralement, d'être issus de la Tribe de Juda, dont ils tiennent que les principales familles furent envoyées en Espagne du temps de la captivité de Babylone, ne peut que les porter à ces distinctions et contribuer à cette élévation de sentimens qu'on remarque en eux."—Pinto [note 610], p. 17.

613. A. Nossig, " Die Auserwähltheit der Juden im Lichte der Biologie," in *Z.D.S.J.,* vol. 1. Cf. in same volume essay of Curt Michaelis ; also his "Prinzipien der natürlichen und sozialen Entwicklungsgeschichte der Menschheit" (*Natur und Staat,* vol. 5) (1904), p. 63.

614. A. Sandler [note 530], p. 24.